PHILEMON OF GAZA

Meditates the Gospel of Matthew

Edited by
DANIEL BOURGUET

Translated from the French by ROGER WILKINSON

Y THE PEOPLE'S SEMINARY PRESS

Edited by Daniel Bourguet

The People's Seminary Press
Burlington, WA 98233
www.peoplesseminary.org
ISBN: 978-1-954387-15-7

Translated from the original French edition.
Le moine Philémon de Gaza médite l'Évangile de Matthieu
Daniel Bourguet, Lyon: Éditions Olivétan, 2023
Copyright @2023 Éditions Olivétan, 2023

Bible passages are literal translations of the French. The author uses
a range of French translations.

CONTENTS

TRANSLATOR'S NOTE

This translation is part of a project to make the works of Daniel Bourguet available in English, and Philemon's work is very much part of that. The translation has kept as close to DB's editing as seemed possible while in a few places adding a little for the sake of clarity. DB's footnotes frequently refer to French translations of the Bible or to the meaning of French terms, and, because his points generally are true of the English too, they have been lightly modified in translation to give the same picture. However, please note that DB's references in the footnotes to other works have often been left as in the French, particularly when the works cited are not readily available in English; "SC" in these refers to *Sources Chrétiennes*, who publish early writings. Where English translations are readily available, the references have been translated. Some of the footnotes in the French refer to other places in the text, and some of these been omitted where they seemed redundant. In a very small number of instances, further notes have been added for further clarity, and in fact, as translator I have taken the liberty of adding one or two illustrative notes of my own; all such contributions are labelled [Trans.]. It's advisable to read DB's introduction since it explains one or two oddities in the text. An account of Daniel's works, biography etc. may be viewed at www.danielbourguet.com

FOREWORD

When Tischendorf, in 1859, made his famous discovery in the monastery of Saint Catherine at Mount Sinai of one of the most ancient manuscripts of the Bible, he left the monastery with a number of other manuscripts; one of these, which was anonymous, did not attract his attention since the Greek script led him to date it to the 11th century. He entrusted this manuscript to a monk friend, an excellent Hellenist, who passionately set about a translation which he made into Latin, as was the custom of the time. Unhappily, because of his age, this monk died before he could finish his work. The manuscript was then stored away in his monastery, there being no other monk to take up the task.

Some decades later, a French monk joined the community and one day came across the manuscript. With his abbot's authorization and helped by the Latin translation, he set to and retranslated the whole work, this time into French. A very good Hellenist and also very humble, he did an excellent job while maintaining his anonymity. It became apparent that the 11th century manuscript in fact contained a text from the 6th century,[1] written by one

1. The dating to the 6th century is due to the authors cited in the text, the most recent of whom undoubtedly belong to that time. It cites Dorotheus of Gaza, Barsanuphius and John of Gaza, all from the 6th century, as well as Abba Seridos, who founded the Gaza monastery at the very end of the 5th century; he entrusted to Philemon the role of gatekeeper. All this enables us to locate Philemon in the first half of the 6th century.

Philemon, a monk from Gaza who, to our knowledge, wrote nothing else. At this moment, there is no other document that mentions this author; the manuscript is the first and perhaps only thing he wrote; he is cited by no other ancient author. Today he belongs to the company of the humble who sing the glory of God in the heavenly choir, but one day this unknown's name emerged when the translator noticed it inscribed in acrostic form in the first letters of the opening chapters. We can imagine his joy when he saw appear before his eyes, little by little, letter by letter, "Philemon of Gaza, servant of God." His interest in the translation increased tenfold and he now had a personal interest in the author, whom he thenceforth considered to be a Church Father.

I met the translator some thirty years ago during a retreat I made in this same monastery; he showed me his work with an enthusiasm which he communicated to me, and I stayed in touch with him through the years until his death. I should own that down these many years, I have become familiar with Philemon of Gaza to the extent of my spiritual walk being significantly affected by him. I owe him a great deal, as will easily be perceived by those who know me. I give infinite thanks to the Lord for everything he has given me through this man. Before his death, the translator asked me if I would be so good as to edit the text, making me promise not to divulge his name, a promise I have respected. As the text is so lengthy, comprising a meditation of the four gospels, I began by publishing the first gospel meditated by Philemon, which is to say, the Gospel of Mark, a particularly interesting text because patristic texts devoted to this gospel are very rare. I am now publishing the next of Philemon's meditations, namely those to do with the Gospel of Matthew.

With the agreement of the original translator, I felt free to insert some biblical references into the text; thus everything in parentheses in Philemon's text is my doing. It also seemed a good idea to add some footnotes as well as a few, minimal, minor alterations, all with a view to making the text more accessible to today's reader. I am happy to now bring this text to the public for its contents to be appreciated by everyone. If God allows me time, publication of the gospels of Luke and then John will follow.

Philemon's text is a collection of meditations, not a commentary; this needs to be borne in mind. The author of a commentary endeavors to make every detail of a text clear; in contrast, the author of a meditation pauses over some one detail which touches and speaks to him. He then takes the necessary time to receive in his heart everything that this detail says to him, taking it as coming from God to help him in his life.

A meditation, then, is always very personal and is not undertaken with the intention of it being shared with others; it belongs to the intimacy of the author with God. A commentary is not intended to be personal and can therefore be passed on to others.

If and when an author sets his meditation down in writing, above all this is going to be for himself. He might pick the draft up later, deepen his thinking and further his conversation with God; whatever the case, modesty forbids that it be made known because the writing belongs to the place of intimacy with God. Philemon was one of those who was not writing for others but for himself; as indicated at the very beginning of our manuscript, his text was only discovered high on a shelf in a monastic cell where it was left long after his death, we don't know just when. Is it perhaps the case that we are betraying him by now publishing it? If so, may he forgive us! Perhaps he would wish to give thanks with us if his meditation helps us too to meditate; he would no doubt be happy to serve us in our walk with God.

While the manuscript is from the 11th century, it is a copy of an older text; the copy was edited very well but we can't know if any errors found their way into the original text between the 6th and 11th centuries because we have no other copy.

There are a number of gaps, due mainly to the poor condition of the lower part of the manuscript. Each of Philemon's meditations begins at the top of a page and closes at the foot of the page with a prayer, so the poor condition of the manuscript explains why these prayers are incomplete or absent. That said, we can still profit from them because we are more or less invited to continue them in our own prayers.

At this point, I yield to Philemon, asking God to bless you in your reading, that it may stimulate and feed your own meditation.

PHILEMON'S INTRODUCTION

This manuscript was discovered high up on a shelf in the closet to a cell; we are unaware who the author was, as are the previous occupants of the cell.[1]

---

1. The XIth century copyist faithfully reproduced this introduction, which is obviously not Philemon's, since, moreover, it's only there in the margin of the manuscript. It is as well to translate it equally faithfully since it is part of the text's history

Through the years, I have prayed, read and meditated a passage from the Divine Scriptures[2] every day, most particularly from the holy Gospels; this is the way I experience the very heart of my life, my attachment to our Lord Jesus Christ. He set his hand on me, touched my heart and led me to this monastery to deepen the bond of love which, by his grace, he has woven with me, unworthy as I am. My joy is in him; he is my light, the source at which I quench my thirst, without whom I cannot live, who loves me with a love which unfailingly overwhelms me in the depths of my being and gives meaning to my life.

2. In the 6th century among the Greek Fathers, the Bible was most frequently termed "the Scripture, "the Holy Scriptures," or, less commonly, "the Divine Scriptures." This is how it is with Philemon too, so when, unusually, he writes here of "the Divine Scriptures," it indicates the importance to him of the Bible as well as his immense and holy respect for the text he is meditating. During the same period, at Gaza, Dorotheus also uses this term, but very rarely (SC 92, *Oeuvres spirituelles*, p387, 513), as does John the Prophet (*Correspondence*, Vol II, Letters 344 and 382). In the 4th century, John Chrysostom speaks of the Bible in terms of "the Divine Scriptures" (*On the providence of God*). However, during this same period, among the Desert Fathers the Bible is rarely referred to in this way, though it is attested to in the following anonymous apophthegm: "An elder said, 'The simple fact of reading the Divine Scriptures makes the demons afraid'" (Apophthegm XXI–44) and also Apophthegm 797 by Abba Paul the Simple). This note provides the opportunity to state the connection between the Gaza monks, the apophthegms and the Desert Fathers. The Gaza monastery was founded at the end of the 5th century, over a hundred years after the period of the Egyptian Desert Fathers. The disappearance of the Desert Fathers was no impediment to the Gaza monks seeing them as their Fathers, and they referred to them all the time, drawing plentiful inspiration from them; witnessing to this is their profound knowledge of the collections of apophthegms which gather their sayings and the stories that marked their lives.

Some years ago, our beloved higumen[3] asked me to prepare myself to come alongside novices as part of their monastic formation by helping them to deepen their understanding of the Scriptures.[4] Since last year, in order to better me in this service, he has also entrusted to me the role of gatekeeper, which gives me much more time to read, pray and meditate the Divine Scriptures, for which I give unceasing thanks. On the day we celebrate the holy evangelist Mark,[5] the thought came to me put my meditations into writing, beginning with his gospel. I had already made a draft of my thoughts and this turned out to be a great blessing because it helped me be more precise in my thinking and go deeper into the text. On that blessed day, I took up a new pen to begin this holy work, but my hand was suddenly afflicted by a fit of trembling! What could I write, I who am neither a preacher nor a man of learning but just a poor monk, a useless servant? Who am I to set my foot in the Holy of Holies of the Divine Scriptures? Without delay, I set off to tell my trouble to our higumen, who listened to me in his great kindness and reassured and blessed me that the Lord would himself strengthen, edify and cause the

3. The higumen is the superior of a monastery in the eastern Church, as is the Father Abbot of a monastery in the western Church. The term comes from a verb ègéomaï, which means "to walk ahead," "to lead," "to command."

4. This perspective of helping novices in their formation certainly impacted Philemon in his meditation. No doubt it's why we find him being very careful about certain details of grammar and vocabulary, as though he already had novices beside him and was commenting on them for their benefit. He may have been unaware of the following point, but it is the case that his meditation is marked by his care to show novices that the closer one's attention to the smallest details of a text, the deeper the meditation.

5. No doubt this was April 25, as it still is today in the eastern Church. Unfortunately, I don't know the year in which Philemon began his work.

love he has given me to live for him to grow in my heart. In my joy and without any further waiting but ashamed not to have done so earlier, I went to share all this with Abba Ireneus,[6] my beloved father in the Lord. Our meeting filled my heart with joy. His holy and humble blessing brought me a flood of peace; I know now that he will be with me through his prayers as I step out; my hand will no longer tremble. As he blessed me, Abba Ireneus invoked the Holy Spirit over me, asking that he purify me and that he lead me into this Holy of Holies of the Divine Scriptures. "In the Holy of Holies," he told me, "the Lord presents himself to our sight (Lev 16:2), and this requires of us the purification of our inner vision. As you know, this purification is the work of the Holy Spirit together with the water of our tears which renew the water of baptism. Therefore go and be seated in your cell, as we are called to do by the Fathers, and weep over your sins in order to prepare yourself."[7]

So here I am in my cell; I am waiting until tomorrow to begin this work which has already filled me with hope. I am choosing to consecrate today to the prayer of repentance so as to place myself before God in my need and thirst. May the Holy Spirit now perform his work and prepare me; and may he continue to work day after day to lead me into the depths of this gospel.

6. The title Abba, which means "father," was not an academic title, nor a hierarchical grade, nor a title a person assumed himself, but a name given a monk by those who recognized in him a real spiritual depth. It is thought by some that the term comes from the Copt *apa*, which also means "father," because the first to receive the title were Desert Fathers, who were nearly all Copts.

7. "Stay seated in your cell and weep over your sins": this was advice very often given by the Desert Fathers to those who were seeking a word. This is the way Abba Macarius spoke to Abba Isaiah (Apophthegm 480) and again to Abba Aio (Apophthegm 494).

Heavenly Father, you are my Father; here I am with my impoverished heart. Please receive my repentance in the tenderness of your mercy and bless me in this new stage of my life. In your infinite grace, obstruct the adversary so that I can walk unencumbered to the source hidden in the depths of the Holy Scriptures and there draw the living water of humble love, and so love you truly and serve you better.

Lord Jesus, beloved Son of the Father, may you too bless me and make me worthy of this work. I pray this of you, who to this day have showered me with the living waters of your Gospel, that, by your grace and day by day, each new meditation will bring if only a few drops of this water drawn from the unfathomable depths of your heart.

O Holy Spirit, Spirit of truth, come in your grace to dwell in my heart, purify my inner vision and shed light upon me so that I don't go astray in the meditation of this holy Gospel. Lead my thinking, and guide my hand as well, giving me the choicest words to set down whatever, day by day, you see fit to give me to live by, I who am so unworthy of your grace.

And every day, without ceasing, the Trisagion.[8]

8. How wonderfully Trinitarian this prayer is. It is highly personal. The final line mentions the Trisagion, which is one of the most ancient of Christian liturgical prayers: "Holy God, holy and strong, holy and immortal, have pity upon us." Every day, Philemon must have spoken or sung this Trisagion and done so "without ceasing," reminding us of Paul's call to unceasing prayer (1 Thess 5:17). Philemon would have prayed the Trisagion not only at the beginning but also during his daily meditation, thereby guarding this unceasing prayer in his heart. This enabled him to experience his walk in fellowship with the whole Church, both on earth and in heaven, given that the Trisagion is a development of the seraphim's praise in the heavenly throne room: "Holy, holy, holy is the Lord" (Is 6:3). Philemon was not doing anything unusual by praying the Trisagion both alone and in communion in his cell. Apophthegem 24 concerning Abba Anthony, the first of the Desert Fathers, teaches us that a doctor in Alexandria chanted it each day at home in the company of angels. This is as much as to say that Philemon must have been encouraged by this knowledge, hoping that he too had the angels for company in his cell as he prayed.

MATTHEW 1

1: 1–17

AFTER MEDITATING MARK'S GOSPEL BUT BEFORE throwing myself into Matthew, I went to see Abba Ireneus to receive his blessing.[1] He asked me to share with him what the Lord had given me in Mark, and then, before blessing me, he spoke a few words:

"You know, Matthew's Gospel is also very beautiful and rich; I pray that you will again receive a wealth of blessings from God as you meditate it. We enter the gospel in the company of all the wonderful descendants of Abraham as they proceeded through the centuries, starting out for the promised land as bearers of God's blessing upon all nations (Gen 12:2–3); and then, from David's time, as they bore the hope of a king whose reign would be eternal, as promised by God (2 Sam 7:16). And so they marched on, transmitting from father to son this promise from God with his blessing, all the way to Jesus, himself a descendant of both Abraham and David.

"But with Jesus something new appears; the genealogy is suddenly interrupted. No longer is it a matter of fathers

---

1. In his meditation on Mark's Gospel, Philemon had already introduced Abba Ireneus as one of the monks in his monastery and his spiritual father.

1

"begetting" sons because the verb for "beget" (*génnaô*) is not now used in the active voice but is passive. Jesus was "begotten,"[2] we are told, without the name of his father being given. His mother, Mary, is named, and, along with her, her spouse, Joseph, who was not the father. This passive verb challenges me, you know, and it makes me wonder too. Matthew wrote his gospel for Jewish origin Christians, like him descended from Abraham and David; accustomed as they were to this usage of the passive, they would have understood that it meant that God was Jesus'

---

2. The Greek verb *génnaô* means both "to beget" and "to give birth to," which explains the different translations available. The official liturgical translation (in French) of verse 16 says that Jesus was "begotten" while others say that he was "born" (KJV . . . "Mary, of whom was born Jesus"). *Génnaô* can certainly be translated both ways, but from the beginning of this chapter it is consistently translated as "begat" (39 times!) since there is always a father mentioned (many modern English translations say "X was the father of Y"). The statement about Jesus is the hinge between the two different ideas since it is the first time "born" is used. It helps if we maintain the ambiguity of the Greek, though this is difficult for us linguistically: Jesus was both "begotten" or "engendered" without the Father being named and "born" of his mother. Abba Ireneus uses both meanings. What we are saying has a further nuance: for the Church Fathers, Matthew wrote his gospel in Hebrew or Aramaean, while Philemon was meditating it in the Greek translation, not the Hebrew original. It would be interesting to check what can be attributed to Matthew and what to his translator (and this might have been Matthew himself), but this curiosity is very much a reflection of modern sensibilities; for the Fathers whether the text was in Hebrew or Greek didn't pose a problem since, for them, all the texts were inspired (2 Tim 3:16), both Hebrew and Greek. Whatever the case, the double meaning of *génnaô* corresponds to the same double meaning of the equivalent Hebrew; it translates the Hebrew *yâlad*, which, in the *qal* conjugation means "to give birth" (Exod 6:20; Ruth 4:13) or "beget/engender" (Gen 4:18; 10:8) according to whether the subject was a woman or a man. Philemon's meditation gives a good account of Matthew's thinking.

Father.[3] That Matthew doesn't name the Father is a sign of his deep respect for he whose name was not pronounced since it is holy. The name of God is holy, and our human lips are too unclean to speak it. The Holy Spirit thus reveals here through Matthew that Jesus, fully man through his mother, was also fully God through his Father, a perfect union within himself of his humanity and his divinity. This union is wonderfully stated here thanks to the double meaning of the verb *génnaô* which signifies that Jesus was both "birthed" by his mother and "begotten" by his Father. We thereby enter this gospel with a revelation deep in our hearts which, in God's grace, the Chalcedonian fathers were able to put into words: they spoke of the double

---

3. In obedience to the divine commandment not to speak the name of God in vain (Exod.20:7), the Jews used the passive voice as often as possible, enabling them to invoke God but without naming him. For example, to say that "the afflicted will be comforted" (Matt 5:4) lets it be understood that they will be comforted "by God." For this reason this turn of phrase is termed a "divine passive." Here, "he was begotten" means "he was begotten by God," revealing God as Jesus' Father. Divine passives are numerous throughout the Bible, which is useful to know if we are to understand passages where they are found. In a similar way, to avoid using God's name, it is interesting to note that to speak of the Kingdom of God, Matthew prefers to say "the Kingdom of heaven" (32 times) and only on four occasions "the Kingdom of God" (12:28; 19:24; 21:31, 43). For the same reason, when Jesus questions the chief priests about John's baptism, he asks if it comes "from heaven" or from men, from God or from men (12:25).

nature of Jesus, his human nature and his divine nature in his unique Person.[4]

"You will note that Matthew lists the human lineage of Jesus at length, showing that this evangelist, himself a descendant of Abraham, was pleased to count Jesus among his brothers; this is all the more true because he was writing for Christians who were likewise of Jewish origin. However, Matthew was extremely discreet in expressing Jesus' divinity; he only suggests it because it is an inexpressible mystery, just as everything to do with God is beyond words. He proceeds in this way because he knew that the descendants of Abraham and David had already received the revelation of this mystery, but as a secret, in a way I will mention to you now.

"Matthew and those for whom he wrote this gospel received from David the psalms in which the revelation of the mystery of the Father of Jesus is found. In these psalms it is revealed to us that God is the Father of Jesus, not just

---

4. Everything Abba Ireneus says lines up perfectly with the fourth ecumenical counsel of the Church, which met in 451 in the city of Chalcedon to discuss the Person (the hypostasis) of Jesus, the mystery of his perfect humanity and his perfect divinity. He is true God and true man. The human nature of Jesus is not erased or absorbed by his divine nature; he is fully human; neither is his divine nature diluted by his human nature; he is fully divine. The two natures don't form a composite nature but are one, without mixture and without change, indivisibly and inseparably one in one unique Person, one of the three Persons of the Trinity (see V.Lossky, *Théologie dogmatique*, Cerf, 2012, p.133). In Philemon's period, this council was not yet unanimously accepted, and Gaza lay at the hinge between Egypt, which had not accepted the council and remained monophysite, and Palestine, which had adopted the council. At the same monastery in Gaza, Barsanuphius, who was Egyptian, chose not to make any pronouncement on this in his letters, but Philemon speaks out clearly, but without setting his thoughts out to the others, given that he was writing his meditations with no intention of publishing.

from his birth in Bethlehem but already from all eternity. Thus, in Psalm 110, God himself says to his Son, "I begot you before the morning star" (v 3).[5] This is wonderful! Here we see Jesus, the Son of God before the creation of the world, before the creation of the morning star, meaning also that he was begotten before the dawn, in the nighttime of our understanding, in a way that will remain to us incomprehensible. And in Psalm 2, God says to his Son, "Today I have begotten you" (v 7). No father could ever say this to his son. It makes no sense unless this "today" lasts eternally, which is the case.

"Finally, as the gospel continues, when the angel reveals to Joseph who the Father of Jesus is, he doesn't talk to him about God the Father but about the Holy Spirit (1:20), whereas neither Jesus nor anyone else ever considered the Holy Spirit to be his Father! This is simply to show us that the mystery of the bond between the Father and the Son is filled with the Holy Spirit in the inexpressible mystery of the Holy Trinity.

---

5. When the New Testament cites the Old, it almost always follows the Greek translation known as the Septuagint, not the Hebrew of the original. Abba Ireneus, like Philemon and all the monks at Gaza, referred only to the Greek. Where the Greek says, "I begot you before the morning star," the Hebrew says, "since the dawn, the dew of your infancy is for you." This Hebrew text is so difficult that the Septuagint just did its best! Perhaps, again, it was translating a slightly different text! What is certain is that Philemon knew no Hebrew, having said so in his meditations on Mark, so he could hardly check the discrepancy between the Hebrew and the Greek. I have a further comment: for Philemon, the psalm here is Psalm 109 according to the Septuagint numbering, which departs from the Hebrew numbering after Psalm 9. I have allowed myself to change Philemon's numbering to facilitate our reading since today we follow the Hebrew. As we continue, each time Philemon cites a psalm, I will follow the same pattern without providing a note.

"The inexpressible mystery of the Holy Trinity: that, my brother is the great door through which you are invited to enter the Gospel of Matthew . . ."

After receiving Abba Ireneus' blessing, I retired to silence and prayer in my cell. It is all so marvelous, and I feel so small before the greatness of this gospel . . .

1:18–25

How wonderful! Joseph was not the child's father but God entrusted the role of father to him, instructing him to name the child. This is a father's role, to name his child.[6] So, if Joseph was to give Jesus a name, it was a sign that he was his father, not the biological father, since Joseph knew very well this was not the case, but father by adoption; this is so good because it was he who would accompany the child into life. What a great task he was being entrusted with! This task was being given him by God himself such that, more than just a task, this was a true mission received from God, a ministry. It wasn't Mary but God himself who was asking Joseph to raise this child. Neither was it Joseph making this decision for himself, but God. What a wonder! In this way God expelled the trouble that had filled Joseph's heart, and not only the trouble but also his suspicions and doubts about Mary's honesty, all of which might have haunted his nights turned sleepless as well as

6. More precisely, in Israel, a child's name could be given it by either the father or the mother. It was Abraham who named Isaac (Gen 21:3) and Joseph who named Manasseh and Ephraim (41:51–52). However, Jacob didn't name any of his numerous offspring; each was named by their mother (29:32–35; 30:6, 8, 11, 13, 18, 20, 21, 24; 35:18). That the task of naming Jesus was entrusted to Joseph is a sign of God honoring him greatly, choosing him as a father for his Son in people's eyes.

his sleep turned nightmarish. It was on one of these nights that he was set free from his torments: an angel revealed to him that God was the real father of the child. So God was himself entrusting his own Son to Joseph's care: what an honor and what trust!

While Joseph was to name the child, he didn't choose the name himself; he received it from God, and the name itself is important: it contains the name of God: "The Lord saves." The angel then comments on the name in a strange way: "It is he who will save the people from their sins." It is "he," says the angel! But who exactly is this "he," the Lord, or the child? Is it the child or God himself who will save the people? The angel doesn't specify and leaves Joseph in a state of deep meditation: what if the child was himself God? This thought was too complicated for him and indeed inadmissible; never in Israel had a human child become God! Joseph therefore preferred to keep all this in his heart without digging any deeper; if God had given him this dream, he would follow through by giving him clarity in due time. For the moment, Joseph was charged with this wonderful mission and knew himself to be infinitely honored: he was to care for this child whose real Father was God. May he be blessed forever!

"It is he who will save his people from their sins": this is really what the angel said! Isn't this even stranger? David, Jephthah, Gideon and other military leaders had saved the people from enemy nations but there had never been any question of a human savior capable of setting the people free from their sins! God alone could do that. But was it of God or the child that the angel had spoken when he commented on his name? Again, only God could clear up this mystery in Joseph's heart, and he would do so in his own good time. For the moment, Joseph could just take hold of the fact that God had entrusted him with a mission that honored him to the highest degree. The night the angel appeared, Joseph felt honored, respected and loved by God in a way he had never previously felt, and from then on, days and nights would have a different savor for him. The love God was bestowing on him was so great that a peace was placed and established in his heart that would enable him to care for the child he was entrusted with.

The angel greeted Joseph saying, "Son of David," and this came as a great surprise! The title was a royal one, reserved for the expected Messiah (cf. 21:9). Joseph didn't know how to reply, but after the angel left, he considered the words and began to think very humbly that the angel was not attributing the title to him but to the child: there could be no doubt that it was the child who would really be the Son of David, the Savior. As for Joseph, he received the title simply to pass it on when the child was older so that he would be plainly written into the line of the Davidic succession. This honor belonged to the child, not to him. Already, in the heart of this father chosen by God a true love was growing for this child who was coming into his life in such an overwhelming way. Not only, now, was it at God's asking but also of himself that he would name the child, and would also present him with the title the angel had honored him with; henceforth the child would be called "Jesus, Son of David" (cf Mk 10:47).

You are blessed, heavenly Father; in your compassionate love you met Joseph in his trouble, in his wounded love and humiliation, and entrusted him with a mission that lifted him up and wonderfully honored him. You are blessed for what you are teaching me through him as he renounced his desire to break off the marriage in order to obey you despite the revolution wrought in his life by the coming of this child. You are blessed for his obedience in love for you, for Mary and for this astonishing child . . .

MATTHEW 2

2:1–12

TO DESCRIBE THE IMMENSE JOY OF THE MAGI AT SEEING the star, Matthew uses a redundancy, a superlative superlative, as though there simply could be no greater joy than theirs: "They rejoiced with a great joy." Even the joy of the women at the discovery of Christ's resurrection is not stated with such emphasis (28:8). After this description of the magi's joy at seeing the star, Matthew continues by telling us that they saw the child, but to describe their joy at seeing the child, he has no words, not one, inexpressible as the joy was. Seeing the child was much more important for the magi than seeing the star. They had undertaken such a lengthy journey just for this, to see the child. Matthew carefully mentions the child first, before his mother, underlining that their objective was indeed the child and not his mother. So here they were, finally in his presence and seeing him: the joy was so inexpressible that they couldn't say a thing, not among themselves, not to the mother and not to God. This child was a king, the king of the Jews, the king they had come to, guided by a star. The star had now gone; it had accomplished the mission God had given it. They saw the infant king; no words could describe their thoughts, their joy or the emotions that filled them. I myself can only be silent with them and then, like them, fall on my knees, bowing down to implore heaven to stop time so that this moment can last forever. I give thanks that I am alone in my cell and can rest in silence, bowed before Jesus, leaving the magi to themselves, and allowing time to unfold. He is the king of the Jews, the king of the whole earth and even of heaven, the one who has a star as his servant.

After opening their treasures, the magi offered the very best they had, gold, to be sure because they were in the presence of a king, but also incense. Why would they offer incense to a king? This incense shows us that, for them, this child was also God.[1] In Jerusalem, they had not said this; neither had they said that they intended to offer him incense. They had only spoken of a king because they discerned that they ought not to say more, but in their hearts they knew that the star had as its mission to lead them to God. Their unspeakable joy once they were with him, confirmed to them that they were indeed in the presence of God; that they were prostrate was also because they knew that's where they were. They stayed silent before him in the way one is silent before the inexpressible, but the incense they offered was enough to speak for them.

Last among their treasure was myrrh. The magi first offered gold and then incense, and then, with some reserve, added myrrh, still in silence since no word could go with such an offering; the mother of the child was there and her soul might well have been pierced by spoken words (Lk 2:35). They said nothing because the myrrh both announced and prophesied the unspeakable. The myrrh could be being given to this child to be used by those who would embalm

1. The incense was presented as an offering to God; the priest would burn it on the altar and the smoke would spread throughout the temple as a perfume of appeasement to God (Lev 2:1–2).

him (Jn 19:39).[2] Matthew too was holding himself back from commenting. The cross is no more than suggested, and the magi were silent.

Matthew then closes his account by telling us with a divine passive that the magi "were warned" in a dream by God. God no longer made use of a star to speak to them but spoke directly so that they would return home by a different route, a completely different way, since for them, thenceforth, nothing would be as it had been. They had seen the child, the king, God; their lives would no longer be the same. I will leave them there on their new way home and remain here in my cell, meditating on their offering of gold, incense and myrrh, and before this child whom I cannot stop thinking of, moved and in a state of wonderment. I am alone before him, in silence, in my cell. I lay my life down at his feet; this is my offering.

Lord Jesus, I have nothing to offer you apart from my life. In your grace, please receive it and do with it what you will. To my life, I add my praise: you are blessed, you who are the master of the stars and of the earth, who lay there on the straw in the greatest destitution, a king without army or escort, with just your mother and father who remained with you in silence at an hour when even the angels and archangels were silent, they too bowed before you. You are blessed for these magi who had come from afar as a sign that the prophecy of David was fulfilled: "All the nations you have made will come and bow down before you, Lord, and they will glorify your name through the ages . . ." (Ps 86:9).

---

2. Myrrh was also used as a perfume (Song 1:13) as well as in the anointing oil (Exod 30:33). As concerning Jesus, it doesn't reappear until the accounts of the Passion, where it was mixed with vinegar as a sort of anaesthetic drink before he was nailed to the cross (Mk 15:23), and then for his burial, as suggested by Philemon.

2:13–18

This page of the gospel is terrible; it opens up to us a dramatic episode which is unhappily written into the long and sad annals of human history, one more among the dramas which are the fruit of human folly and the work of the prince of this world. We cannot nor should we deny this reality, but I give thanks to God for the manner in which Matthew lit upon this episode and was enabled to present it; it leads us into the divine depths, providing us with a wonderful teaching to edify our faith.

Without denying the reality, Matthew takes no pleasure in the horror; with great wisdom, he chooses another way, one of reserve and discretion. He does report Herod's murderous decision but without describing its fulfilment, which must have been horrible. He instead replaces any such description with a lamentation, not that of the mothers who lived through this event but of their ancestor Rachel, who wept with them (Jer 31:15); this brings a further depth to the drama. With this lament, Matthew steps back and humbly gives place to the prophet Jeremiah, and, through him, to God, returning the massacred infants to him and placing them, with their mothers, on his heart. Matthew's self-effacement allows us to marvel at the immense love of God, who received these children and their mothers in all their suffering. Blessed indeed is the prophet Jeremiah for inserting in this oracle a divine passive which discreetly and magnificently reveals God's reaction. Speaking of the tears of Rachel, Jeremiah says, "A voice was heard in Ramah"; this leads us to understand that the lament "was heard . . . by God,"[3] as confirmed in the rest of the oracle: "I have

---

3. This is clearly a divine passive.

heard," says God to Ephraim, Rachel's grand-child (31:18). What comfort for Rachel, for all the mothers of Bethlehem and all the mothers of the world who weep over murdered babies or victims of human folly: God hears!

To demonstrate that God does more than just hear and that he intervenes, Matthew inserts another quotation into his account, another prophecy; the reference for this, in my poverty, I am unaware of, but am confident that Matthew was not making a mistake. This prophecy conveys the following word from God: "Out of Egypt I have called my Son,"[4] a wonderful statement that reveals Jesus, the child refugee in Egypt, as none other than the Son of God. Thanks to this blessed revelation, Matthew leads us to read this story at another level: we are dealing here not just with the story of the infant Jesus being exposed to the folly of a tyrant but with the story of the Son of God who, in his divinity, came to expose the foolishness of tyrants like Herod, and, through them, the foolishness of Satan himself, who, in his pride, wishes to take the place of God. It was for this that the Son of God became man, to deliver men from their sins, as the angel had told Joseph (1:21). However, for man to be delivered from sins, it is primary that the Son of Man attack the very one who is the source of human sin, Satan himself. Also, to bring us into the depths of this and to show that God remains the master of human

4. Philemon was unable to find this reference because it isn't there in the Septuagint. The reference is to Hosea 11:1, which was poorly translated in the Greek, but which Matthew, who wrote his gospel in Hebrew, simply copied from there: "From Egypt I have called my son." The Septuagint says, "From Egypt I have called back his children," referring to the children of Israel. Bless Matthew for having it in his heart to restore these magnificent words from God. This verse argues strongly in favor of a Hebrew original for Matthew's Gospel without, however, entirely resolving the issue of its original language.

history, Matthew constructs his account by prioritizing not Herod but the angel of God: in the first place (2:13), the angel reveals Herod's plot to Joseph so that Jesus would be safe, and then, as the account continues, he announces the tyrant's death (2:19). With Satan's servant now eliminated, Jesus the Son of God would then face Satan himself head on when, immediately after his baptism (3:13–17), Satan attacked him by putting him through temptation (4:1–11). Jesus' victory there would excite still further the rage of the Adversary, who would work through other men to set off his final assault, which would play out on Golgotha; Jesus would emerge as the definitive victor, as is revealed to us in the Resurrection.

The massacre of the Bethlehem infants therefore has to be placed in the larger context as an episode in which, while bearing in mind the weight of human suffering, hides God at work: in his love, God was preparing the way for his victory over the Adversary. This massacre needs to be examined in the light of God so that we see that Jesus himself became an innocent victim on the cross, and that he too heard the tears of mothers, including his own,[5] he himself going down into the depths of human suffering, the deeps of human hell.

---

5. John's Gospel is alone in mentioning Mary's presence at the foot of the cross (19:25), without stating specifically that she wept. Very quickly, though, Christian tradition added this feature of her tears, and no doubt Philemon was referring to Apophthegm 718: "Abba Joseph recounted the following from Abba Isaac: 'I was seated one day beside Abba Poemen and I saw him go into an ecstasy. I was very free and open with him so I bowed and asked him, "Tell me, where were you?" Constrained by me, he replied, "My thoughts were with saint Mary, the mother of God, as she stood in tears near the Savior's cross; I wish that I could always be in tears like her."'"

When the infant Jesus left for Egypt, it was "night," we are told;[6] but mysteriously at the heart of this night was the light that would illumine the world on Resurrection morning . . .

You are blessed, Lord Jesus, you who are already causing your light to shine in the darkest of our nights . . .

2:19–23

We know of three episodes in Joseph's life, and all three are recorded by Matthew at the beginning of his gospel. I am struck by the fact that on all three occasions an angel appeared to Joseph, and that each time Joseph responded by evincing entire obedience; on each occasion he applied what the angel told him to the letter. On each occasion, Matthew carefully describes in detail what Joseph did to follow the angel's instructions, thereby emphasizing his obedience. His obedience is indeed exemplary, and Joseph is a real model for we monks, particularly engaged as we are in obedience; for us, obedience to our higumen or one of the other brothers is obedience to an angel and so to God himself.

6. To frame the mention of night in 2:14, Philemon says "we are told," which should certainly be understood as a divine passive. This is of great interest because it shows that he was aware of divine passives to the point of using them himself; we find that Philemon was so respectful of the mystery of God that he would resort to this usage. For him, the mention of nighttime wasn't Matthew's doing but the Holy Spirit's through him. It was the Holy Spirit discreetly making a connection here with the darkness of the Passion with Christ at its heart, the light of the world. There are other divine passives of Philemon's production. At the start of this meditation, he writes, "It was given to Matthew . . ." which means that it was given to Matthew by the Holy Spirit; it follows that for Philemon the gospel was genuinely inspired (2 Tim 3:16). I won't point out any further such instances; the reader is well able.

In the first episode, when Joseph hears the angel, he renounces his intention to break off with Mary and obeys without argument (1:24). His obedience meant that he set aside his own view to follow God's. There can be no doubt that he reaped the rewards in full because in the following episodes he no longer had to change his own plans but was fully open to what God was asking of him. This is great!

All the more remarkable is that Joseph always obeyed without discussion, without questioning, and without a moment's hesitation. Unlike Mary (Lk 1:26–38), and unlike Zacharias (Lk1:5–20), there was no dialogue with the angel; he remained completely silent. He accepted in whole and completely the word that was spoken to him and then put it into practice without delay. He thus allowed himself to be entirely led by the word of God. He really is a perfect example of obedience, particularly to me since I am not always silent when something is asked of me! I am definitely both amazed and instructed by this!

I might stop my meditation here in order to prepare myself to diligently follow Joseph's example, but I am struck again that in what follows, the gospels just don't mention him again. However, it is good that we not forget that Jesus grew up alongside him. He too had opportunity to consider this man of perfect obedience to God, a wonderful silent obedience that gave no place to the slightest doubt or the slightest disobedience. What a joy this must have been for Jesus, not so much to hear Joseph give some teaching on obedience but to simply see him living out obedience to God. Example is so much more beautiful than a discourse! Further, though, to Joseph's obedience, Jesus would also have admired his humility; as Abba Moses says, "obedience begets humility,"[7] and how true this is. In fact, the more we obey God, and Joseph did nothing else, the more humble we become; and the humbler we are, the easier it is to obey God. Jesus grew up alongside this humble man who had no need to preach about humility because it could be seen in his life. How blessed is Joseph to have had in his care and to see growing up our Savior, who is gentle and lowly of heart. He is blessed, and is now with him in inexpressible light near to the Father.

This adoptive father was a wonderful support for Jesus, who was already humble and obedient of himself, as we see perfectly in the gospels, and as Paul was pleased to emphasize in his letter to the Philippians: "He humbled himself, becoming obedient to the point of death, to death on a cross" (2:8). "To the point of death": indeed, there is no end to being obedient and humble; it is a pathway to be pursued with perseverance to the very end.

We will never know just what Jesus received from Joseph; however, it is always wonderful to contemplate the magnificent harmony between these two humble men who walked in obedience to the heavenly Father, and also to say that the two lived under the same roof as Mary, who was also wonderful in humility and obedience. The holy family is truly a model not just for Christian families but also for monastic communities.

The secret of the exemplary life is revealed to us by Jesus himself on the day he was told that his mother and

---

7. "Abba Moses said to a brother, 'Let us acquire the obedience which gives birth to humility and brings with it perseverance, long suffering, compunction, brotherly love and charity; these are our armor for the fight'" (Apophthegm XIV–6). It is beautiful to see here Abba Moses, the former bandit, speak of a different fight to his earlier practices before becoming a monk. Note also that in this meditation, Philemon mentions perseverance.

brothers were there seeking to speak to him; he opened up and extended his family, telling us how to become members of it: "Whoever does the will of my Father who is in heaven, he is my brother, my sister, my mother" (12:50). This is the secret of both humility and obedience: doing the will of the Father.

You are blessed, heavenly Father, to have chosen Joseph, to whom you entrusted your beloved Son, one who was able to persevere alongside him through so many blessed years on the way of humble obedience . . .

MATTHEW 3

3:1–12

JOHN THE BAPTIST'S MESSAGE IS VERY CLEAR: HE WAS announcing the immediate coming of the Kingdom of heaven and was calling for repentance; nothing else. This was the only attitude to adopt: repentance. However, John the Baptist also saw the Pharisees and the Sadducees coming to him and requesting baptism but not in a state of repentance. Shocked by their attitude, he vigorously opposed them, asking them, "Who has taught you to flee?" and speaking of them as "vipers." For clarity, he expanded on this with two images which both end with the mention of fire: there is the picture of the landowner who comes with his axe to chop down and throw into the fire all the trees that were not bearing fruit, and then, at harvest time, the chaff being thrown into the fire. The two images both present a division, between the trees that bear fruit and those that don't, and then between the wheat and the straw. Both also evoke places, orchards and fields, frequented by vipers, which, as we know, flee from fire. "Who has taught you to flee?" the Baptist asks of those he is calling vipers. The answer is evident: it was not God, who is the owner of the orchards and fields, but Satan, who is the "fleeing serpent" (Is 27:1). It's Satan who has taught you to flee,

Satan, who flees before the fire of God just as enemies flee before the face of God (Ps 68:1); you flee in vain because the fire will pursue you, will overtake and consume you. This is "the fire that burns and is not quenched," "the eternal fire prepared for the devil and his angels" (Matt 25:41).

All this is terrible, but John the Baptist's message remains an invitation to repent, but this repentance is not because of the fire and the anger of God since this fire is not for everyone; it is intended neither for the fruit producing trees nor for the wheat. In fact, the Baptist's message is not a bearer solely of anger and fire; while God is angry with the vipers, he is not when there is a good harvest of fruit or wheat; his anger then gives way to joy. The announcement of the coming of the Kingdom will certainly bring fear to some and joy to others.

Can it really be that a call to repentance produces joy? Yes, John the Baptist tells us. Listen carefully to his message. As he expands his image of the trees and speaks of those who produce fruit, he says of this fruit that it is fruit "worthy of repentance." It follows that there is a repentance that bears fruit! What might this fruit be? For a moment, I was perplexed by this question, but then I suddenly remembered some words of Abba Ireneus which brought me light: "The first fruit of repentance," he said to me one day, "is tears." That's the truth! A person who truly repents and becomes aware of having offended God, sheds tears, the tears of compunction. A person shedding tears is not fleeing like a serpent from God but, on the contrary, is drawing near to him like the sinful woman who came to Jesus spilling tears of repentance on his feet (Lk 7:36–48). She drew near without saying anything, but her tears spoke for her and told Jesus of the depth of her repentance, a repentance in which Jesus discerned genuine love. A person who repents sheds tears of love for the person he has offended. Such tears are received with mercy and forgiveness because they touch God viscerally, and he is quick to forgive. As Abba Hyperechios says, "He who sheds tears of compunction[1] causes the heaven of mercy to come" (Apophthegm III–35). This is just what John the Baptist would have us understand: when the Lord comes to chop down the trees, he sets his axe aside when he sees trees that bear fruit, and his harvest of fruit brings him joy. Moved to the core, he forgives with joy, and his forgiveness is a source of joy to the penitent. The tears of repentance are wiped away by divine mercy (Rev 21:4) and give way to other tears, sweet, deep tears of joyful thanksgiving.

Repent, says John the Baptist, the Kingdom of heaven is drawing near, with anger for those who fear and flee without repentance, and with mercy for those who repent in tears. Then, as Abba Ireneus said to me, I believe that in the Kingdom of heaven, when repentant people fix their eyes on the Lord, they will discover other tears in his eyes, tears of joy like the father in the parable when he welcomes home his son and takes him in his arms, hiding his tears of joy (Lk 15:20).

O my soul, when the father shed tears on his son's shoulder, the son shed his own tears on his father's shoulder, and

---

1. Compunction (*katanuxis*) is the pain felt in one's heart with the awareness of having offended God. The word is taken from the account of Pentecost, where the crowd was "pierced to the heart" (*katanussô*) on hearing Peter tell them that they had wounded the heart of God by crucifying his Son (Acts 2:37; in the Latin translation *compuncti sunt corde*, from which "compunction." When he speaks of tears of compunction, Abba Ireneus specifies that they are the "first" fruit of repentance; that is, the very first fruit because the tears don't so much follow repentance as go along with it. Other fruit follows: good works and changed behaviour attest to the repentance being deep rather than superficial and passing.

the tears mixed together in their hearts, just as the tears of God are mixed with ours in the waters of baptism, giving us a taste of the joy of the Kingdom . . .

3:13–17

After all the crowd had come to John the Baptist to be baptized by him (3:5), now Jesus does the same; he too presents himself, which surprised the Baptist, as it does us. The baptism, in fact, was accompanied by a confession of sins and was only granted to those who were repenting, as preparation for God's forgiveness. So what was Jesus doing when he hadn't committed any sin (Heb 4:15; 1 Pet 2:22)? John the Baptist's initial refusal is easily understood. Moreover, Matthew carefully avoids telling us that Jesus confessed sins in the way others had (3:6). Why was Jesus acting as he was?

This passage also discreetly makes it apparent that Jesus was the last to come seeking baptism, after the crowd of people had confessed their sins; this implicitly leaves us to understand that, not having any sin to lay down, he was coming to take on himself all the sins the crowd had confessed and left behind in the Jordan. Matthew made sure to say the crowd had come from *throughout* Judea and *throughout* the Jordan region; thus, Jesus was taking upon himself the sins of *all* who were baptized. He wasn't preaching and said nothing, but in silence took on the sins of everyone. He was behaving as the servant of God of whom the prophet Isaiah speaks, bearing the sins of the multitude (53:12).

This was Jesus' first appearance in his office, and Matthew is already giving a glimpse of the mystery of this person whose path led to Golgotha, bearing our sins to deliver us from them as the angel had announced to Joseph before his birth: "It is he who will save his people from their sins" (1:21). Thus, without a word, Jesus came to accomplish his mission; he took upon himself the sins of his people, our sins, "the sins of the multitude," as announced by the prophet (53:12), and as the Baptist would say after baptizing him (Jn 1:29). What an extraordinary text!

However, Jesus was doing more than this. Long before this crowd, another person had been baptized in the Jordan, to dispose not of his sins but his sickness. During the time of Elisha, Naaman had left his leprosy in the waters of the Jordan (2 Kgs 5),[2] and Jesus was taking sickness upon himself too, as Matthew will say, citing another prophecy of Isaiah. It's not too serious that I can't find this prophecy because Matthew knew what he was telling us when he cites Isaiah as speaking of Jesus, "It is he who took our infirmities and bore our diseases" (8:17),[3] not just Naaman's but all of ours too. In this way, in his baptism, taking upon himself in silence not only the suffering for which we are blameworthy, but also the suffering of which we are victims, Jesus saved his people from their sins and their diseases. God alone is capable of this. In this way, Jesus divinity is impressed upon us, in his infinite humility

2. The Septuagint here uses the word *baptize* in the sense of immersing or dipping to describe Naaman's actions: "He went down and dipped in the Jordan seven times" (2 Kgs 5:14). No doubt it was this verb that led Philemon's meditation along these lines.

3. The reason Philemon was unable to find the citation is that it isn't there in the Septuagint. Only in the Hebrew that Matthew was using is the verse expressed in this way; it is taken from another excerpt from Isaiah's passage on the suffering servant (Is 53:4). The Septuagint translation is incorrect, perhaps to avoid theological misunderstandings by gentile, Greek speaking readers. This is the translation: "He bears our sins and he suffers for us." In this passage on the servant of God, the Septuagint removes everything to do with sickness, retaining only the aspect that relates to sins.

going down to the deepest depths, to the point of being immersed in our sins and sicknesses, bearing them himself and setting us free from them. In his baptism, Jesus' ministry is already summed up and the cross is announced along with the resurrection.

As he went down into the Jordan, taking on himself everything its waters contained, Jesus cleansed them and sanctified them, as the one that is pure and holy. He took everything that followed from Adam's sin, and he cleansed the waters so that they would be ready to receive us in our baptism, that we too might be beneficiaries of his saving work, we too being saved by him. He did this for us, his people, in the profound silence of his humble love. What goodness and what grace![4]

God then opened the heavens[5] which Adam's sin had closed. The Kingdom of heaven had come near, John the Baptist tells us; the heavens were now opened for all who repent. The Holy Spirit then descended onto Jesus, and also onto all the baptized. The word of the Father was now heard from heaven, pointing to Jesus, and in his grace, to every baptized person: "This is my beloved Son, on whom my love is set" . . .

---

4. Philemon charges Matthew's text with the whole of Christian theology despite it not being explicitly stated, and he was right to do so. His sense of wonderment is also well-placed: Matthew wrote his gospel with the same theology in his heart. Much more than Mark, who was more the contemplative, Matthew was a pedagogue who took care to present a text which was an open book for Christian theology. I note that today Matthew is preached from much more often and more easily than Mark.

5. Without saying so, Philemon develops what Matthew had only suggested in the divine passive, "The heavens were opened," a passive which unhappily is not always respected by translators. The heavens did not open on their own; they were opened . . . of course, by God.

Lord Jesus, you said nothing and stepped forward in the greatest humility, the only one who had no need to be baptized; but in your infinite mercy and infinite compassion, you took upon yourself all our sins and all our diseases in order to give us a share, with love, in your new life, your life in the Holy Spirit and in the immense love of your Father who became Father to us all. You are blessed for so many benefits of which we are unworthy and do not merit. Before you now, I fall to my knees, bowing down to adore you. In your immense grace, please bless me again and enable me to contemplate you now as you stand humbly in silence before the Father and the Holy Spirit, in the unfathomable depths of the mystery of the most holy Trinity . . .

MATTHEW 4

4:1–11

WHO COULD HAVE TOLD MATTHEW ABOUT THIS EVENT? No human witness was present. Only Jesus himself could have told how he was tempted; this shows us the great humility of one who had been publicly declared to be the Son of God. Why, then, did he recount it? His humble love leads me to say that he spoke of this to his disciples after Matthew had joined them in order to edify them and help them in their own temptations. He therefore had no need to tell them anything other than what would concern them since he had not come to earth to satisfy our curiosity but to teach us. He is our true teacher, and Matthew, as teacher, was acting as his spokesman. If the purpose was to help us, then it is good for me to hold on to only those elements that really help me to face my own temptations.

Jesus was tempted just like every one of us, says Paul (Heb 4:15), which for me is very comforting; he knows what temptation is, and more, he was tempted "in every point" (Heb 4:15; Lk 4:13).[1] He can therefore perfectly

---

1. These two texts go together: "He was tempted in every point" (Heb 4:15) and "the devil exhausted every form of temptation" (Lk 4:13). Jesus knew by experience all the tricks of the Adversary, but he didn't tell the disciples every one of the temptations he was subjected to. This is doubtless why Philemon says above that Jesus only told the disciples "what would concern them."

27

understand and genuinely help me. O my soul, what a blessing! He was tempted and "was without sin," as the apostle continues. What a further blessing it is to know that to be tempted is not a sin. Jesus didn't sin in listening to the devil's suggestions; he didn't sin when he disputed with him or when he refuted the suggestions. He would have sinned had he acceded. It is precious for me to understand this: we only sin when we acquiesce, as Adam did (Gen 3:6); to refuse the suggestions is to stay connected to God, obedient to his word.

The devil spoke about food when Jesus was hungry; he knows how to insinuate his suggestions into just those areas of human weakness that will awaken or respond to a desire. Gently here, he awakens the desire. This is nothing like the violent struggles such as Abba Anthony knew.[2] The devil tempted him, but without inducing fear or by a show of strength, just by very subtly prompting desire. Do you see, O my soul, how extremely careful I have to be and how I need to lean on the Holy Spirit if I am to see clearly; no doubt this is why Matthew specifies here that Jesus was accompanied into the desert by the Holy Spirit.

To each temptation, Jesus responded with a word from God (Deut 8:3; 6:13,16); he was therefore constantly relying on his Father, not his own understanding. He was relying not on prophecy but on the Law, on what is required of man if he is to humbly obey God. The devil's objective, in fact, is to have us disobey God, but Jesus remained humbly obedient: what a beautiful lesson this is for me! He replied by quoting the Scripture from memory, not by consulting books! He had memorized it all; the Holy Scriptures were alive in him. Another beautiful lesson!

2. Here, Philemon is alluding to Athanasius of Alexandria's record of Anthony the Great's temptations in his *Life of Anthony*.

Satan counter-attacked with the word of God, which he knows well (Ps 91:11–12), but in a way which made the word a servant to Jesus, whereas for Jesus it was to be used to serve God. It's for me to discern whether I am turning to the Scripture to put it to my own uses, to establish my own might, desires or will, or in order to obey the will of God alone. May the Holy Spirit help me to know!

Where was God? He was watching! Indeed, if finally he sent the angels, this is because nothing gets past him; he was ready to intervene, as Abba Anthony learned for our instruction.[3] Another beautiful gift! The closeness of God is a great blessing, to be called on at any time. Jesus is strong enough to fight, but I am not. Further to this, he counselled his disciples to pray when faced with temptation (26:41). Instead of disputing with the devil, it is preferable to pray to God, the surest of all refuges. O my soul, isn't it a sign of my pride if I converse with the devil?

To the weapon of the Word in the battle, Jesus added fasting, which helps us be discerning; Satan, however, can also turn this against us and have us fall into vainglory (6:16–18), in the same way that he knows how to slip a suggestion into the Word, as he did here with the psalm.[4] How despicable! He can turn everything against us, at times prodding us to use the Scripture to pressure God, saying to him, "You have said such and such, now put it

---

3. After another particularly trying temptation, Anthony questioned the Lord, asking him where he had been since he had felt alone. Athanasius continues: "Then a voice came to him, saying, 'I was here, Anthony, but I was waiting so that I could watch you fight; I will always be your defense . . .' Hearing these words, Anthony stood up and prayed. He was so comforted that he physically felt much stronger than before."

4. Psalm 91, quoted by Satan in his own way.

into action!" If we try to have God serve us like this, we are tempting him, while Jesus warns us here against doing this.

Jesus didn't go into the desert to be tempted of his own choice but was led there. Neither is it for me to go into places where I know I will be tempted; it's not for me to presume on the basis of my own strength; this again would be pride. More, Jesus put an end to the dialogue with authority: "Get behind me, Satan!" I too must know to repel the Adversary without delay because he will never let up!

When the Holy Spirit leads us into the wilderness, it is to have us grow and bring us light.[5] It is there that I can check whether my love for God is big enough to help me resist everything Satan can set before me to flatter my self-love.

4:12–17

"Repent because the Kingdom of heaven is at hand," was now preached in Galilee of the nations, by the way to the sea and in the lands of Zabulon and Nephtalim, the message that Judea and the Jordan region had already heard when John the Baptist called us to repent and receive

5. "Jesus was led by the Spirit," Matthew tells us. The verb for "lead" (*anagô*) means more precisely "to lead upwards," which is difficult for translators to convey. It must mean the Holy Spirit lifts us, causing us to grow spiritually; while this is true and good, it is something we only come to realize later; that in one way or another we do emerge from temptation having grown. In Deuteronomy we read that, "God will cause you to pass through temptation to know whether you truly love the Lord your God with all your heart and all your soul" (13:4). Here, the unstated subject of the verb "know" is ambiguous; it might be either "God" or "you." However, it is not difficult for God to know, so above all it is we who are instructed by temptation. The verse is therefore best understood as saying, "God will cause you to pass through temptation so that *you* may know whether you truly love God . . ."

baptism. Who then was now proclaiming the same message? It could not be the Baptist, who had recently been arrested and thrown into a prison dungeon. Of course, it was not him but another messenger from God, another, the one the Baptist himself had announced but whose sandals he was unworthy to remove (3:11).[6]

The one now preaching is the same one who, for forty days and forty nights, had confronted the Tempter so as to know all his ruses, the one who through the length of Lent went down into the depths of the lie but came out alive. His word now shone as a great light to call all to repentance who sat in the darkness and in the shadowy land of death. The call to repent knocks at the door of every heart so that they may open to the forgiveness that he alone can give, having received from his Father all authority (28:18). Thanks to him, the doors of heaven, shut since the fall of our ancestor Adam, were opened to receive those who hear the message of grace and who allow the light to perform its saving work in their hearts. This is he who came to earth to save his people, as the angel of the Lord had announced to Joseph, the son of David: his name is Jesus (1:21).

This Jesus who was now preaching is the beloved Son of the heavenly Father, the one who knows the depths of divine love and who came to spread it abundantly into the

6. The verb *bastazô* which Matthew uses here means both "to carry" and "to take off," which explains the various possible translations. The context invites us to understand John the Baptist as seeing himself unworthy to take off Jesus' sandals. The more important a person was, the greater the demands of protocol for a servant to remove his sandals, for example to enter the temple. John was so humble that he found himself unworthy even to be a servant, given the grandeur of the one he was announcing. In their parallel accounts, Mark (1:7) and Luke (3:16) use another verb (*luô*) which points in the same direction: "I am unworthy to undo the straps of his sandals."

hearts of all who hear and open up to be healed of wounds caused by the Tempter. His message is a song of love sounding out in the night of sin, spreading a light as beautiful as the light of the Paschal morning. His invitation to repent is not a warning, a threat or condemnation but a song of mercy, a prelude to the forgiveness which would be planted in the hearts of those who weep over their sins. His appeal is a song of hope in our nights of despair, a word of light in the heavy silence of darkness, an open door to the Tempter's captives. The night of sin is not eternal for whoever hears and welcomes the word of the Beloved, the word which lifts the downtrodden, the light which the darkness cannot dim (Jn 1:5) and which blots out confessed sin. His message is not that of a judge who condemns but of a judge proclaiming God's forgiveness, the message of one who undoes the bonds of sin and loosens the Adversary's grip, the message of the physician of our souls who spreads over our wounds the balm of divine grace.

O my soul, when John the Baptist called us to repentance, I was seated in darkness so deep that I was unable to see the multitude of sins that had accumulated in my heart and was incapable of lifting myself up to go and confess before him. But now, the Son of God shines a light so great that it shines right into the bottom of my heart and reveals to me the real depth of my faults. There is so much there of which to despair, that would stop me from standing up and make me ashamed to present myself to him. But his voice is so gentle that it encourages me to do it, to rise and come to him. I believe that he will receive me with mercy because the prophet has told us that he "bore the sins of the multitude" (Is 53:12). O my soul, I will go and lay down all my sins before him. Never before have I seen a light as beautiful as that which is shining today. I will not be able to hide any of my failings from him; I thirst to receive the forgiveness of God from him, to be cleansed, to be loved with the eternal love of God (Jer 31:3). Let us run to him who has risen as a great light at the dawn of a new day and lay before him everything that has darkened my heart, bowing down before him. His light is so full of life that it dazzles my still diseased eyes. But let us not fear, he will care for my eyes just as he cares for my heart, with the gentleness of his mercy. He will wipe away the tears I am shedding as I weep over my sins. The angels and archangels will then be silent to allow him to announce my pardon; I am not worthy of it, but I believe that his forgiveness will have the beauty of a love song.

Lord Jesus, here I am before you, my heart bruised to have offended you in a thousand ways; I am so ashamed that I fall at your feet, my eyes full of tears. In your grace . . .

4:18–25

At the end of this brief episode concerning the calling of Peter and Andrew, Matthew concludes with the words, "They followed him." At the close of the following episode, to do with James and John, he tells us the same thing, "They followed him." Then, in the verses about the multitudes who were drawn to Jesus, he tells us again, "They followed him," always with the same expression. The term disciple is not used here, not for Peter and Andrew, for James and John, and not for the crowds, but they all followed Jesus. It's certainly true that we habitually regard as very important the four fishermen Matthew tells us about; this is readily understandable because they played an important role in the life of the Church, but what of the others? All these crowds that came from Galilee, the Decapolis, from

Jerusalem and elsewhere, what became of them? They had heard Jesus preach the gospel of the Kingdom and been witnesses to the numerous miracles he had performed. There is no doubt that many of these people heard the call to repentance and indeed repented in the secret of their hearts before God. What became of them? We will surely meet most of them again on the mountain where they come to hear Jesus' lengthy teaching as recorded by Matthew; they make up the listeners to whom Matthew refers as "crowds" (5:1), in the same way as he speaks here of the "numerous crowds" that followed Jesus. Matthew is very reserved when it comes to these crowds, but nevertheless has no hesitation in saying the same thing about them as about the leading disciples, that "they followed him." What became of these people? I really have a lot of difficulty believing that they went back to their daily lives as though nothing of Jesus' message had stuck, or that they had not seen his miracles. It is certainly possible that some of them might simply have disappeared, but not all, surely. Not all that Jesus sowed was eaten up by the birds (13:4). I would say of these people that they formed the Church of the people, made up anonymous disciples of Jesus, disciples who are not made known by the gospel authors but who nevertheless continued to follow the Lord through good and through ill, each in his or her own way. It was to this Church that Jesus spoke the Beatitudes, and for this multitude that he gave his life (20:28); it was for this Church that he went out into the wilderness to pray (Mk 1:35), and for whom he multiplied and distributed the loaves and fishes, these thousands who had listened to him for several days without eating (Matt 15:32). To the same Church, he will say on the last day, "You gave me drink, and you visited me" (25:35), and on behalf of the same anonymous disciples he said on the cross, "Father, forgive them, they don't know what they are doing" (Lk 23:34). He prayed like this for Peter, Andrew, James and John, who likewise didn't know what they were doing, but also for the people in the crowd, who, just like them, didn't know what they were doing but nevertheless had both followed him and then denied him. It was for everyone that he died and descended into the depths of darkness in order to deliver them.

This Church of the multitude still exists today, and I am a witness to it. I see these anonymous disciples at the monastery gate,[7] so cautious and timid that they don't even greet me as they pass, but who I then find in the church during the next service, deep in prayer which has nothing of the hypocrite about it. I have returned to the church an hour later and seen the same person, unmoving, in the same place, still withdrawn in prayer. It's enough for me to see such people for me to wonderingly give thanks to the Lord for them. I don't know their names, but Jesus knows them and receives their prayers. I think of the man who comes to the church each year at the same time, and has at last responded to my greeting, but continues reserved as ever and still without giving a name. This is the Church of the people to which the Alexandria doctor belonged, the doctor who Abba Anthony never met but whose existence was revealed to him by God; he gave everything extra away to the poor and sang the Trisagion together with the angels every day.[8] Athanasius, although a native of Alexandria,

7. In his meditations on Mark's Gospel and in the foreword to the manuscript, we learn that Philemon had committed to him a ministry as doorkeeper to the monastery. This is why he mentions the monastery gate, where he served visitors and passers-by.

8. As mentioned in note 8 to the foreword.

where he had spent his whole life, first as a deacon and then as archbishop for many years, doesn't so much as mention him in his *Life of Anthony*. Perhaps he never met him, but the angels knew him, singing the Trisagion with him every day!

O my soul, Jesus most certainly loves all these anonymous disciples with an infinite love. I am happy to now think in my meditation that Matthew was speaking of them when he wrote, "They followed him," and to know that I am in communion with them when, in the solitude of my cell, I bear them up with love in my prayers.

You are blessed, Lord Jesus, to have also given your life for those who followed you without saying they did so . . .

MATTHEW 5

5:1–12

THIS IS THE FIRST TEACHING THE DISCIPLES RECEIVED from Jesus. To this point they had only heard the call he had spoken to them beside the sea (4:19, 21); they were now to hear his first teaching. In order to emphasize the event, Matthew abounds in preliminary details: "Jesus went up into the mountain; he sat down and let the disciples draw near; then he looked at the crowd and opened his mouth . . ."

When preparing to listen to a master for the first time, we are particularly attentive to their opening words. It is just these first words spoken by Jesus that hold my attention and lead me in my meditation.

"Happy . . . ," he said: in front of him, Jesus had a crowd drawn by what they had heard and seen of him, and by what they had witnessed; it was a crowd that had come from different areas, a composite crowd. "Happy . . . ," he said: who was it though his gaze would be fixed on first, honoring and highlighting them by calling them "happy" and granting them a place in the Kingdom he had said was at hand? Who was he going to name? A surprise! "The poor in spirit": how amazing is Jesus' way of seeing! The ones Jesus had his sight fixed on were the "poor in spirit,"

37

not the people dressed in purple and fine linen (Lk 16:19), and not the pious with their long fringes (Matt 23:5). Since this was also a teaching, in this beatitude Jesus was setting about educating his disciples. You, my disciples, are to learn to have your eyes fixed above all on the poor in spirit because these are the first for whom the Kingdom of heaven is destined; it is these that the Father wishes to welcome and have enter first into his Kingdom. It is at them that he looks first, wanting to honor them by opening the door of the Kingdom to them, and it's as of now, because the beatitude is not in the future but the present: "the Kingdom is theirs." Jesus' mind, set on the poor in spirit, is the outlook of God who draws near to them, even searching them out to bring them in since, of themselves, they humbly hang back, not daring to approach.

Who, however are these poor in spirit? This is a very important question, since we can easily be mistaken at this point. Nowhere else are they mentioned in the Holy Scriptures. Yes, the poor are there, but never the poor in spirit. So who was Jesus speaking about? I give thanks for the golden-tongued Patriarch[1] who God blessed and to whom he gave the explanation: the poor in spirit are the humble, not the poor who are forced to beg because poverty has been imposed on them, a poverty that does them harm, wounding or angering them. No, though God takes care of them. Jesus is speaking here of those who, in their spirit, think of themselves as poor, not poor compared to those richer than themselves because we all have someone richer than we are, but because they are poor before God. He

---

1. Philemon is talking about Saint John Chrysostom, born in Antioch, 349, and dying in exile in 407. He was the Patriarch of Constantinople from 397 until his death. He was known as "the golden-tongued" (*chrusostomos*) while still alive and declared to be a saint a few years after his death.

is speaking of those who carry themselves as poor before God and may even become poor voluntarily. It is they, the humble, since they don't look at their smallness or their poverty but only at God. They have no pride to call on; they are not vain or pretentious but humbly abase themselves before God.[2]

If this is so, then why not say, "Happy are the humble because the Kingdom of heaven is theirs?" Because the word "humble" is reserved for Jesus; only he is truly humble and indeed humble of heart (11:29), to the depths of his heart; we, however, always retain a substrata of pride. It is factually true that Matthew keeps the word "humble" for Jesus, and that he never uses the word for "humility" because the only real humility is Jesus' humility, which is God's. Divine humility is entirely beyond words, indescribable. This is also why Jesus didn't use the word "humble" here and preferred to say "the poor in spirit." He was looking, then, at these poor who saw themselves as small, poor, wretched and needy in the eyes of God and in their own eyes too. Happy are they because it is they whom God will bring into his Kingdom. If this is so, our place is to become poor in spirit ourselves as well as having our eyes open to such, to see them in the way Jesus sees them, the way he saw the poor thief crucified beside him, to whom he said, "Today you will be with me in Paradise" (Lk 23:43).

---

2. John Chrysostom preached sermons, among his many others, on Matthew's Gospel. In one he says this: "What is meant by 'the poor in spirit'? The humble, those whose hearts are contrite . . . those who humble and abase themselves voluntarily . . . those who, in accordance with Isaiah's prophecy, God welcomes with love: 'The one upon whom I will look is the poor and quiet of spirit (*hèsuchios*) who trembles at my word'"(Is 66:2, Septuagint). From *Homilies on Saint Matthew, Homily XV–1.*

Happy are the humble because God himself draws near to them to bring them to himself. If the Kingdom of heaven has come near, it is in order to open its doors above all to the happy ones on whom Jesus fixes his gaze and whom he contemplates wonderingly: come, you who are beloved by my Father, you who the world thrusts aside and mistreats; God welcomes you into his Kingdom . . .

5:13–19

"You are the light of the world": these words of Jesus left me stunned for a whole day and unable to put behind me this state of mind into which I was plunged. What over-whelms me is that Jesus says of us what he says of himself: "I am the light of the world" (Jn 8:12). It's certainly true that this expression fits him perfectly because he is indeed the light of the world, of both heaven and earth, the true light (1 Jn 2:8); he is this eternally, and heaven and earth are united eternally in acclaiming and glorifying him without whom the world would be nothing but darkness. But we, poor Christians, how laughable is our light on this earth . . .!

Even as he speaks these words to us, Jesus guards us against any pride because he makes sure to add images which point us back to our lack of importance: firstly he gives the image of a city which, even though standing on a mountain, can hardly light up the whole world, and then the picture becomes a simple lamp in a simple room, and when finally he speaks of glory, the glory is not ours but God's. We are thus called to a salutary sense of humility; we are lamps in the room of a house!

Jesus always speaks of us in the same way as he speaks of himself, which always challenges me. By what mystery are we the light of the world in the way he is? By what grace are we likened to him? Not seeking to tease out some ground for pride, I continued to be stunned at these surprising words he, the true light, speaks to us, we who are nothing without him . . . To look into this more clearly, I finally went to speak to Abba Ireneus, hoping he would help.

"You see," he explained, "that it is because he is God that Jesus said, 'I am the light of the world.' He says 'I am' in the way only God can speak, as he did from the burning bush to Moses, saying, 'I am the One who is' (Exod 3:14).[3] Jesus says 'I am' many times in this passage from John's Gospel, at the close of which the Jews gather rocks to stone him.[4] What to them was a blasphemy, for us is the truth. It is also because he is God that Jesus says he is light, because God is light (1 Jn 1:5). You see, by telling us that we are the light of the world, he is in his grace making us participants in his divine nature (2 Pet 1:4); this is tremendous grace, from which we can extract nothing for our pride, we who are weak little lamps somewhere in a house. The great question before us today is

---

3. In the Hebrew text, God says of himself, "I am who I am," but in Greek the translation is, "I am the Being." No doubt this modification was made to fit with Greek philosophers who termed God, "the Being." A literal translation like this means we don't see the distinction here: the Greek philosophers would speak of "the Being" as neuter (*to on*) whereas the Septuagint uses the masculine form (*o ôn*) meaning that God is a person ("the one who is") and not an abstraction ("that which is").

4. After saying, "I am the light of the world" (Jn 8:12), Jesus says "I am" three further times (8:24, 28, 58) and on the third of these the Jews gathered stones to stone him; stoning was the prescribed penalty for blasphemy (Lev 24:16). To say, "I am," was to blaspheme the name God revealed to Moses; it was to put oneself in God's place since only he could say "I am" in this way; this is shown again in the reaction of the chief priest who denounced it as blasphemy when Jesus again said "I am" (Mk 14:61–64).

how to remain light. He is our source of light, and through contact with him, we are light in the same way a lamp receives light from a flame which is its source. Jesus, the source of light, communicates his light without losing his own, and our place is to remain in contact with him so that our lamp is fed. We can do this through contact with his Word, which is light (Ps 119:105), receiving this Word to live by always, every day, day and night. In this way we can remain in contact with him and even united with him as we commune in the Holy Mysteries;[5] Isaac the Theban understood this very well when he told his brothers that in this communion he received a tiny flame which he then tended carefully so that, in the narrow space of his cell, it would shine (Apophthegm 423).[6]

"I would add too that in order to remain as light we have not only to be in contact with him but attached to him, the true light of the world. With respect to this attachment, I marvel at the psalm in which David says with such propriety to the Lord, 'My soul clings to you' (63:8). He says this with thanksgiving because this attachment is a grace. In the same psalm, he says to the Lord, 'My soul thirsts for you' (63:1), as though it was far from its source. This is how things are: we are at once both attached to the Lord and thirsting for him, both very close and yet removed!

5. "The Holy Mysteries" was a designation for the bread and wine of the Holy Supper in the Eastern Church dating to the time of the Desert Fathers (Apophthegm 542) and perhaps earlier. The expression uses the plural because the bread becoming the body of Christ is one Mystery and the wine becoming Christ's blood is another. To speak in this way of "Mysteries" is much more fitting and humble than to try to explain the bread becoming flesh and the wine blood; this is not accessible to reason.

6. Jesus spoke first of the light of the world, then of a city set on a mountain and then of a lamp in a house; Isaac took this trend towards humility further by speaking of a little lamp in his cell.

This great mystery is a mystery of love. Our attachment to the Lord comes from the love he gives birth to in us by his touch, enabling us to be in communion with him. This love also makes us thirsty for him, for his love. This is how it will be for us throughout our days. Our thirst can produce in us fear of being separated from the source; and at the same time we can say with Paul, 'Who will separate us from the love of Christ?' (Rom 8:35). And you know the great assurance and thankfulness with which he cries out, 'Nothing can separate us from this love' (v 38–39)."

"And now," Abba Ireneus told me, "go back to your cell and drink from the source of light . . ."

You are blessed, Lord Jesus, for what Abba Ireneus has been telling me. You are blessed, you who are the true light without which we are nothing. You are blessed for the immense grace you do us by making us participants in your divine light. Grant that I may remain attached to you every day . . .

5:20–32

Can anger really be murderous? Surely this is an exaggeration? Can we likewise say that an insult amounts to murder? I am perplexed! For sure, anger and insults can wound deeply, but are they so serious as to cause death? O my soul, I repent of thinking like this when the one who is speaking of anger and insults in this way is the Lord himself. His discernment is perfect and his word the standard of truth. I should humble himself because of this thought that he exaggerates and must also open myself up to him and let him lead me into the depths of his word.

In order to confirm the thought that the word of the Lord is the truth, I have immersed myself in the Divine

Scriptures, and this has been a great benefit to me. The result is that I am now clear, reassured and convinced that anger and insults can indeed be murderous.

David was the first to challenge me when I found a statement of his in the psalms about men's anger that "their anger is like the anger of the serpent" (58:4).[7] What exactly was he saying? Is the serpent's anger so formidable? Then James came along and added his light, stating that the human tongue is "full of murderous venom" (3:8). David and James thus made the Lord's word clear, that insult is murderous and can indeed bring on death like snake venom. Man is well able to bite with his words and inject the venom of his insult or anger into a brother's heart. Paul confirms this in his letter to the Romans when he too says of men that "the poison of the asp is on their lips" (3:13). The comparison he makes here about the poison brought me a little more light. He says in the same verse that the poison is none other than a "curse" as well as "bitterness" (3:14). What truth! Man is indeed well able to pronounce curses or bitter words which are so full of evil that they can wound to the point of death. The human tongue can certainly be full of deadly venom.

Thanks be to God, these texts from Scripture lead me to understand what the source is of the terrible words that men can speak. The fact that they can be compared to poison is undoubtedly because they come from that formidable serpent, Satan (Gen 3). That man is capable of speaking words that are murderous is because he is impelled by

7. "Their anger is like the anger of the serpent." This is just what the verse says in the Septuagint. "Anger" here translates the Hebrew (*hémâh*) which has many meanings: heat, venom, pain, anger. Hence the variety of translations.

44

Satan, who comes along to insinuate his deadly poison into human words. This is terrible; it links up with the Lord himself revealing to us that there is one thing Satan seeks, human death. He is "homicidal," Jesus says with this perfectly precise word (Jn 8:44). The whole thing is clear to me now: a simple insult can, just like anger, bear the Adversary's deadly venom, and the death that results above all is spiritual death; unhappily, this is all too true. In fact, I have seen a Christian deny the Lord and destroy his own life after being violently insulted by a Church leader . . . Lord Jesus, have pity upon us!

However, this is not what the human tongue was made for. Certainly, people can insult, lie and curse but they can also rejoice, speak truth and bless, just as James tells us (Jas 3:9–10); they are then wonderfully led by God who has given the tongue for this end. James brings further light when he compares the human tongue to a wild animal; he uses the word "tame" (3:7–8), implying that we are really wild beasts who are incapable of taming our own tongues (3:8)! This is terrible but so true. I have become aware of this as I observe others as well as myself. It's with consternation that I note the way I cannot control my tongue, which suddenly comes out with something terrible which I immediately regret but have nevertheless said; too late, because it has unhappily injected its venom into a brother's heart. James takes this no further because for him it was all clear: while mankind is unable to tame its own tongue, it is possible to entrust it to the only one who can; to God, of course. I marvel to hear David handing his tongue over to God: "Lord, you open my lips and my mouth will announce your praise" (Ps 51:7). Such is my prayer too; each morning I say this prayer that leads me into repentance. With my whole heart, I say at the same time, "Have pity on me, my God, according to your great mercy . . ." and "Lord, open my lips and my mouth will announce your praise."

To you, heavenly Father, I entrust my lips, that they may bless you and celebrate you . . .

5:33–48

"You have heard that it was said, you shall love your neighbor and hate your enemy; but I say to you, love your enemies and pray for those who persecute you." I don't know how the crowd and the disciples received these words from Jesus, but clearly they must have acquiesced in the first part since they would often have heard that enemies are to be hated; they would have heard it in the streets, at home and perhaps in the synagogues. As for the last part, "love your enemies," they would not have heard this on any street, in any home or in any synagogue. They had never heard such a thing and must have been asking themselves, "Why have we never been told this?" Today we are convinced that this commandment is from God, but God himself never said this in the Law or ever instructed a prophet to say it. Why were we not told this before Jesus?

Jesus has told us what the two greatest commandments are (22:37–39), but this new commandment is surely greater still. It is certainly much more difficult because, as Jesus said, it is easy to love a neighbor who loves us, who is open to our love and receives it. The same goes for God; he is open to our love and welcomes it, and he loves us infinitely. But to love our enemies who are closed off to our love, who hate and persecute us, this is altogether more difficult. Why wait until this day to require such a thing of us, we who are so small? Couldn't this have been asked of Abraham, Moses and David, or those who were more capable, greater and more holy than us?

The two great commandments are made easier in that they are presented to us in the future and not the imperative; they are therefore easier to put into practice because the future tense transforms them into promises which God will fulfil by helping us to perform them.[8] But the love of enemies is not asked of us in the future but as an imperative, setting aside any help from God and confronting us again with our inability. Who will help us?

O my soul, it all suddenly becomes clear: Jesus alone can help us, and this is why it was not required before his coming. Not Abraham, not Moses, not David, no one can help us, but Jesus, he can because he loves us and has even loved us first (1 Jn 4:19); he loved us before we loved him, even when we were indifferent to him, strangers and even his enemies, with Paul as an example, who Jesus loved when he was persecuting him. However, why doesn't Jesus say that he is there to help us love our enemies?

O my soul, he doesn't say this because he has such humility that he has no wish to push himself forward by proposing to lead us in this way of loving enemies. He doesn't say it, but he does wonderfully help us when we see him wash the feet of Judas; I can see him at Judas' feet, and his example fills my heart with strength. He helps us still more when we see him on the cross, giving his life and praying for everyone, even his persecutors (Lk 23:34).

O my soul, isn't it our place to witness to the love of Jesus for his enemies? While no one witnessed in his favor

---

8. Philemon had previously discussed the commandments as future or imperative in his meditation on Mk 12:28–34, where he noted that a commandment stated in the future also constitutes a promise from God, implying that he will one day meet its conditions.

during his trial, some of his enemies witnessed for him after his death through the grace of the Holy Spirit. Paul is undoubtedly the best example; after persecuting Jesus, he testified before everyone (Acts 9:21–22) and in his letters; he bore witness to Jesus' love for him (Gal 2:20). When Jesus asked him on the way to Damascus, "Why are you persecuting me?" he didn't know what to say, but he was asked the question with infinite love. It was only later that he responded, when he had understood how much Jesus loved him; he then understood that this love had disarmed him and reconciled him to the Father. This is love for enemies, disarming them and reconciling them with the Father. It is a love so strong that it disarms the enemy, not in order to kill him but to reconcile him in love to God. The strength of this love does not lie in swords but in humility; the strength of humble love disarms the enemy by touching his heart through the grace of the Holy Spirit. To touch the heart in this way, you would have to be God since he alone can touch the deepest place in the heart and bring someone back by his humble love.[9]

O my soul, Jesus requires us to love our enemies and to pray for them. Love and prayer are inseparable because our love alone is not enough; it has to be accompanied by prayer since our prayer invites God to join his love with ours to get to the unfathomable depths of the enemy's heart, to disarm him and open him up to the endless divine love so that he can be reconciled to him in a wonderful communion of love. O my soul, take courage, the Lord is with us . . .

9. The phrase "to touch the heart" (*aptô tès kardias*) that Philemon uses is only found once with a positive meaning in the Bible, and in this instance it is indeed God who touches the heart (1 Sam 10:26). There is another instance, but this time negative, speaking of evil touching (KJV "reaching") the heart (Jer 4:18).

MATTHEW 6

6:1–6

MY FATHER, I HAVE SHUT THE DOOR OF MY CELL; I HAVE no closet (taméion)[1] or any room other than this. Here it is that I sleep, that I read and write, that I meditate; it is here that I pray. I don't receive anyone here,[2] yet here you are. What grace! I welcome you with infinite thanksgiving. You are blessed! You were already here even before I came in and shut the door. You were waiting for me! What goodness! My Father, I have so many things to tell you that I don't know where to begin. So many emotions are stirring in my heart that I prefer to be quiet for a moment.

My Father, your presence alone is for me a gift beyond price. You who live in the inaccessible heavens, you have come to my home, to simply be with me. Knowing you to be here with me now overwhelms me. Your humble presence,

---

1. Philemon picks up on the term *taméion* used in the gospel (6:6) which refers to a room that is difficult for us to identify, though it can mean something akin to a cellar or pantry; it is translated in many ways. Clearly, though, Philemon had a simple cell which had no sort of annex to it. It was enough for him to retire to his cell and close the door in order to pray, just as Jesus says.

2. This was the rule in Abba Seridos' monastery where we find Philemon: a monk was not to receive another person into his cell. Other places were available for talking.

your humble Father's love overwhelms and amazes me. You who cannot be named, whose name is so full of mystery that it is not to be pronounced, have been revealed to me by Jesus as my Father, and I as your child. You are the one that knows me better than I know myself, and you love me more than I love you, you formed me and have laid your hand upon me (Ps 139:5) and have cared for me from my mother's breast (Ps 139:13).[3] You have always been there, welcoming my prayer like a father full of love welcoming his child's first words, even better than my physical father ever knew to do. But my love for you is so wretchedly weak! You are blessed, present despite everything.

My Father, I am filled with shame and confusion before you because so often and so easily I get distracted in prayer although you are there awaiting me. Even in the midst of praying so often I run away, my spirit scattered and absent; but you know this and in your infinite goodness you don't blame me at all! I pray that you forgive me though I offend and wound you by my innumerable distractions. In your great mercy, please forgive me and keep me close to you so that I don't flee; my desire and my good is to remain with you. You who know my heart, please care for it, purify, transform and attach it to you in the way you are attached to me, I pray.

My Father, I also wish to thank you for everything; it is good for me to do this but the list is so long that I will never be able to manage it. You have filled me with benefits from the time I left my mother's womb, you who have always been my Father. Before I even knew it, you loved me, and throughout my life, each and every day, your love has never

---

3. It is lovely to see these two verses from the same psalm rise up in Philemon's heart; this psalm is undoubtedly the one which manifests the greatest wonderment at the mystery of God.

ceased to surround me and fill me without ever dominating me. You know how to love me infinitely better than I can love myself. I can now rest in silence before you, before your benefits which are as countless as the stars of heaven and the sand in the sea (cf Gen 22:17). I can but contemplate their immensity, and this is enough for my heart to never cease to marvel. I close my eyes before you who shine more brightly than the sun and fill the silence with your radiance, a silence that means you can draw near to me and work in my heart unperceived. There is then only you and me, a heart to heart that leaves me speechless. The noise of silence is like the murmur of a bubbling spring, like the song of the stars in the sky; my heart vibrates and sings with them a song of love that unites us with you. You made us for this. I don't know if you sing with us or if your heart just listens; no doubt one day you will tell me. At times I sing in harmony with heaven and earth and at times I just listen to the harmony. Perhaps you are the same; I have no idea, it's just beyond me. The song of your creatures is thanksgiving and at the same time is full of hope and open to your love.

My Father, the song also carries the world's pain, and I join in with my poor compassion. The song is open to your perfect compassion; it is also full of your children's repentance and open to your infinite mercy, and all this it sings at once. Heaven and earth unite in this song and lay it before you in the unfathomable depths of your tenderness. You are Father to all and Father to each individually. I have closed the door of my cell to be alone with you and I find that you are here with, together in your heart, all your children. Here I am before you, in communion with heaven and earth and I drop my prayer into your heart: my Father, may the day come in which your song and ours are just one throughout the ages. Amen.

6:7–15

What a mystery! Jesus instructs me so wonderfully here. First of all he puts me on my guard against the vainglory which so quickly gets me stuck on the praise of others; then he calls me to retire to my cell as protection against this same thing. He carefully tells me to close my door and so be alone before God in the secret that suddenly and wonderfully reveals itself: "Your Father is there in secret." What a revelation this is. Me, alone in the presence of my Father; my heart then readies itself for prayer with fear and trembling. However, before I even start to pray, Jesus gives me a final word about prayer in solitude, a final surprising piece of advice: "You, therefore, pray like this: Our Father who is in heaven!" How can this be? What a mystery! I get ready to say "my Father" and Jesus invites me to say "our Father." I prepare to say "my Father here in my cell," and he tells me to say "our Father who is in heaven." What am I to understand? Jesus sets me up to say "my Father" but then holds me back; further, in a psalm addressed to anyone who might pray it, the Father himself says, "He will say to me, 'You are my Father'" (89:26). The Father himself thirsts for me to address him in this way and Jesus is calling me to the same, but then stops me. I receive Jesus' invitation as a lesson in humility. Prayer to the Father in heart to heart intimacy is a wonderful grace which, when undertaken with humility, calls me to enter this heart to heart while making room for others, entering into my cell, shutting my door against vainglory, keeping others in my heart and saying "our Father" with them; it is to enter my cell while making enough room in my heart to pray in communion with heaven and earth. The more I open my heart while integrating others into my prayer, the more I can truthfully say "my Father." The Father himself is alone with me, but he is carrying in his heart the multitude of his children. His love is so great that he excludes no one, and this is the way he comes to me in my cell. He comes with this great multitude in his heart and yet is here, alone with me, calling me to be fully present with him while I carry others in my heart too.

Humility also calls me to recognize that the only person who can really say "my Father" is Jesus, the beloved Son. Only he is worthy to pray this way in the heart intimacy deep in the Holy Trinity. Who am I to say "my Father"? But then, leading me further along this path of stripping things away and humility, the Lord Jesus invites me to say "my Father" in such a way that I say it as I say an "our Father" which includes the Son and the Holy Spirit. It's because I am confessing their presence that it does me good to say "our Father." It's then, knowing myself to be accompanied by the Son and the Holy Spirit, in the wonder of the Mystery of the Trinity, that I can say "my Father."

So which expression is more accurate, "my Father" or "our Father"? "My Father," in the way the Father longs to hear and as the Son indicated, or "our Father," in communion with heaven and earth and in communion with the Son and the Holy Spirit? I find myself asking if I will be able to avoid stumbling over this difficulty, but I don't doubt that with God's help things will be fine; the silence of my cell and the silence of God himself will lead me to discover that the silence opens onto silent prayer, and there I will be able to say just, "Father," simply, "Father." "Father" is the word passed on to us by the evangelists as most often spoken by Jesus in his prayers.[4] In this way, I can hold back from complications and stay focused on the one essential: "Father," mine for sure, but the Father of others too, as well as of the Son and the Holy Spirit, without either our communion being impeded by the personal bond or the communal invading the personal intimacy.

Father, you are blessed, you who receive me with so much love here in my cell and who also reign in the inaccessibility of heaven. You are blessed, weaving with me bonds of incomparable intimacy. You are blessed, at the same time forming the bonds of an incomparable communion with all your children, those in heaven and those on earth, those who belong to yesterday and those who belong to today. You are blessed, you, who in your grace, also receive me into the infinite mystery of love that ties you to the Son and to the Holy Spirit, unworthy though I am. You are blessed, desiring as you do that I should humbly say "my Father," without leaving aside the extraordinary beauty of saying to you "our Father." O Father, you my Father, our Father, may the Holy Spirit lead all your children into the depths of the mystery of your fatherhood, and may he enable us to enter there bowing before you in the silence of worship and of . . .

4. On two occasions Jesus says "my Father," using a vocative as he prays (Matt 26:39,42); elsewhere, he says simply, "Father" (Matt 11:25; Lk 10:21; 22:42; 23:34, 46; Jn 12:27, 28; 17:1,5,11.). When he says "Abba," there is no possessive (Mk 14:36).

6:16–24

"Your Father who sees in secret will give back[5] to you . . ."

O my soul, have you understood that Jesus is speaking to you here personally? Have you understood that he is confiding in you, indeed for the third time (6:4,6,18)? No doubt this is to make sure you have understood and that you realize the wonderful gift this is. In fact, this passage is the first time he has spoken to you about God while saying that he is "your Father."[6] What grace this is, flowing from infinite love, a love which is for you personally, a love from the Father who is in heaven and who comes to your cell to deposit in your heart that love which surpasses all other love. His coming into your poor cell is also an expression of his humility which surpasses all other humility. He doesn't come to receive anything from you since he has no need of anything you have. He comes because he loves you, as simply as that; his love has no self-interest. He comes solely to demonstrate that your prayers are not falling into the void and that he receives them deep in his heart. He receives your prayers in silence so as not to interrupt you and so that you pursue to its end everything you have to say to him. He is silent because he doesn't want to miss the least word of your prayers, the least groan or sigh. And when you have finished your praying, he will remain in your cell

---

5. The Greek here is *apodidomi*, usually translated in English as "reward," but "give back" translates the French (*rendre*) better and perhaps the Greek. [Trans.]

6. Never, other than in these few verses from the Sermon on the Mount, does Jesus say to us that God is "your Father" (6:4,6,18). He is not speaking here just to the disciples but to the whole crowd gathered around him on the mountain.

in silence to welcome your silence into his and so unite you with him in this silence of growing intimacy.

O my soul, the one who is listening to your prayer is "your Father"! Have you understood that you are his son; that he is your Father, and you his son! No one has ever revealed this in such a personal way. And the one who thus reveals this bond of love you never suspected is Jesus, his beloved Son. He is revealing to you that you are the son of the Father just as he is the Son of the Father. He is honoring you as no one has ever honored you. You are a son and no longer a servant! What a revelation! You might be a king or a prophet, but this is nothing compared to the rank of a son being granted you here; you are above even angels and archangels.

Now that you have begun to be aware of the revelation made to you, perhaps you can understand the other particular feature of Jesus' confidence, that, "Your Father who sees in secret will give back to you . . ."[7] Why is this saying incomplete? It means simply that the word that is missing doesn't exist. It is a word that doesn't belong to our human languages, a word from heaven, a word from the realm of the inexpressible. What your Father will return to you is beyond everything that you can think since what he will return he will draw from his heart, from the unfathomable depths of his heart. You know, the heart of the heavenly Father contains much more than a treasure; it is a treasure house of infinite love. It is this love that he will give you and it's not just a part of his love but all of it because when the Father gives, he gives everything. He is not like Herod, who

7. Somewhat strangely, a description is lacking of what the Father will give. This is sufficiently troubling for the some translations to try to complete the sentence, but it is better to stay with Philemon, leaving the phrase as it is.

promised to give up to half of his kingdom (Mk 6:23), but is like the father in the parable who says to his son, "All that is mine is yours" (Lk 15:31). But this word "all" is still far from the inexpressible reality. What the Father will return to you is beyond any and everything; it is his being that he gives you; it is his heart that he gives you.

O my soul, why do you give alms? Why do you pray? And why do you fast? If it's to receive something then you are the worst of mercenaries; but you are much more than a mercenary expecting his pay, you are a son, a son of the eternal Father. So don't look for pay like those who fast or give alms and pray in public places, expecting recompense from men. Don't expect payment from your Father or some other recompense because you are neither a servant nor a mercenary. A son never waits on his father for pay; whatever he does for his father is done out love and out of love alone since he does it for his father whom he loves; it's only for love. Your Father likewise has no self-interest; he simply loves you. Love doesn't negotiate, sell itself or count costs, not in terms of money or anything else. Love is beyond any form of calculation. That Jesus doesn't finish his statement is to open your heart to an infinite silence. The Son is silent now, just as the Father is, united with him in the silence; the Holy Spirit is silent too and is gazing at you in your heart to heart communion. The silence of Trinitarian love is the silence of an infinitely deep intimacy. This silence of divine love is now enveloping you and immersing you in the fathomlessness of the inexpressible. O my soul, your Father is here; he sees in secret all that your prayer is unable to say. The Son is here, imparting to your heart a secret, eternal love. The Holy Spirit is leading you into the mystery that the Son reveals and into which the Father receives you. So be silent.

6:25–34

This text is extraordinary because it is filled with the extraordinary and inexpressible humble love of God for us. It is filled with love but without using the word since love is beyond anything Matthew, I, or even Jesus can say; they can only hint at it, and my best is to try to highlight it. The noun for "love" and the verb "to love" are only found in this gospel to speak about human love and never of divine love, quite simply because divine love is beyond words. Nonetheless, this text is so filled with it that it overflows.

When Jesus tells us that our Father "feeds the birds," his expression wonderfully evokes the God whose love is so great and so humble that he cares for and provides food to every little bird. Jesus speaks here in the present tense in order to show how this daily reality has lasted from the first day of creation and will last to the end of time. If we marvel at a saint feeding the birds, how much more should we marvel on learning here that God has always fed every bird![8] And how much greater should our wonderment be

---

8. I don't know just who Philemon was thinking of when he mentions the saint who fed the birds. At any rate, it certainly wasn't Saint Francis of Assisi. Many must have done this before Philemon's time, but I am unable to name any one in particular. Saint Blaise (IVth cent.) blessed and cared for wild animals (lions, tigers, bears, wolves . . .) but birds are not reported in relation to him (*Synaxarium* for February 11). There is also Father Gerasimus (Vth cent.) and the lion, near the Jordan river and therefore closer both in space and time to Philemon (*Synaxarium* for March 4). The Synaxarium is a compilation with the sub-title "Lives of the saints of the Orthodox church," which gives a sufficient idea of its contents. There is a 6 volume French edition (*Le Synaxaire*) edited by Father Macarius from the Simonos Petra monastery on Mount Athos. The lives of the saints are set out according to the days of the years on which the memory of each is celebrated.

when Jesus adds that in the heart of our Father we are of much greater value that the birds (Lk 12:24). What indescribable humble love our Father has for us!

Jesus continues his teaching by evoking at length the same love of God for the lilies of the field and for every blade of grass that he has arrayed in splendor since time began. Jesus himself marveled at this and, as it seems to me, could find no words to express the way the same is true of us, each of us.[9]

Jesus concludes in such a way that we can perceive in him the same humble and inexpressible love for us. Indeed, it is with just the same extraordinary love that he is at pains to reassure us, freeing us from any disquietude when it comes to food and clothing. Your Father is wonderfully concerned about these matters: "So don't worry!" He states and restates this imperative, using both the present tense and the aorist[10] with an insistence overflowing with love. This too is stated with inexpressible humility, addressing us with an infinitely delicate term but without insisting on it lest it be wounding: "people of little faith."[11] His teaching here is not for Abraham, Moses or those who are great in faith, but for us, poor little chicks, so that we can grow in faith.

9. Jesus uses a verb for "dress" or "array" when it comes to plants, but there is no such description for people (v 30). Perhaps the same verb can be understood, or perhaps we are left with the inexpressible.

10. "Don't worry/don't be disquieted": three times in this passage Jesus uses the same verb in the imperative, firstly in the present (v 25) meaning that we should never worry, and then in the aorist (v 31 and 34) which emphasizes not worrying at each particular moment. The nuance of meaning in the Greek is beyond either French or English.

11. To speak of "people of little faith" as a "term" falls a long way short but it is adequate for the Greek, in which the phrase is one term, *oligopistos*.

Thus discharged of any worry about food or clothing and strengthened in our faith, what does there remain
for us to do? First, we are to open up to the idea that this
humble love of God for us is the same for all time and for
all his children. David wondered to see that God gives food
to even the young ravens (Ps 147:9), to birds that were
declared unclean by the Law (Lev 11:15). And God feeds
them! We also wonder to see him carefully making clothes
for Adam and Eve though they had brought him pain by
their disobedience and had not even repented (Gen 3:21).
Our Father, in unspeakable humility, made himself a tailor
who sewed clothes for his children! How can we not marvel
again when we see him for forty years giving the bread of
angels as food to his rebellious people (Ps 78:25)?[12]

Again, what does there remain for us to do? Just what
Jesus asks of us: to seek first the Kingdom of God and his
righteousness, which is to say to have the Kingdom of
God as our first objective, and thus have our hearts turned
unceasingly away from ourselves and to God who loves us
infinitely, loving him with all our heart, all our soul and all
our strength, as he commands us. Certainly, loving in this
way demands infinite effort, energy that is beyond anything
we are capable of, but God himself expressed the commandment in the future, making it a promise that he will accomplish in us and with us.[13] It remains for us to open our

12. "The bread of angels": in the psalm, this is a term for the
manna given to Israel as they passed through the Sinai desert. In the
Hebrew, the expression is less precise; translators hesitate between
many options, in English the main ones being "the bread of angels"
and "the bread of the mighty."

13. Philemon is referring to the way the commandment to love
God (Matt 22:37) is not expressed as an imperative ("Love the Lord
your God") but in the future (You will love the Lord your God with
all your heart . . ."), making the commandment a promise as well as
an instruction. As noted previously, Philemon developed this further
in his meditation on Mk 12:28–34.

hearts and put ourselves to work without delay, together with the Father whose joy it is to establish his Kingdom in us, with the Son whose desire is to live the Kingdom in the midst of us, and with the Holy Spirit who is already at work within us for the Kingdom. It simply remains for us to begin today and then begin again and again, just as our fathers in the faith applied themselves indefatigably to constant renewal.[14]

You are blessed, heavenly Father, you whose love for us is so humble that I am sometimes unaware of and forget about it even though each and every day you care for my food and clothing. Please make me humble enough to love you and to love all your children . . .

14. The call to continual renewal of the spiritual life is a recurrent theme with the Desert Fathers. Abba John Colobos began again "each day at dawn" (Apophthegm 349) and Abba Pior "each day" (Apophthegm 659). Abba Moses asked Abba Silvain, "Can a man start over every day?" The Elder replied, "If he is a workman, he can start over every hour" (Apophthegm 866). Abba Silvain was close here to the psalmist who said (77:10), following the Greek, "I am beginning now" (the Hebrew and our translations are very different eg "this is my infirmity"). One day, as he prayed, Abba Arsenius cried out, "O God, in your kindness, let me begin" (Apophthegm 41). As he was dying, Abba Pambo said, "I am going to God as if I had never yet begun to serve Him" (Apophthegm 769). And Abba Sisoes, at the hour of his death, "I have no sense of even having begun to repent" (Apophthegm 817).

MATTHEW 7

7:1–11

AS HE SAYS FURTHER ON IN THIS GOSPEL, JESUS IS THE SON who reveals the Father to us (11:27), and this is what he has been doing so wonderfully step by step from the beginning of his teaching on the mount. In the few verses here, he goes a step further, and we do well to pay close attention. He opens with the two verbs, "ask" and "give," the second of which is a divine passive: "Ask and it will be given you" (v 7). A little later he reuses the same verbs but now without the divine passive: "Your Father who is in heaven will give to those who ask him" (v11). He thus reveals who is hidden behind the passive, and it's not exactly "God" but "your heavenly Father." This is really wonderful, opening up to us the mystery of the divine and revealing the divine fatherhood. This revelation adds to our understanding from earlier in this teaching; we now see that God is both "our Father" to everyone, with the plural "your Father" here, as well as "our Father" to each individually as found previously (6:4,6,18),[1] and that he is also truly in heaven as much as in our cells. This is the paradox of the Father

---

[1]. Greek and French both have singular and plural forms of "you"; the only way to get this across in English would be to revert to using "thee" and "thou" for the singular. [Trans.]

who is both inaccessible and very near, the Father whose love is beyond words; this is the Father Jesus wonderfully reveals to us.

Jesus continues the revelation here by contrasting the divine Father with human fathers, qualifying human fathers as "evil"; this may seem abusive but is entirely just since the contrast enables him to reveal the divine goodness beside which all human goodness is evil. How true this is! To underline the contrast further, at the very moment we would expect to find the adjective "good" to describe the Father, Jesus doesn't use it; he leaves it as understood so that we would understand that this goodness is beyond words and truly inexpressible. He thus reveals the Father while also keeping him hidden in the secret of his inexpressible mystery; how wonderful this is.

O my soul, from now on we should understand that when Jesus uses the divine passive, he is speaking of our inexpressibly good Father who is hidden in the inaccessible depths of heaven, and who is also in our cell where too he remains inaccessible.

"Ask and it will be given you": now that we know who lies behind the divine passive, we are here invited to receive the promise Jesus is making to us, a promise that calls us to total trust in our Father because his infinite goodness will be manifest in answering our prayer. It's a wonderful promise that nevertheless runs up against the reality of life which says that our prayers are not always answered. This is a delicate point and we need fine discernment here. This reality of life ought not to make us doubt the divine goodness but instead lead us to carefully reconsider Jesus' words. He tells us that our Father will give "good things," and it is these "good things" that we need to reconsider.

If the goodness of God is beyond our understanding, this also means that what he considers to be good is beyond what we might consider to be good. Certainly, we always ask God for good things; if he doesn't give them, this would mean that the things requested are not good in his eyes. He may give them to us later when they would really be good, just as certain foods are not good for an infant but become good when the child is an adult. In fact, if something is given to a child too soon, this may turn out bad although the thing itself is good. Thus it is when particular answers are delayed. Further, God at times doesn't give what we have asked but something else which later turns out to have been better. God's discernment is infinitely more accurate than ours, and this is not something we should be upset about. It is fundamental that we must never cease to trust our Father and humbly accept that our discernment is fallible. Lastly, it may be that God doesn't meet our requests because we are not in the right state or are unworthy to receive the answer. Thus, I know I should never ask to be made higumen because I am neither worthy nor able. The Tempter may well tell me the opposite, but I know that he is not the one who will teach me good discernment! Under the Tempter's influence, my requests may be foolish; I therefore need to ask God for discernment.

O my soul, may nothing subdue my trust in the inexpressible goodness of our Father, who always gives what is good for us, the "good things" as Jesus puts it.

7:12–20

"Enter by the narrow gate": this laconic saying will leave us perplexed if we isolate it from the rest of the teaching on the mount. Just where is it that Jesus is inviting us to enter?

Is the door[2] open or closed? Why say "the" door rather than "a" door? And what door exactly? The vagueness here impels us to go back over what Jesus has already said in his teaching. Indeed, it then becomes clear: the one use of the word "enter" at the beginning of the teaching gives us to understand that we are to enter "into the Kingdom of heaven" (5:20). Furthermore, Jesus had just been saying, "Knock and it will be opened to you" (7:7), so we understand that the door was shut; the use of the divine passive also indicates that it will be opened by "our Father who is in heaven."[3] What a revelation! The one who will open the door to us is not an angel, not some mere doorman, but our Father himself . . . What joy! Our Father will be there close behind the door to hear our knocking and open to us with the infinite love that is his. But what a surprise it is also to learn that "the" door to the Kingdom of heaven, "the" door as in the only door, this door is "narrow." Jesus says no more, but while it might at first appear that God is distrustful and poor, in fact he is humble: the door to the Kingdom is not like the door of kings or emperors but is the door of a humble God. "Enter by the narrow door," Jesus tells us, dropping into our hearts these astonishing words which call us to prepare to be welcomed by our heavenly Father, who, in his inexpressible humble love, is waiting for us by the door of the Kingdom to welcome us, just as he is waiting for us and welcomes us when we go to pray in our cell (6:6).

2. Most English translations have "gate" rather than "door," but the French *porte* here is more naturally translated as "door." [Trans.]

3. From the preceding meditation, it is evident that the divine passives are understood to be enacted by "our Father who is in heaven."

Jesus tells us again that the way which leads to our Father in the Kingdom is again narrow and constricted and yet leads us to life because it is life that truly awaits us there. What more precisely is this way to which we should give ourselves without delay? Nothing is told us about this early in the teaching, though we are told to whom the teaching is addressed, which is to say, those who "follow" Jesus, both the disciples and the crowd, since they were all following Jesus. This is enough to bring light: the way of the Kingdom is the very same as the way walked by Jesus. There is nothing more for us to do than to follow Jesus; he himself leads us to the Kingdom, to life, to our Father. The way is "narrow," he states; it is not the way of ease. It is demanding, challenging, like the whole of the opening of the teaching; it is a way on which we are to master our anger and stray desires,[4] and to love our enemies; a difficult way with few following it. Saying this, on Jesus' part, is a way of preparing us for and sparing us from disappointment and discouragement when trouble comes. We must not lose Jesus from our sight as he leads us through trials and battles.

That the way of the Kingdom is a way of humility lines up with the Scriptures which never fail to set before us humility as the way; and that Jesus is the humble master who goes before us on the same path doesn't surprise us either; he himself specifies, "I am meek and humble of heart" (11;29). But what overwhelms and amazes me is to know that the one who is waiting to open the door and receive us is a Father of inexpressible humble love.

O my soul, follow Jesus all the way to our Father who is so humble and loving; this is the right way; I have no

4. The French here is *regards impudiques*, presumably referring to 5:28. [Trans.]

desire for any other and I entrust myself to him and his help through his Holy Spirit.

I give thanks that the Chief Elder[5] prepared me to open up to the humility of God when he drew my attention to the passage in the Holy Scriptures where this wonderful and astonishing humility is revealed. At the close of the period of the Judges, when the people of Israel were asking Samuel to set a king over them, Samuel was hurt because in their request he perceived that the people were slighting him, but God said to him: "It is not you that they despise but me, I who am the true King; therefore, do what they are asking of you" (1 Sam 8:6). "You see," the Elder said, "God is so humble that he renounces his own will to satisfy the will of the people who nonetheless were turning their back on him .. !"

O my Father, I am overwhelmed by this revelation of you from Jesus in his teaching; I marvel to learn that you are waiting in your Kingdom for us, to so humbly open the door. You are blessed for your beloved Son who leads us along the way of humility.

5. "The Chief Elder" was the title given by the Gaza monks to Barsanuphius. I don't know when he communicated with Philemon, who was his contemporary, but he did write the same thing to the bishop of Gaza, calling him to humility. He wrote this: "It is most useful for us to recognize that there is still within us the human nature so that we then know our limitations, where we stand with regard to this, and that it is as we humble ourselves that we receive the grace of humility. We have asked God that, in the same way he gave the Israelites a king when he saw that this was their desire, he would condescend to the desires stemming from our weakness. And indeed his kindness has stooped so low as to pull back from his own will to please us. (*Correspondence*, Letter 811). Barsanuphius lived as a recluse in a cell near the monastery. He received no visitors and communicated by letter through Abba Seridos, the higumen of the monastery. Where Philemon refers to what Barsanuphius "said" to him, this could only have been through one of his letters.

7:21-29

Here we receive the final words of Jesus' lengthy teaching spoken to us on the mount, a teaching which speaks constantly of God, essentially as Father, the Father Jesus knew he was loved by (3:17), and who we learn later, on the eve of his death, Jesus loved too; this was something he would only say to his disciples, reserved as he is (Jn 14:31). Here, this reserve holds him back since he was speaking to a crowd of people he didn't know; however, his love is so fully implicit that I receive the teaching here as a veritable song of love from Jesus in honor of his Father; what we have now is the song's final strophe.

An astonishing element of this song is that the Father celebrated by Jesus is revealed as particularly humble, which therefore sets us squarely before a great question: how could Jesus honor his humble Father, thereby bringing him to the fore, when he, who is so humble, continually wishes to keep out of sight? This requires us to listen particularly carefully. May the Holy Spirit help me to look further into the Son's song of love in honor of the Father.

Prior to Jesus, the word "Father" had never been used to designate God;[6] here Jesus uses it frequently but not to the point of excess, which would never do to celebrate a humble person. To avoid this, Jesus preserves the humility around his Father by using a large number of divine

---

6. In the Old Testament, the use of "Father" to designate God is most exceptional; to my knowledge, it is found nowhere other than in Ps 89:27, Isa 63:16 and 64:7. We might also note that it only appears five times in Mark's Gospel and sixteen times in Luke, but in the Sermon on the Mount alone "Father" is used for God seventeen times.

passives,[7] and this enables him to discreetly point to him without the naming of him which would contravene his humility. It is precisely thanks to these divine passives that he reveals to us the humble love of the Father who consoles the afflicted (5:4), who fills those who are hungry and thirsty for righteousness (5:6) and who opens the narrow door to the Kingdom (7:7);[8] and let us not forget that the humble Father does all this and feeds the birds (6:26) and forgives those who forgive (6:14).

In this final strophe, concerning the last judgment,[9] the humility of the Father is revealed again. In fact, when the time comes for the Father to take his place as judge, we suddenly find that he steps back and cedes this role to his Son. In this way, those who come to plead their cause saying, "Lord, Lord," find themselves not before the Father but before Jesus.

More, this song has the singular quality of being composed by a humble person who, like the Father, unfailingly effaces himself. We thus find that in order not to keep this love of his Father to himself alone, Jesus only once says "my Father" (7:21) and keeps restating "your Father," prioritizing us.[10] He so effaces himself as to prioritize each of us individually by telling us that God is "your (singular)

---

7. In the Sermon on the Mount, I have counted twenty six divine passives, a more discreet way of designating God and so preserving his humility.

8. "Open" here is a divine passive, so it's understood that it is God who will open.

9. Verse 22 has the phrase "on that day," which in the Old Testament already referred to the end of time, the last judgment (Isa 2:11; 10:3; 49:8 . . , as well as here in Matt 24:36; 26:29).

10. 5:16,45,48; 6:1,8,14,15,26,32; 7:11 just in the Sermon on the Mount.

Father" (6:4,6,18). "When you pray, go into your cell; your Father is there in secret": what an extraordinary revelation!

Never had anyone in the Scriptures spoken like this about personal prayer; never had anyone experienced such great intimacy with this Father who seems to leave heaven and come down humbly into our cells to be there personally with us and listen to us in magnificent humble love. Jesus humbly effaces himself to leave each of us in deep heart to heart intimacy with the Father.

In this final passage, we note again that while Jesus exercises the judgment entrusted to him by his Father, he also sets as the rule an obedience not to his will but to the will of his Father. Jesus thereby effaces himself again before his Father, always humbly, having specified that he was devoted to accomplishing the entire will of his Father (5:17): this is a humble and perfect obedience to the will of his Father which Jesus would pursue all the way to the cross (26:39 and Phil 2:8).

Lastly, this song was particularly composed for the humble and was addressed by Jesus to those who had come up the mountain, humbly following him.[11] For these people, in the last section, Jesus emphasizes obedience to the will of the Father. Those who will be honored and given entrance to the Kingdom are those who will obey the least of the commandments (5:19), who give charitably (6:3–4), who pray (6:6), who fast (6:17–18), and who do so as humbly as possible, while those who will be cast away are those who point to their prophecies, exorcisms and miracles. Prophecies, exorcisms and miracles are not, indeed, human works but the work of God through men; but to appropriate

11. Everyone on the mountain who came to listen to Jesus had set out to "follow" him: the disciples (4:20 and 22) and the crowds (4:25).

them and despoil God of his work demonstrates a vanity which shines a light on our pride and our thirst for vainglory! The humble disciple is the one who, in the strength of praying "Our Father, may your will be done" (6:10), applies himself to doing the will of the Father on earth as it is done by the angels in heaven, and who will have humbly practiced obedience with all the love that the Holy Spirit has brought to birth in him.

MATTHEW 8

8:1-4

Go ahead, brother leper, and do everything that Jesus has just told you; go and seek out Moses' prescription for your healing: two birds, cedar wood, scarlet thread and hyssop (Lev 14:4), and don't tell anyone. Go and show yourself to the priest and present your offering. Obey Jesus and Moses perfectly and your obedience will take you along the road of humility (Phil 2:8); it will purify your heart. You will then be perfectly clean, declared clean in your body by the priest who examines you, and clean in your heart, as the Holy Spirit will bring you to understand as a result of your humble obedience.

Go, brother leper, make your offering in the presence of the priest and may your offering truly be to God; it is intended for God as thanksgiving for your healing because it is he who has healed you and not the priest. The cleansing ritual will take you many days (Lev 14:8), and when these days are past, be sure to guard your heart with thanksgiving. After offering the requirements of the Law, if your heart is still occupied with thanksgiving it will call you to offer your whole being to God. Never say anything to anyone and continue to follow the teaching Jesus gave us on the mountain. Don't forget that he has also called on you to pray humbly in your room. Then, when you are cleansed and return home, go and pray in your room where your heavenly Father is to be found, and he will welcome you and receive the offering of your life.

Go and say nothing to anyone of what Jesus has done for you; don't seek to bear witness to it because others will do so in your place. Your healing took place before numerous witnesses; a whole crowd was there, and the crowd will witness for you, knowing that it was indeed Jesus who healed you. Say nothing to anyone; just pray humbly to the heavenly Father in your room and humbly offer him your life.

One day, the disciples of John the Baptist will come to question Jesus, asking him if he is really the Messiah that was to come (11:2). They will be told that the lepers are cleansed (11:5), and others than you will confirm it. John the Baptist will understand and tell his disciples that Jesus is indeed the one who was to come; he will tell them that this was confirmed both by the Holy Spirit who descended on him the day of his baptism and by the Father, who designated him as his Son. Then, in their turn, the disciples of John the Baptist will also bear witness on your behalf

On still another day, Jesus' disciples, those who were witnesses, will retell the story of your healing; they will be speaking to Matthew as he composes his gospel. Then everyone who reads his gospel will receive your healing as a witness, and you can be certain that today in my cell in Gaza, this gospel is witnessing for you; it tells me that it was surely Jesus who healed you, and this healing tells me that he is God because only God heals lepers, as witnessed to by Miriam (Num 12:10) and Naaman (2 Kgs 5). You know this yourself, you who humbly bowed prostrate before Jesus in the way we prostrate before God. Similarly, I find that, inspired by the Holy Spirit (1 Cor 12:3), you addressed Jesus as "Lord." You are blessed, brother leper, in that the one who led you to Jesus is the heavenly Father (Jn 6:44), the one who testified to Jesus on the day of his baptism, telling us that he is his Son. Go then and humbly pray to your heavenly Father in your room, and one day there will be revealed to you the work of the Holy Spirit within you, the work of the Son for you and the welcome the Father gives you in your privacy. Then say nothing to anyone because words will fail to express just how, along the road of obedience and humility, the mystery of the Holy Trinity has begun to work for you. Humbly obey everything that Jesus tells you as well as the prescriptions of Moses in the Law because it is to humble people that the Holy Trinity is revealed, perfectly humble in a humility that surpasses every other humility.

Go, brother leper, say nothing to anyone, go and present your offering to the priest for your healing and your cleansing. Your life belongs from this moment to the one who has healed you; give it to him with your whole heart and pursue your path in humble obedience to his word. The offering of your life will witness for you silently; and the Holy Spirit will add his witness, witnessing on your behalf, through the crowd, through the disciples of John the Baptist and through the disciples of Jesus, including Matthew, who, by his gospel, will witness for you throughout the earth.

Go, brother leper, say nothing to anyone. Simply offer your life to the thrice holy God and allow him to fill your heart with his infinite love; he will make your life a song of love.

8:5–13

Jesus' humility has no need of further demonstration; it comes across so magnificently and I always contemplate it with wonder; I happily do so here too as we listen to Jesus speaking to the centurion, as he says of his servant, "I will come and heal him." The verb Jesus uses here (v 7) is wonderful; *thérapeuô* means firstly "to serve" and "to tend" and only took on the meaning of "heal" in the New Testament.[1] In the Old, it never has this meaning.[2] The fact that it takes this meaning in the New is to emphasize the humility with which Jesus healed. Alongside *iaomaï* and *sôzô*, which also mean "heal,"[3] *thérapeuô* is the one term which shows Jesus working a healing humbly, as a service.

This humility did not go unnoticed by the centurion, who marveled at it and responded in turn with humility; he was humble himself, declaring himself unworthy to have Jesus come to his home. In the conversation between these two humble men, the centurion goes on to his express his wonderment at the way his soldiers obeyed him, marveling because in his eyes the authority he could exercise over them came from a superior authority to which he was himself submitted. According to him, when the soldiers obeyed him,

---

1. In the Bibles of today, translations all use the word "heal" because we don't have any choice; both French and English are less rich than Greek with its nuances to express healing. I have used "heal," but this hides the fact that in verses 8 and 13 a different verb is used in the Greek (*iaomaï*); Jesus used *thérapeuô* of himself not *iaomaï*.

2. In the Old Testament, *thérapeuô* means "to serve" (Is 54:17) or "to tend" (2 Sam 19:25), never "to heal."

3. Iaomaï does mean "to heal" in the Old Testament (Gen 20:17; Exod 15:26) as it does in the New (Matt 8:8,13; 15:28). *Sôzô* also means "to heal" in both the Old Testament (Ps 6:4) and the New (Mk 5:28).

in reality they were obeying the superior authority through him; he humbly saw himself as just a relay station for the authority. On this basis, he believed that the same was true of Jesus, so that the authority Jesus had over sickness came to him from the God who alone heals. This is why he said to Jesus, "Simply say the word and my servant will be healed": he didn't pick up on the word used humbly by Jesus, but chose a less humble synonym, *iaomaï*, but with a divine passive, meaning that it was God who would heal. We see that this man believed that God would heal the servant with Jesus as the intermediary; nevertheless, respectfully not wishing to lessen Jesus' status, the centurion consistently addressed him as "Lord" (8:6,8), in the way one addresses God. The man marveled at the mysterious bond which unites God and Jesus, a bond which no doubt was beyond his understanding but caused him, at all events, to see how the humble Jesus remained obedient to the one greater than himself, the one who gave him authority to work healings. No doubt, the centurion had heard the teaching on the mount and understood that Jesus was putting into practice what he taught; he said that the Kingdom is for those who do the will of the Father (7:21), and he calls us to pray, "Father, may your will be done" (6:10).

Jesus marveled too, marveling at the faith of this man who had been enabled to understand that his humility was linked to his obedience to the Father. Indeed, this would be precisely Jesus' experience in Gethsemane: "My Father, not what I want, but what you want" (26:39).

O my soul, the Jesus we are contemplating here is indeed the humble one who obeys his Father and does so to the utmost, as the Apostle tell us (Phil 2:8), but there is something still deeper to consider here. In his humble obedience, Jesus reveals that he is the image of his Father, who himself is humbly obedient. What an infinite mystery this is! Can God have a superior authority who he obeys? Not at all, and it would be blasphemous to say such a thing! Nevertheless, our heavenly Father is so humble that freely, in his grace, he commits out of love to obeying others, but only the humble, and in this way he lifts up the humble in accordance with his promise (Job 5:11; Matt 23:12). He does not obey the prideful, who, on the contrary, he pulls down; but he does lift the humble, obeying them in his inexpressible humility. This truth is not directly attested, but it is experienced by the humble to whom it is given; David, for example, discovered this on an occasion of which he doesn't speak, guarding it in the profound secrecy of his love for God. He stated it with infinite, wondering thankfulness, but only to God: "Your obedience has made me great" (2 Sam 22:36).[4] We will ask nothing further of David about this, a humble one who God in his grace obeyed. This experience is granted humbly by God to the humble who can then only marvel, unable to find words to express it, belonging as it does to the inexpressible mystery of the divine.

I marvel in the same way at the words of Abba Mios, a humble man who was also honored by God and never spoke of it. He has left us only the following without commentary, wonderfully nourishing my meditation and calling me to

---

4. While the Greek *upakoué* is easy to translate because it corresponds closely to "obedience," it is difficult to find a close correspondence to the Hebrew, which is why there is considerable diversity in modern Bibles. The diversity is very unusual: gentleness, help, obedience, propitious dealing, mildness, condescension ... The text from Samuel is almost identical to Psalm 18, in which the equivalent verse (v 36) doesn't use the same word but the translations are just as varied. In its translation, the Septuagint opted for *paideia* ("pedagogy") rather than *upakoué*.

unfailing obedience: "Obedience for obedience: if anyone obeys God, God obeys him" (Apophthegm 539).[5]

You are blessed, heavenly Father, for the inexpressible humility you show towards the humble . . .

8:14–17

"It is he who has taken our infirmities and was burdened with our sicknesses": this is a strange quotation which I can't find in the book of Isaiah or anywhere else in the Divine Scriptures, but in my incompetence I receive and marvel at it because it contains an incomparable treasure. I have already pointed to this text;[6] it is good, however, to return to it and pause over it at length, even though the words I use are so poor. May the Lord help me!

"It is he": this is certainly Jesus and no one else since he alone has taken our infirmities and borne our sicknesses. This doesn't mean that he became physically sick with our sicknesses since none of the gospels describes him as ill or sick. It does instead tell us that he took our sicknesses upon himself in some mysterious way, no doubt in the same way that he took upon himself our sins as the lamb that bears the sins of the world (Jn 1:29) but without becoming

---

5. This apophthegm is given twice. (There are two collections; those cited in both are considered to have heightened importance [Trans.]) Philemon cites it here as found in the alphabetic collection, but it is repeated in the systematic collection but with a modification, no doubt to obviate poor interpretations: "Obedience for obedience: if anyone obeys God, God answers him" (XIV–9). In a psalm, we find a statement very close to this saying of Abba Mios: "God will do the will of those who fear him" (Ps 145:19). The "will" is *thélèma* in Greek and *râtson* in Hebrew. We can understand that "to do the will of" is indeed "to obey," knowing also that, for their part, those who fear God do obey him (Ps 128:1).

6. See the meditation on Matt 3:13–17.

a sinner. How then were they laid on him unless by his bearing his cross? In favor of this meaning is that the two verbs in the quotation are both used of carrying a cross,[7] and more precisely, not Jesus' cross but ours, the cross Jesus calls us to carry. In fact, in Matthew's Gospel, the first use of the word "cross" comes later on and points to our cross (10:38), with the first of the two verbs used here. It is therefore clear that the cross evoked here is ours as borne by Jesus. By bearing our sicknesses with infinite compassion, he bore our cross which was laid on his. What love!

The wonderful thing here is that Matthew speaks of Jesus being charged with our sicknesses, not in the future as an announcement of the Passion, but in the past. Already, then, in healing the sick, Jesus took on our sicknesses and our cross without yet telling us this; this means that when he calls on us to carry our cross, we know that he himself carries it with us and before us! This doesn't mean that Jesus bears our cross in our place in order to remove it from us, but that he bears it with us, together with us, as a yoke which he takes on to bear as a team, with each of us. When he takes our sicknesses, it is in order to experience them with us, in perfect compassion for us, as no one else could. What a wonder this is!

Before I bear my cross, Jesus has already borne it with wonderful compassion, but when was this? It must certainly have been long centuries ago because Isaiah spoke of it, speaking not in the future in the form of a prophecy, but in the past, as a reality long established in his era, from time both immemorial and incalculable. Already in his

---

7. The first of the two verbs, *lambanô*, commonly translated as "take," is found in Matt 10:38 in the phrase "take his cross." The second is *bastazô*, translated in Lk 14:27 by "bear," in the phrase "bear his cross."

time, the prophet witnessed that his sicknesses and those of his people were being borne by Jesus. Already, as only the prophets could, Isaiah saw Jesus voluntarily weighed down with their sicknesses and ours, of his own initiative, his own will, in inexpressible, compassionate love.

Many centuries later, Matthew picked up what Isaiah had said, and we today can do the same and experience his words as a reality that spans the centuries since our first father, Adam, a reality that no doubt is actually eternal. Thus, not only did Jesus bear the sins of the world on the cross but also the world's sicknesses; as much the sins of which we are guilty as the sicknesses of which we are innocent. How wonderful!

We are given this quotation by Matthew to shed light on what he had just said of Jesus, that "he healed all the sick" (v.16). The word for "heal" used here is again the one that speaks of great humility (*thérapeuô*); he presents this healing as a service, and Jesus as a servant, the servant of God who makes himself a servant to us, humbly, by bearing our sicknesses with us. Thus, the cross of Jesus is healing for the sick, inexpressible healing which we must receive in faith as a wonderful truth. O my soul, he did this for us, to serve us and to serve God: this humble Jesus! How wonderful!

Matthew introduces the passage like this: "When evening had come," an expression which he returns to further on in his gospel to frame the whole Passion; that is, the Passion takes place between the "when evening had come," which introduces the Supper (26:20) and the "when evening had come," of Jesus' burial (27:57). He could hardly improve on this as a way to link the prophecy here with the Passion and to set it before us to feed our contemplation of the crucified one: "It is he who has taken our infirmities and who was burdened with our sicknesses" . . .

"It is he": this designation for Jesus is the most beautiful there could be; it suggests in an inexpressible way the one whose name is not to be pronounced, so far above all other names as it is . . .

8:18–27

Before going any further in my meditation of this passage, it seems important to understand why it differs from Mark's account. I am thankful on this point for the commentary lent me by Abba Ireneus, which cleared the question up beautifully. The commentary drew my attention to the fact that neither Matthew nor Mark actually experienced the storm: Mark was not in fact a disciple, and Matthew was not one yet but became one later (9:9). The two of them were therefore informed by different witnesses, which explains the differences in their accounts.

Mark's informant was Peter, his spiritual father,[8] a professional fisherman, well qualified to provide the precise details Mark reports, and a disciple of such humility as not to hide the lack of faith stated in Jesus' reproach.[9] As for Matthew, we are told by Clement of Alexandria that he was informed by Philip,[10] who could not have given such details, knowing nothing of fishing or the sea; to cap it all, Philip was still in mourning for his father, since he is

8. Mark is undoubtedly the same "Mark, my son" who Peter mentions at the end of his first letter (5:13).

9. This is certainly the biggest difference between the two accounts. According to Mark, Jesus said that the disciples didn't have faith: "Do you still not have faith?" But according to Matthew, he saw them as "men of little of faith."

10. Clement of Alexandria was certainly well informed, though, living at the end of the 2nd century, he was at something of a distance compared with the first witnesses; I don't know where he would have found the information he gives in his work.

the disciple Matthew mentions just before the account of the storm, and was humble enough to ask Matthew not to name him.[11] With this I fully understand the differences between the two accounts and can now proceed with my meditation on Matthew, appropriating it by putting myself, in a way, alongside Philip.

Philip's greater attachment to Jesus than to his own father led him to renounce important family duties concerning mourning. This attachment explains the wonderful respect he had for Jesus which meant that he didn't name him; not once in this account does Philip name Jesus — he recognized his divinity but dared not yet say anything openly for fear of being accused of blasphemy. For Philip, Jesus was God; this is why the prayer addressed to him is genuinely prayer, asking something that could only be asked of God: "Lord, save . .!"[12] This great and humble prayer in no way suggests to Jesus how he should save the disciples. "Save!" was enough; there was no point telling the Lord how to do it, he would know. Prayer like this reveals real faith in Philip's heart, even though, for Jesus, it was "little" faith.

---

11. Matthew calls him here a "disciple" since he already was one. The account of Philip's calling is found in Jn 1:43, the day after Andrew, Peter and John were called. Matthew's account here can be considered as confirmation of Philip's vocation.

12. There is another big difference in the two accounts at this point. In Mark, when the disciples spoke to Jesus, they called him simply "Master" (4:38), a term never used in the Bible for God and which could be applied to any man at all: "Does it mean nothing to you that we are perishing?" In contrast, "Lord, save!" is spoken only to God, in fact a good dozen times in the Old Testament (Ps 106:47; 118:25 . . .). It should also be noted that this request of Jesus makes explicit his own name, "the Lord saves" (1:21), and also that Philip addresses Jesus calling him "Lord" (8:21), whereas the scribe in the preceding passage calls him "master" (8:19).

Philip really believed that Jesus would save them, but we can also feel that his faith was fragile because of his grief. His spirit was still attached to his family, who would be burying his father without him. His spirit was so occupied with death that he feared for his own death in the storm, which for him, with his lack of knowledge of the sea, was beyond measure. The storm was so terrifying to him that it was like an earthquake.[13] He was even more scared because he could see Jesus sleeping! Seeing his own death approaching, Philip began to pray with his whole heart, "Lord, save!" However, everything changed when he saw Jesus rise and stand up, as he did on the Paschal morning,[14] imposing silence on the wind and the sea, revealing his perfect divinity.[15] In the great calm that followed, Philip found that the fear had disappeared from his heart. Death had been repelled and silence reigned, a majestic and inexpressible silence, the same silence as the human heart feels when prayer is answered by God, and a silence that here opens us up to contemplate Jesus in the mystery of his divinity answering his disciples' prayer . . . May he be blessed . . .

"The men marveled," Matthew concludes. Why say "the men" rather than "the disciples"? Well, it underlines that Jesus was not one of those who marveled; in his inexpressible mystery, he is more than a man: he is God, a wonder to men.

13. The word translated here as tempest or storm is in fact *séismos*, usually, an earthquake; it is never used elsewhere for a storm, which explains the difficulty translators have. They use "tempest," "storm," "commotion," "a great moving," " a great quaking" . . .

14. Here, Matthew uses the same verb égeïrô ("to be raised") as at the end of the gospel where it refers to Jesus as risen (28:6–7).

15. In Scripture, only God calms storms (Ps 107:29 . . .).

The great calm rested on the sea but also in Philip's heart. This great calm invited a deep inner silence before Jesus, the better to contemplate him, a silence which stayed until little by little the question emerged, "Who then is this . . ?"

The account opens onto silence, giving space for the Holy Spirit to pursue his work in us until he has laid down in our hearts the answer to the disciples' question, wiping away all fear they might blaspheme and strengthening our feeble faith so that it would grow to the point where we confess, "You are the Christ, the Son of the living God . . ." (16:16).

In truth, Lord Jesus, you are the Christ, the Son of the living God, you who are in the Father and in whom the Father is, in the light of the Holy Spirit. You are there, standing in the boat, radiant as in the early Paschal morning; I gaze at you and worship, you before whom our fear of death disappears like darkness before the rising sun. I pray, please fill my heart now . . .

8:28–9:1

Very little information is given us about these two demoniacs, but there is enough for us to understand the essence of the miracle Jesus did for them. They are presented to us as "difficult" (v 28)[16] without further precision, but the

16. The Greek here is *chalepos*, which does mean difficult but with a number of forms of difficulty according to the context: "difficult to effect, difficult to traverse, difficult to understand, to bear." It seems to me that Philemon was right to understand that the demoniacs were difficult to bear with, in particular their loud crying. The primary meaning of *chalepos* according to Danker is "troublesome," and to Strong as "difficult," but it is usually translated here in English as fierce or violent, terms which suggest that the demoniacs were dangerous. The same is true of the French, where, like Danker, the authoritative Bailly dictionary gives "difficult" or "hard work."

context makes clear that they were difficult to bear because of their loud cries whenever anyone dared approach them. Anyone who has heard demoniacs crying would understand that there are no words to describe it; their cries express terrible suffering that makes us suffer too in a way that is disabling. These two demoniacs were so unbearable that the people of the area did everything they could to keep away from them; in order not to hear them they no longer went that way. What exactly was their suffering? Well, it was the oppression inflicted on them by the demons. Demons inflict suffering on their victims no one can cure; here, they had led their two victims into the tombs where they experienced the pains of hell, as indescribable as hell itself is indescribable. And as no one could stand to hear them, they were abandoned by everyone.

But now Jesus was passing the way of these unhappy individuals and, seeing him, they came to meet him. The verb "came to meet" (*hupantaô*) doesn't express any aggression.[17] The demoniacs therefore came to him without any malicious intent. They began to cry out as they normally did when there was any passer-by; it wasn't threatening cries but cries of pain, hoping for a little of the succor or compassion no one had yet been able to offer them. They cried as you would cry in hell. Something that tends to confusion here is the words that are reported since they were the words not of the demoniacs but of the demons. As gentile pagans of the Decapolis,[18] the two demoniacs had no knowledge of Jesus; however, as for the demons,

17. Matthew reuses the same verb (*hupantaô*) to describe the risen Jesus "coming to meet" the women with their spices (28:9). There is no hint of aggression in the verb.

18. Gadara was in the region of the Decapolis, a gentile territory to the east of the sea of Galilee in present day Jordan.

they recognized him and knew he was the Son of God since their chief knew him and had informed them all.[19] The dialogue recorded here is therefore between Jesus and the demons, who knew themselves to be in danger in the presence of the one who had all authority to drive them out and who would punish them on the last day.[20] This is why they begged Jesus, in a sense negotiating the terms of their expulsion, themselves choosing their new victims, the pigs. In a preceding passage, Jesus had cast out the demons with a single word (8:16), and that is confirmed here when he simply says, "Go,"[21] just as he had said to Satan in the wilderness; and the demons left.

However, I am less interested in the demons than in the two unfortunate Gadarenes whose suffering was all the greater in that they had been deprived of speech, able only to cry out in their unbearable way. However, by driving out the demons, Jesus had returned speech to their victims; he had snatched them out of the grasp of their oppressors and delivered them from hell, and all that with a single word. He had heard the cries of these oppressed men, the cries of these two gentile pagans, and had saved them. What a compassion filled miracle! How wonderful!

But what was Jesus even doing in this pagan area? The account is so well constructed that we can tell because, as

19. In the account of the temptation, Satan also addresses Jesus using the term "Son of God."

20. When they say "before the time" (8:29), they are referring to the end of time when Satan and all those who are his are to be consigned to eternal "torments" (as in Rev 20:10, with the same verb for "torment," *basanizô*, as here).

21. This "go/be gone" is *hupagé*, spoken by Jesus to Satan at the close of the temptation (4:10). The same word in plural form, *hupagété*, is applied here to the demons (8:32). Other translations are possible so long as the connection with 4.10 is maintained.

soon as he arrived in the Gadarenes, Jesus saved the two afflicted men and then left; he got back in the boat and went home. This is to say that his only business there was the miracle; however, Jesus never took the initiative to go anywhere to perform a miracle but was always invited by the sick person or by his friends, so, who was it that had called him to go among the gentile pagans for this miracle? There is only one possible answer: God, his Father. He it was who charged his beloved Son with this miracle. God had heard the cries of these two unfortunates just as he had heard the cries of Israel oppressed by the Egyptians (Exod 3:7), and in his immense compassion he had sent Jesus, just as he had sent Moses, to free the oppressed. How beautiful this is! What is even more beautiful is that the cries of the demoniacs were not even prayers addressed to God but were merely cries of pain to passers-by. However, God hears the cries of the unfortunate, the cries of the oppressed, even the cries of pagans who don't pray! So Jesus, sent by the Father, crossed the sea, enduring a terrible storm and came to save them since they too, even as pagans, were children of God . . . What infinite love! Jesus was immediately driven away by people who were more attached to their pigs than to two sick men, but this matters little: for him, as for the Father, the lowliest pagan who suffers is of greater price than all the animals in the world.

You are blessed, heavenly Father, you whose heart overflows with love as does your Son's . . .

MATTHEW 9

9:2-8

"THEY BROUGHT A PARALYZED MAN TO HIM": THE OPENING of this account fits in perfectly with the structure of this gospel, even though the healing of this man has nothing particularly surprising about it. Matthew had in fact already spoken of similar healings in the same words: "They brought paralytics to him and he healed them" (4:24). Such miracles are wonderful and it can never be too soon to go over them again; they add to Jesus' renown. Nevertheless, the welcome Jesus reserves for this paralytic has a surprising aspect, something that it is really new. "Take heart," he says to him: Jesus had never previously said this because he had never before been faced with a sick man in such a state of discouragement.[1] He "saw the faith" of the man, we are told,[2] and this touches on his divinity because only God can see into men's hearts (1 Sam 16:7); but he also saw the discouragement, which no one, not Matthew, not the sick man himself,

1. Jesus will say to others "take heart" (9:22) or "take courage" (14:27; Mk 6:50; Jn 16:33) but this is indeed the first occasion. [Translator's note: the French is literally "take courage"; there are numerous English renderings; the Greek is *tharseô*.]

2. More precisely, the text says "he saw their faith," pointing to the faith of the paralyzed man and his bearers. Philemon focuses on the paralyzed man.

89

nor anyone else had mentioned because discouragement too is lodged in the heart and can hide there. Jesus saw it, just as he had seen the sick man's faith; may he be blessed. What, though, was the source of the discouragement?

"Take heart, your sins are forgiven," says Jesus. Clearly, Jesus discerned that the man was discouraged by his sins, whether because he considered them too serious to be forgiven or because he thought sins didn't lie within Jesus' competence. Indeed, at the beginning of the gospel account, Jesus' fame was as a healer (4:24) and not as someone who forgave men their sins. He called for repentance (4:17), but had granted forgiveness to no one. But now, he affirms to this paralytic that his sins were forgiven. The scribes reacted immediately, thinking he was blaspheming since it is only God who forgives; for them, if Jesus was forgiving he was taking himself for God. To this Jesus replies, "The Son of Man has authority to forgive sins." The scribes didn't insist and fell silent, but a question arises: what is the connection between the Son of Man and Jesus? It matters little what the scribes thought, but, for Matthew, as for us, it is Jesus who is the Son of Man and so there is nothing blasphemous here. To say that Jesus is the Son of Man is a discreet way of saying that he is God, having in himself the very authority of God.[3] In fact, Jesus doesn't say that he "received" authority but that he "had" authority to forgive. Clearly,

3. In the gospels, Jesus is alone in speaking of the Son of Man, initially in an imprecise way as here but then identifying the figure with himself; at 16:13, he refers to the Son of Man and then at 16:15 to "me." That is, he reveals that he is the mysterious figure who appeared to the prophet Daniel (Dan 7:13–14) in a heavenly vision, a person so closely tied to God that Daniel didn't know whether the figure was also God: the prophet just says that he was "like a son of man." By revealing himself as the Son of Man, Jesus help us understand that he is both man and God, the Son of Man and the Son of God.

he is God. Some heretics may set themselves against such a statement,[4] but here again, that matters little. What matters to me is to understand the source on which Jesus drew to grant his forgiveness. This attracts my full attention.

"My child, your sins are forgiven," says Jesus to the sick man. "My child": these words reveal the source of forgiveness. If in fact Jesus was able to forgive the man's sins it is because he had a particular relationship with him, the relationship of a father with his son; this relationship reveals a deep love, a love that is all the deeper because it is divine since Jesus is God. The source of forgiveness is here, in divine love, the merciful love that forgives and the compassionate love that restores courage to a suffering invalid; this indeed is God, merciful and compassionate (Exod 34:6). I wonder at this man saying nothing, not about his sin or his discouragement, not even his suffering; he says nothing because he had no words to express the extent of his sins, discouragement and suffering; there were no words to express the great thirst, hope and confidence that went along with the suffering; no words to express all that was buried in his heart after years and years of waiting both for healing and forgiveness; there were no words because the paralyzed man knew that only God could hear and understand all that was inexpressible in his heart that suffered and hoped within him. O my soul, the wonder here to me is that Jesus hears and understands the inexpressible in our prayers, and that he replies, "Take heart, my child, your sins are forgiven . . ."

4. Philemon was no doubt thinking of the followers of Arius, who denied Jesus' divinity. Arius, a 4th century priest in Alexandria, stated that Jesus was a being created by God and not God himself. His theology was condemned at the first Ecumenical Council convened at Nicaea in 325. The theological conflict was not completely resolved, which provoked the meeting of further councils; it continued into Philemon's time, with him clearly following the Nicaean line.

The scribes and the heretics must be silent. Jesus pours his love into this man's heart and performs the extraordinary miracle of taking away both his sins and his paralysis; he heals the man in his body and in his soul, through his whole being. He has to be God to have accomplished such a miracle; his renown as a healer is now expanded: he is God. Matthew at this point speaks of the fear[5] experienced by the witnesses, the fear born in the human heart in the presence of God when he manifests his glory.[6] I marvel at the way the witnesses are designated here with such finesse: the text doesn't speak of a crowd but of crowds, by this evocative plural suggesting both the crowd of earthly witnesses and the crowd of heavenly witnesses uniting to acclaim the Son of Man come to save people on earth, he who . . .

9:9–17

This passage is altogether exceptional because it is the only one written by a disciple to recount his own calling. This invites me to read and meditate with particular attention.

I am also touched by Matthew's humility in not telling us anything about his life before meeting Jesus, as though his life only really started with this encounter, and this is confirmed when we note that he doesn't tell us his father's name, Alphaeus, or the name he received from his parents,

5. The standard French translation uses *crainte*, "fear" in v.8, where English translations, more accurately, tend to render *thaumazô* as "marvel." [Trans.]

6. Philemon discusses the "fear of God," which is to say, respect for God, in his meditation on Matt 10:24–33.

Levi, but only the name he received from Jesus, Matthew.[7]
Thus, he considered Jesus as his father, the one who gave
him life. What a lesson this is for me! Should I now say that
my life began with my encounter with Jesus when he led me
to become a monk and then receive a new name?[8]

"Jesus saw a man," Matthew tells us; this is magnificent! If everything began for Matthew with a look from
Jesus fixed on him, this "look" is presented as the same
as that God fixed on his creatures at the beginning of the
world.[9] In fact, Matthew picks up the verb *oraô* used to
express the way God saw his new creatures each day before
he states his pleasure in their beauty. Who did Jesus see at
the tax collecting post? "A man." Not a tax collector, not
Levi, as the other evangelists say,[10] but a man (*anthrôpos*),
the word which exactly designates the man created by God
(Gen 1:26, 27). This is wonderful! Not only did Matthew
see Jesus as his father but also as God, his creator. What
a lesson again for me! This exhorts me to hold on to the
way Jesus has his eyes fixed on the depths of my heart,

7. Thanks to Mark, we know that Matthew was first called Levi
and was the son of Alphaeus (2:14). The name Matthew was given
him by Jesus in the same way Simon was given the name Peter. It is
wonderful to see that both Mark and Luke (5:27) preserve his name
as Levi, but Matthew himself only uses the name Jesus gave him.

8. This tells us that the name Philemon was given him when he
became a monk; it was the name of the first bishop of Gaza. Tradition
says that the Philemon Paul addressed in the letter we find in the New
Testament was consecrated as the bishop of Gaza by Paul himself. He
is celebrated on November 22 in the Orthodox calendar. What was
the Philemon of our text's birth name? We know nothing; perhaps he
was following Matthew's example in not telling us either the name his
parents gave him or his physical father's name.

9. In the first chapter of Genesis, the refrain to each day's work
is that "God saw that it was beautiful."

10. Mark says, "Jesus saw Levi, the son of Alphaeus" (2:14);
Luke says that Jesus saw "a tax collector named Levi" (5:27). Only
Matthew says that Jesus saw "a man."

not to see the sinner that I am but the created being, good, indeed very good,[11] as issuing from the hand of God; and he does this with the same infinite love with which the Creator contemplated his work. This is the way, with his inexpressible divine love, that Jesus looked at me when he called me to follow him and that he still sees me, the same way he carefully contemplated Matthew and, now, each of us. What could be more wonderful than this!

Yes, Matthew, like Adam and each of us, had become a sinner. This was what struck the Pharisees about him, and it was all they could see. It must have struck Matthew himself, having humbly to recognize himself as a sinner and even a friend of sinners since he presents himself here among the sinners he invited to his home. While this is so, it is evident that while Jesus saw in Matthew a sinner, he also looked at him in a way that was wonderfully full of mercy (v 13). Indeed, it was in his divine mercy that he stopped in front of the tax desk to call him. He called him to follow him in obedience to his Father, who had always said through his prophets that he wants mercy and not sacrifice (Hos 6:6). Humbly, Jesus was obeying his Father, so it was with mercy that he called Matthew the sinner to follow him. What good news this is for me! It is with his inexpressible mercy that Jesus calls me too to follow him and that he forgives my sins, just as he forgave the sins of the paralytic when he fixed his gaze on him (9:2). O my soul, what extraordinary and unfathomable mercy there is in the gaze Jesus fixes on us!

---

11. The refrain in Genesis about the goodness of the creation as contemplated by God eventuates in an important modification after the creation of the man and the woman: "God saw that it was *very* good" (1:31).

But this is not all! In his grace, Jesus came not to condemn the sinners that we are but to care for us, as he himself said when he came to Matthew's house; he had come not for the whole but for the sick, because the truth is that when our sins are oft repeated they become passions which require the care of a physician. O my soul, how happy we are to have as our physician the best there could ever be: Jesus himself!

In this wonderful account, Matthew tells us the discovery he made as he began to follow Jesus; he discovered his father, his creator, a father full of mercy as well as a physician full of infinite compassion, a God who alone is capable of being so full of mercy, compassion and love. And to what did it all tend? To lead back into life his creature who had fallen into sin. Matthew tells us this so magnificently. In fact the first thing he did on hearing Jesus' call was to "rise." "He arose," he says, with the same verb used to describe Jesus' resurrection.[12] Thus Matthew rose, in newness of life; like us, he had been seated in the valley of the shadow of death but had seen the great light of Christ (4:16) come among us to save his people, as the angel said to Joseph (1:21). Matthew knew that Jesus had come to save him; this is why, without hesitation, he answered the call. How wonderful! And what a magnificent lesson for me!

9:18–26

There is great sobriety in this text in which Matthew leads us with no detour to the heart of the matter, without

---

12. The same verb, *anistèmi*, is used for Jesus in 17:9,23; 20:19.

the abundance of details provided by Mark and by Luke.[13] This sobriety is focused on prayer because the essence of the text lies in the man bowed to the ground, not getting up until his prayer is over;[14] his face is to the ground, no doubt to hide his emotions or else in an effort to control them. What he had to say is certainly very painful and moving. He doesn't know what to call the man he is praying to; he doesn't know what title to give him, but he does pray and this is the essential thing. Everything centers on his daughter, who he lays on Jesus' heart with great confidence. He can't bring himself to say that she is "dead," because this is too hard a word to speak;[15] he risks being overcome by emotion. So he speaks in a different way, more simply, but just as clearly, without fear of being misunderstood. How difficult it is for a man who has just seen his daughter dying to control his emotions! This man believed in resurrection; he believed that his daughter would be raised, not by Jesus but by God, who would answer Jesus' prayer. His request is clear; allusive but clear: when he speaks about "laying on hands," everyone understood that this liturgical gesture would be accompanied by prayer, even though this

---

13. Not counting the verses about the woman with the issue of blood, the account concerning Jairus only takes up six verses in Matthew, compared to thirteen in Mark and eleven in Luke.

14. The Greek word for "bow down" is in the imperfect, that is, it expresses the length of time; then, the verb for "say" is a present participle, meaning that Jairus' words were spoken while prostrate and not after.

15. There are two verbs in the text that mean "to die." The more classical term, *apothenèskô*, is found on Jesus' lips ("she is not dead," v 24); the other, spoken by Jairus in v 18, *téleutaô*, is less specific and less overwhelming because it has a number of meanings: "to end," "reach a conclusion," "end up," as well as "die." The nuance here is difficult to convey in translation, and almost all say either that the girl was "dead" or had "died."

was not spoken.[16] Jesus would understand; he would pray and he is so close to God that his prayer would be heard just like Elijah's (1 Kgs 17:21) and Elisha's (2 Kgs 4:33), the two prophets whose whole beings were given over to prayer, in both word and deed.[17] Thinking of Elijah and Elisha encouraged the man: God had answered them; he would answer Jesus. The man believed this to the point of certainty. Here, then, we have this man whose prayer was the supplication of his whole prostrate body.

Jesus didn't reply; his heart was already filled with the man's prayer and so he humbly followed him home.[18] Along the way, a woman interposed herself and stopped their progress, but this didn't distract the man from his prayer; he was thinking only of his daughter, was there only for her. Jesus' words to the woman, "Take courage, my daughter, your faith has saved you," could serve only to encourage the man in his faith since he could apply them to his daughter. When they arrived at the house, Jesus' words to the crowd of mourners are magnificent. What he said suddenly reveals the great affection he felt for the child; so tenderly he says, "the little girl, the maid."[19] What a balm to the father's heart! "She is sleeping," he stated. This is

16. The laying on of hands is a liturgical act accompanied by prayer. The prayer is often made explicit, as in Matt 19:13 or Acts 6:6, but more normally it is left understood as here, in Mk 6:5; 8:23,25 and in many other places.

17. Neither Elijah nor Elisha laid on hands as they prayed; their whole bodies were involved.

18. The word for "follow" here (*akoloutheô*) puts Jesus on the same level as the disciples, as though he was taking the position of a disciple of this man who Matthew presents to us as a leader.

19. While Jairus speaks of his daughter using the most common term, *thugatèr*, "a girl," Jesus uses a more unusual term, *korasion*, "a small young girl," a diminutive of *korè*, "a young girl," which, like most diminutives, is very affectionate.

overwhelming! Had Jesus' prayer already been answered? Had God already snatched the child back from death?

Once beside the child, Jesus did not lay his hands on her! Neither did he pray! He neither said nor did any of what Elijah and Elisha had said and done! He just gently took the child by the hand to reassure her[20] and then called her to arise. And then the miracle . . . she got up! This act speaks of the almighty power of Jesus over death, which withdrew without resisting, like night before the rising sun. A great silence filled the house. God was there. The child rose and shone with the light received from the Lord Jesus.

O my soul, how good it is to be silent before the Lord and to contemplate him restoring life to a child. I am silent and allow to rise within me the impulse to meditate this miracle. What wonderment: Jesus didn't behave like Elijah or Elisha; he didn't act like a man of God, but like God himself. This is why he didn't pray: he is God! How utterly wonderful!

O my soul, how overwhelming this all is! The man had asked one thing and Jesus did another. My thoughts are running over each other: what good is there in telling God he ought to act in a certain way to answer our prayers if he fulfils them quite differently? What good is it to tell him our will when he knows better than us what he should do? O my soul, it seems that this man had given God instructions, but the instructions were useless! Could it be that

---

20. The verb for "take" (*kratéō*) followed by the genitive case of "hand" is not a liturgical but a protective action. In the same way, God took Israel by the hand as an act of reassurance: "I am the Lord your God; I am taking hold of your right hand, and I am telling you, 'Do not fear, I am coming to help you'" (Isa 41:13).

the instructions we give him in our prayers somehow upset him and then he has to answer us in a different way? Not at all! The Lord our God is too good to look down on our awkward prayers; no, his gaze is fixed with love on the depths of our hearts; he doesn't hear the instructions we give him but the faith with which we address our prayers to him and the love we have for those we are laying on his heart. This is what he hears and what he answers.

You are blessed, Lord Jesus, you who pass no judgement on our awkward prayers but receive them . . .

9:27-38 (A)

Jesus went round all the towns and villages unfailingly preaching, teaching and healing; this intense activity confronted him with the suffering of the crowds. The word "suffering" is not used here because it is a suffering of unfathomable depth, including the suffering of the body, the spirit and the soul. The issue here (v 36) is not just one of "fatigue" or being "beaten down,"[21] of a flock or harvest ready to perish without a shepherd or harvester, but of suffering seen by Jesus that is beyond any of that and inexpressible. It is the inexpressible suffering of the world . . .

Jesus was also confronted by the lack of workers who could help him in his service to the suffering crowds. Such service requires one to be like him, full of compassion, but, according to the gospels, Jesus is of such compassion that no

---

21. "The crowds were tired and beaten down." The two verbs used here are never found together anywhere else in the Bible. The first, *skullô*, ("to grow tired," "to be pained," "to be discomforted," "to be disturbed") is rather rare and points to inner fatigue; the other, *riptô*, ("to be beaten down," "to be prostrated") is a more intense, more physical tiredness.

one except God resembles him.[22] He would therefore have to teach compassion to his helpers. We now find Jesus with his disciples, who he would shortly be sending out into the harvest among the crowds, but curiously, he doesn't teach them compassion; indeed, nowhere in the Scripture is any such teaching given, not by Jesus, nor by God through the prophets. Why would this be? Well, it's because compassion can't be taught! What a mystery!

While Jesus didn't teach compassion, he did incessantly teach humility. Humble himself without equal, he was well able to do this; he taught humility by his words and his deeds. But why speak here about humility when the issue is compassion? Well, it's because truly compassionate people are first humble. Faced with the suffering of others, we are brought low because we don't know how to genuinely show compassion; a humble person has been similarly reduced, but this doesn't mean the compassion of God can't flow through them. Humility impels us to stay in the background, to be quiet and make our heart available to listen to the sufferer. A humble person thus allows the sufferer to speak out his suffering and makes space for God to deposit his compassion in his own listening heart; then, mysteriously, the compassion of God flows through

22. The term for Jesus' compassion is *spanchnizô* ("to be moved with compassion"). In the Gospels of Mark and Luke, Jesus is the only subject of this verb, so he is the only truly compassionate one (Mk 1:41; 6:34; 8:2; 9:22; Lk 7:13; 10:33; 15:20). The same applies to Matthew, except that here God is also compassionate in the same way, as in the parable which speaks of him in these terms (18:27). According to the interpretations of the Fathers, Jesus is again compassionate in the parable of the Samaritan (Lk 10:33) since he is the good Samaritan; and in the parable of the prodigal son, the compassionate father is the God (15:20). The verb is not found in John's Gospel. In the Old Testament, God's compassion is frequently mentioned, but a different, synonymous verb is used, *oikteirô* (Exod 34:6 . . .).

the humble person and brings comfort to the sufferer. This is how God conveys compassion through the humble. The proud don't know how to be compassionate, even if at times they propose that they do; such a person cannot be compassionate since they are overly self-centered; pride fills the heart and prevents it being open to another's suffering.

If this is so, how are we to learn humility? The answer is clear: through obedience and through prayer since these lead to effacement of self and so to humility. "Pray," Jesus says to the disciples here, without giving them any teaching. He simply asks them to pray and then to obey him by praying in the way he asks: "Pray, asking God to send laborers into the harvest"; pray this while, to be sure, making yourselves available to God. The issue here, then, is for us to practice obedience and prayer, but with the risk that our prayer be answered, which is to say, that we get sent by God into the harvest! And this is what will happen. In the following verses, we are told that Jesus sends out the disciples, in fact, the apostles.[23] The more humble they proved, the better would be their work. I will say no more of this here because it is the subject of the next passage; but if we don't discuss the apostles now, we will instead speak about certain others. Who? Those who were not sent but stayed beside Jesus without leaving him. Among them we find monks. In the remainder of the gospel, Jesus continues to teach the apostles, not monks. He only makes one short statement about the latter when he speaks about voluntary eunuchs (19:12), and he leaves the task of teaching them to

23. Jesus does exactly send out the disciples in the next verses (10:5), where they are presented to us now as "apostles" (10:2), meaning "sent ones." This is the first time they are named "apostles"; to this point they had been disciples, which is to say they had stayed close to their master to receive his teaching. The moment they were sent, they became apostles.

the Holy Spirit, which we then see him doing throughout the history of the Church. What I can say now is that apostles and monks are to obey and pray, and that without ceasing; without ceasing, because otherwise they will no longer be compassionate; without the bond of prayer with God, God will not extend compassion through them, and their compassion will be extinguished. In common for apostles and monks are obedience and prayer; the difference is that the apostles go out to the suffering whereas the suffering come to the monks. It is true that the suffering come to the monks; they are mysteriously drawn by them; and through them, God in his grace, mysteriously exercises compassion.

O my soul, I contemplate Jesus, the perfect one, full of compassion, perfectly obedient, praying perfectly, perfectly humble, the perfect apostle sent by God to go round the towns and villages; and the perfect monk to whom the suffering come, flowing to him and preventing him from even withdrawing into solitude to pray. May he be blessed, the true model of apostles as well as monks, teaching both groups by his life and making them workers in his harvest. O my soul, what joy and what grace for me to bear the apostles and the crowds with love in my prayers . . .

9:27-38 (B)[24]

"Pray the master of the harvest to send workers into his harvest."

Heavenly Father, today as we go through the towns and villages, we find houses filled with a spirit of humble love and those who stay faithful to you. I don't know the man

24. This is the first time that Philemon has two meditations on the same text; however, when we look a little more closely it seems that really one meditation is spread across two pages.

who stops by the monastery each month for a moment of prayer and who each evening in his home gathers his family and with them recites with great devotion the prayer your Son has taught us. I give thanks for this family and others like it who are ready for the day of the harvest.

Heavenly Father, today as we go through the towns and villages, you know that there are also many homes that have not yet heard the Gospel of our Lord, or have left it aside and gone astray; so many homes in which egoism and pride reign, gripped by the spirit of the world, where people are sick in their hearts and in their souls. In your grace, heavenly Father, please send workers into these shepherdless homes, which also belong to your flock.

Heavenly Father, today as we go through the towns and villages, we find families struck by the sickness of one of your children and yet remain faithful to you, with great confidence welcoming the trial which causes their souls to grow. The body is sick but the spirit remains attached to you with a great and humble love which makes them shine with your peace. I thank you for these families. But you also know that there are so many families in which sickness brings bitterness and rebellion to birth in their hearts. In your grace, heavenly Father, please send workers to these homes to speak into the hearts of your children to bring them under your wings, and according to your will, please heal whoever is sick in their body or their spirit.

Heavenly Father, as we go through the towns and villages, we find priests and deacons who are faithful to you, who correctly teach the Gospel of our Lord and who celebrate the Divine Liturgy[25] shining out your light and

25. "The Divine Liturgy" is the Orthodox Church's term for the Holy Supper or Eucharist.

spreading around them a spirit of humble love. I give thanks for your servants who are ready for the day of the harvest. But you also know that there are servants who bring you shame and cause you suffering by their hypocritical lives and their teachings that are full of heretical thought. In your grace, heavenly Father, please send faithful shepherds who will bring back your flock that has been scattered by such servants.

Heavenly Father, as we go through the towns and villages, we find priests and deacons who are magnificently faithful to you but can do no more because they are worn out and no longer have the strength to fulfil their ministry. In your great compassion, have pity on these suffering men and in your grace please send workers to care for your flock.

Heavenly Father, as we give ourselves over today to the monastery, we find monks and nuns who pray faithfully as Jesus calls us to, and who with great compassion ask you to send workers into your harvest. But you know too that not all are faithful to you. You know our struggles against the enemy who wishes to discourage us from unceasing prayer for your flock. In your grace, please have pity on us and cause the fire of your Holy Spirit to burn without ceasing in our hearts so that we stay attached to you in love for all your children, in compassion for your flock and in contemplation of you in your mystery.

Heavenly Father, you are blessed for your Son and the Holy Spirit who unceasingly pray beside your (Rom 8:26,34) for us all and who thus join us in a magnificent communion until the day when you yourself come to celebrate with us all the day of your harvest. You are blessed, you to whom belongs all honor and all glory along with your Son Jesus Christ and the Holy Spirit, now and throughout the ages. Amen.

MATTHEW 10

10:1–16

"Go rather to the lost sheep of the house of Israel," says Jesus to those he sends; not to the gentiles and Samaritans, people unknown and strangers to Israel, but to those closest since the disciples too belonged to the house of Israel. More precisely, he sends them to those who were close but lost, in danger, exposed to death.

As this mention of sheep is an image, it seems a good idea to pursue the image and see what the disciples are being compared to. At first, it looks as though Jesus is comparing them to shepherds, but the continuation of his instructions very quickly set me right because he specifies, "I send you forth as sheep" (v 16). What a surprise! There is no flattery of our pride by making us shepherds with great responsibilities; he sends us out as simple sheep to other sheep which are lost. This is magnificent because a lost sheep which comes across another sheep of its own flock will be quickly reassured and calmed; it will docilely follow the way back to the flock.

Our mission is genuinely important, of course, but it needs to be kept humble, always as a response to the urgency of the situation caused by the wolves: "I send you forth as sheep in the midst of wolves." If the mission is important,

105

the danger is too, both for the lost sheep and for the sheep that go out to look. This perspective of danger disquiets me, but the rest of the gospel reassures me since Jesus is himself revealed as "sent to the lost sheep of the house of Israel."[1] What a blessing. We will not be alone on this mission; Jesus will be there with us (28:20). He will know better than us how to drive off the wolf when it approaches. We can therefore give thanks for these verses that lead us to meditate on both our responsibilities towards the lost sheep and our confidence in Jesus, our true shepherd (18:12), as well as on our fear of finding ourselves alone on our mission to others and yet safe in the mysterious, reassuring presence of the shepherd. He is blessed for his presence alongside us.

But what really is a "lost sheep"? It's a sheep that's suffering because it is separated from the others. It is frightened; in need of being reassured and not judged. It needs compassion, and this is what Jesus felt when he compared the crowd of people to "worn out and beaten down sheep" (9:36). Faced with them he was "moved with compassion." This is the important word for us. When he sends us to the lost sheep, he is looking for compassion in us towards them. This is so important! A compassionate person judges no one. In the presence of lost people, he sees deeper than their failings; he sees in them children of God who are suffering from being lost.

However, compassion is not learned in books; no, it's learned by going to the school of the one true compassionate person, Jesus. May this meditation of the gospels be all the more precious to me! It helps me see how Jesus behaved with those who excited his compassion, like the leper (Mk 1:41) or the hungry crowds (Matt 15:32). But

---

1. "I was sent only to the lost sheep of the house of Israel." The same term is used here for "send" (*apostellô*) as in 10:5,16.

the best apprenticeship is undoubtedly when we ourselves benefit from the compassion of Jesus through the course of our lives. On this, Matthew's Gospel is exceptional. It is the only gospel to record these words of Jesus as he sends us out to the lost sheep, just as it is the only one to record that Jesus himself was sent to the lost sheep of Israel (15:24). I understand by this that Matthew was particularly touched by the image of the lost sheep. He knew what it was to be a lost sheep because he had been one! In fact he is alone in describing himself as still a tax collector even though he no longer was,[2] and he places tax collectors right there in the list of sinners (9:10; 11:19) such as prostitutes (21:31, 32). He knew that the day Jesus called him, he had called a lost sheep. "Follow me," Jesus had said like a shepherd speaking to a lost sheep he had long sought with all the love a shepherd can have for his sheep, and all the compassion he has for one that is lost! What joy for the lost sheep to now follow the shepherd who had come looking for it! Matthew knew deep in his heart what the compassion of Jesus is! With how much love could he now live the mission being entrusted to him: "Go, Matthew! Go to the lost sheep of my flock!" What joy for him to go and give to others what he had received from Jesus, even though his portion might be much smaller.

You are blessed, Lord Jesus, you who came to seek with your marvelous compassion the lost sheep that I am, and who now call me to act with compassion to other lost sheep. May your compassion be added to mine to lead them to our Father . . .

---

2. In the list of disciples, Matthew adds "the tax collector" after his name, though he no longer was one. In the parallel lists in Mark (3:16) and Luke (6:15), as well as in Acts (1:13), there is no such addition.

10:17-23

What a terrible passage this is, announcing as it does the great evils which are happening in our day; they are not just for the distant times of the world's end but are going on now. This is why we need to be particularly careful and watchful, and all the more because these evils will be inflicted not by strangers but by our neighbors and those closest to us: by a brother, by a child or by our own father. We will be handed over to political authorities who will condemn us to death. In order for this somber future to touch us a little less, Jesus describes it in terms which are the same as those of his own Passion.[3] Everything that he suffered will be inflicted upon us in his cause; this is our bond with him which makes us participants in his Passion. Jesus begins, then, by putting us on our guard against men, without leaving us any hope that some of them might separate from the crowd and help us. In fact, he continues with a terrible phrase that tells us that the danger will not come from just a few but from them all: "You will be hated by all." This perspective is really terrible because it leaves no room for any love; awaiting us is the hatred of everyone! A terrible solitude is set before us. Not only will we be hated by our own, by our family, but also by the Church. "Hated by all": all means all! When Jesus speaks about what we will suffer at the hands of our brother, our child or our father, he is speaking of family bonds but of also of spiritual bonds within the Church . . . O Lord, take pity on us!

3. The verb "hand over" (*paradidômi*), here in 10:17,19,21, is one of the more important verbs in the Passion and is found again concerning Jesus in 17:22; 20:18,19; 26:2,15,16,21,23,24,45,46,48; 27:3,4,18,26. The verb for "whip" (*mastigoô*), here in 10:17, is found again of Jesus at 20:19. And "condemn to death" (*thanatoô*), 10:21, is applied to Jesus again at 26:59 and 27:1.

The passage is both terrible but also magnificent because, while no good can be expected from men, we do have support, and this, our sole support, comes from God himself. Jesus talks about God here in very sober terms because it touches on the inexpressible, but he says enough to reassure and strengthen us. What he does is to speak to us about the Holy Spirit who, in the very worst moments, will come and speak for us, in our place, even "in us," as Jesus says. It is wonderful to know that the Holy Spirit will be in us! What love! No one could be closer to us than he who is in us. No man, however close, could be in us in the way the Holy Spirit will be, and that not, of course, to tip hatred all over us but to fill us with his love. Jesus doesn't actually state the word "love" here because this love is beyond measure and the word is too insufficient and poor to tell the riches of the Holy Spirit's love for us. Jesus specifies that this Spirit is the Spirit of our Father. He says nothing more about the Father because, again, this touches on the inexpressible. He says, "Your Father," and that is enough. It speaks of the inexpressible bond of love between the Father and us, and it speaks of our inexpressible divine sonship. He doesn't here say, "Your Father who is in heaven," but "the Spirit of your Father," which enables us to understand that the Father, like the Spirit, will also be in us! What love! After speaking like this about the Father and the Holy Spirit, Jesus then talks about the Son, announcing his coming, not now at the end of time but at the end of our trials, before our death: before we finish our pilgrimage on earth, "He will come." What love! This promise has the power of the presence of the Father and the Holy Spirit, an inexpressible power, because where the Father is, there the Son is. If the Father and the Spirit are in us, the Son will be too, the one who is in the Father and the Father in him

(Jn 14:10). Jesus is setting out an inexpressible love, the love of the most Holy Trinity for us! What infinite love![4]

With the perspective of such love, what does there remain for us to do? "To persevere," Jesus says.[5] This is the important word in this passage, so important that Jesus will repeat his call to perseverance in his teaching on the end times: "Whoever perseveres to the end will be saved" (24:13). This word "persevere" was so important that all the Fathers in the faith understood, received, welcomed and made every effort to live it out with infinite trust; it is one of the master words of the spiritual life. It is so important that I am always hearing it in the mouths of the venerable monks here. It's a pleasure to repeat an apophthegm with which Abba Ireneus often counsels me: "Abba Poemen said to Abba John Colobos that he had prayed to God and that his passions had been lifted away so that he no longer had any cares. He then said to an elder, 'I find myself entirely at peace and without any struggle.' The elder then said to him, 'Go and petition God for the struggle to come back to

---

4. "What love!" Philemon exclaims concerning the love of the Holy Spirit, then of the Father and then of the Son, before finally, "what infinite love," concerning the most Holy Trinity. He makes it a sort of refrain to his song. It seems to me that Philemon had run out of words; he himself says that the word "love," beyond any other, is too poor and utterly insufficient; love is inexpressible. No doubt each time he penned these words it was with infinite thanksgiving coming from the very depths of his heart.

5. Here, as in 24:13, most translators use a future simple tense for "persevere" (*upomeïnô*) when the Greek is in fact an aorist. Because of the future tense that follows it ("will be saved"), it would be better to translate with the French Jerusalem Bible by a future perfect to keep the proper concordance of time ("whoever will have stood firm"). Here, "persevere" is a participle, so to me it seems best to translate "whoever will have been persevering."

you along with the affliction and humility you had before; it is through struggles that the soul progresses.' He did then petition God and, when the struggle came, he no longer prayed for it to be taken away but said, 'Lord, give me perseverance through the struggles.'" (Apophthegm 328). How true this is! I now bless the Lord for the fruits with which he has graced me since I followed Abba Ireneus' counsel and took this apophthegm for my own. I cannot also . . .

10:24–33

"Rather, fear him who is able to destroy both soul and body in Gehenna."

Heavenly Father, it is you of whom Jesus is speaking here; it is you whom he calls us to fear, you who can destroy both our body and our soul in Gehenna. I now turn to you in my prayers after reading, rereading and meditating the psalms, in order to meditate these words of your Son and gain a better understanding; at first they hit me hard, filling me with fright at the thought you could destroy my soul and body in the house of the dead. I trembled as I opened the Psalter, petitioning the Holy Spirit to bring me light in my meditation, immersing myself in the Psalms, to discover everything they say about you and your attitude towards those who fear you.

Heavenly Father, this meditative reading did me so much good, reassuring me and filling me with joy. In fact, I couldn't find a single verse in the Psalms that told me you lack love for those who fear you, and I believe that if I read the rest of the Divine Scriptures, I would surely reach the same conclusion: your love for those who fear you is infinite. You are blessed.

As I read, meditated and prayed the Psalms, my fright slowly melted away, like wax near a fire, mysteriously turning into a peaceful fear that is open to your blessing, as stated expressly in one verse" "The Lord has blessed those who fear him" (115:13).[6] How good it is to find that your blessing here is more than a desire but is a statement of fact; you really do bless such people! Better still, this goodness is presented as a beatitude: "Happy are those who fear the Lord and walk in his ways" (128:1). What a relief to read that for those who fear you, you are full of fatherly compassion: "As a father has compassion on his son, the Lord has compassion on those who fear him" (103:13), and that you also have mercy on them eternally, as we find in the same psalm: "The mercy of the Lord towards those that fear him extends from eternity to eternity" (103:17). Father, this reading has filled me with peace and strengthened my love for you. How good it is to read and to meditate on the verse that says "the Lord has pleasure in those who fear him" (147:11), and then to understand that the Holy Spirit addresses the following prayer to you: "As for me, I am the companion of all those who fear you" (119:63).[7] How much encouragement I have received thanks to

6. In the Septuagint of Ps 115:13, "bless" is in a past tense whereas in the Hebrew, it is future.

7. "As for me, I am the companion of all those who fear you," is from the lengthy psalm 119. Who would this companion (*métochos*) of all be? In an apophthegm, we read the following: "One of the Fathers said to Abba Poemen, 'Who is it that says I am the companion of all those who fear you?' The elder replied, 'It is the Holy Spirit'" (Apophthegm 710). Abba Poemen, himself enlightened by the Holy Spirit, had noted the word "all"; no mere man could be the companion of "all" others. Only the Holy Spirit is capable of this. Abba Poemen was doubtless relying on a verse in Hebrews which says something similar: "Those who have received light and have tasted the heavenly gift are become companions (*métochos*) of the Holy Spirit . . ." (6:4).

meditating the psalms and the wonderful closeness of the Holy Spirit in prayer; he has slowly opened my heart with great gentleness and enabled me to understand quite differently the words of your Son in this gospel text: "Fear him who is able to destroy both soul and body in Gehenna."

My Father, I understand now that your Son didn't say this to produce fright in us, but as a call to fear you since this fear brings to birth in us the repentance that leads us to you. It is the Evil One who brings fright to birth so that we would flee you and hide ourselves from your sight; this is just the way he sowed fear into the hearts of Adam and Eve (Gen 3:10). Those who hold you in reverential fear are not frightened of you; they know how much you love them and how great your mercy is towards them. These who fear you rightly but have hurt or offended you have only one desire, to seek your forgiveness, since the Holy Spirit is their companion and lives in them to accompany them along the way or repentance.

And now, Father, as I listen to your Son and with the help of the Holy Spirit, I come to ask forgiveness for all the times I have hurt or offended you, in whatever way.

O my Father, it is with tremendous gladness that I now hear the Holy Spirit speak to me, through David,[8] about you with this promise which completely sets me at ease: "He will do the will of those who fear him; he will answer their prayers and save them (145:19).[9] My Father, God of mercy and compassion (Exod 34:6), please, in your infinite tenderness, receive my repentance and grant me the grace

8. Philemon was aware, as this shows, of David saying, "The Holy Spirit has spoken through me" (2 Sam 23:2).

9. In this psalm (145:19), the Greek speaks of "prayer" where the Hebrew says "cry"; no doubt this should be understood as a cry of prayer.

of your forgiveness, and teach me to forgive all others, keeping me close to you with your Son and the Holy Spirit, today and throughout the ages. Amen

10:34–42

"Whoever loves his father or his mother more than me is not worthy of me." These words were not spoken to the crowd but only to the disciples (cf. 10:1ff); they are not spoken in the plural form but in the singular, the "whoever" is "that person who," and are for each disciple to receive into his heart, to examine himself and his love for Jesus.

Jesus spoke these words at a particular moment, not when he called the disciples on the sea shore or from beside the tax collector's desk, but later, when the disciples had already been with him a good time. He said this when he was sending them out on mission, which supposes that they had already acquired a certain amount of experience (10:1,5). As he sent them, Jesus was confirming that they were indeed his disciples, that he was placing his trust in them and that he loved them; and he was inviting them to see if, for their part, the trust and love were reciprocated. This is important because once they had left, they would find they were on their own without him alongside them, on a difficult mission, exposed to wolves (10:16) and hatred (10:22). In such difficulties, without him, they would be exposed to the Tempter who would weaken them with questions about their love for Jesus. It is the same for each of us: it is easy to love Jesus when he is there, but when he is not, when we don't feel his presence, it is more difficult because the Evil One sidles up and tells us, "He isn't there anymore; he has abandoned you; you don't love him enough; you are unworthy of him . . ." Love for our family then rekindles in our heart and we are tempted to go back to them. Therefore, it's prior to such a trial that Jesus calls us to consider carefully: "He who loves his father or his mother more than me is not worthy of me." Before sending us out, Jesus broaches another important topic, one he had never mentioned before and which the disciples had not discussed, not among themselves or with Jesus: each person's individual cross! In fact, each disciple already carries his or her own cross, though we do so secretly because it is difficult to talk about, even to Jesus. This cross is made up of secret thoughts tied to the love of money, pleasure, glory or some other attraction . . . Each disciple bears, often from well in the past, their own cross, and, according to Jesus, it turns out to be ever present; it has not disappeared. Each disciple was still carrying it, in secret, and no doubt with a certain sense of shame, not daring to confess it. However each one was now to set out with their cross on a mission; and here was Jesus talking about it! What a relief! And what grace![10]

What grace it indeed is to hear Jesus speak to us about our cross, and for him to speak about it as a present reality and not as a distant memory. He was so right to speak about this before the disciples found themselves on their own, without him, with their cross always on their shoulders; once alone, they would meet that most difficult moment, the moment of truth and temptation when the Evil One draws near and speaks of their cross in a tone of reproach: "What are you doing there with your cross? Are you still carrying it? Hasn't Jesus set you free from it? Your cross makes you unworthy of him, unworthy to follow him! The others don't have such a thing and are more worthy than

10. The word "cross" does not appear again in this gospel. It is not a matter for discussion, not even Jesus' cross.

you; they are following him in purity of heart. You are unworthy of Jesus. Go back to your people, who doubtless love you more than he does; go back to those who love you and who you love . . ."

This moment of temptation is wonderfully anticipated by Jesus here. What grace! He talks about our cross before Satan does, and he talks about it quite differently: "You are carrying your cross, I know, and I have chosen you just as you are; I love you as you are, with your cross. Keep going as you are, carrying your cross. Go out on mission, even though you are still carrying it; it doesn't make you unworthy of me, but it does make you more humble, and that is very important. Your cross will be a great school of humility for you and will always make you more humble; and the humbler you are, the more worthy you are of me, worthy of the mission I am entrusting you with . . . Your cross will also be a great school of prayer for you because you will be opening up to me, always, talking to me about the passions that make it up and which crucify you . . ."

So, it is in the context of being sent on mission that Jesus speaks to us in this way, helping us to truthfully check on our heart, with our cross on our shoulders. What Jesus has not said yet, because the moment to do so had not yet come, the great secret that he will open to us, is that he will help us bear our cross, that he will help out of love for us as no family member ever could. He will help us bear it until the day when he will take the full load, but this is later because the way of humility and prayer is still lengthy; later, because it is with him alongside, beneath our cross, that we will always be discovering more of how he helps us and loves us, and how our love for him is strengthened . . . May he be blessed!

MATTHEW 11

11:1–15

"ARE YOU THE ONE THAT SHOULD COME?" JOHN THE Baptist had already received the answer to this question the day of Jesus' baptism when he saw the Holy Spirit descend upon him and heard the Father say to Jesus that he was his beloved son, which is to say, the one that should come. From that day, the Baptist had never stopped going over in heart this dazzling revelation: it was him, Jesus, who was the one that should come, the Son of God! And now that he was in prison, he continued to hear at all times in his heart the witness of heaven and to think of the Spirit who settled like a dove on Jesus. Nonetheless, as he felt his death draw close, it seemed a good idea to send his disciples to Jesus so that they too could receive a testimony that would reveal who Jesus was, that they too might be touched and convinced by what they would see and hear for themselves. This is why he sent them to ask Jesus the central, vital question and receive from him the confirmation that he truly was the one that should come; this was now their moment to ask, "Are you the one that should come?"

Jesus reply is wonderful, as wonderful as his silence the day he was baptized, when his silence was so humble that the heavens opened (3:16). At this moment, his reply to John's disciples was full of the same humility, a humility that is more than human. "Are you . . .": this question was asked in such a way as to expect an answer beginning with "I am." It's marvelous! The question invited Jesus to say "I am," the "I am" that belongs to God alone.[1] I marvel to see that in having them ask this question, John the Baptist was "preparing the way of the Lord" (3:3) in his disciples' hearts for them to receive the "I am" which would reveal Jesus' divinity to them. But Jesus didn't say it! No doubt he discerned that it was not the moment to reveal this mystery to disciples who were not yet ready to receive it. Jesus responded in a different way, but always with extreme humility. He didn't say, "I am," or, "I did this and that: I restored sight to the blind, I made the lame walk, I cleansed the lepers, I gave hearing to the deaf, I raised the dead and announced good news to the poor." No, there is none of that! He recounts the same miracles but says nothing of himself, not pointing to himself, and without even suggesting that the miracles were performed by him . . . Jesus' response is most surprising; asked about himself he doesn't mention himself, as though he didn't wish to be seen as having anything to do with it; he didn't wish

---

1. The first words of the question "are you" (*su ei*) have the same redundancy as God's "I am" to Moses at the burning bush (*ego eïmi*). In the Judaism of Jesus' time, to say "I am" was considered blasphemy. For John the Baptist, however, for Jesus to say these words was not a blasphemy but him revealing himself as God. Before the Sanhedrin, the chief priest would ask Jesus a similar question starting with the same words, "Are you" (*su eï*, Mk 14:61). Jesus replied very clearly, "I am." This reply was right in line with the divine revelation at the burning bush, so much so that the chief priest reacted immediately by denouncing it at as blasphemy. "I am" was therefore a revelation of Jesus' divinity, a revelation the chief priest could not cope with. With John the Baptist's disciples, Jesus guarded against any possibility of causing them trouble.

to be the occasion of anyone stumbling or falling. This, then, was his response, one of perfect humility. Jesus didn't even mention himself when asked about himself, and I now understand why he repulses those who speak about themselves saying, "Lord, we have prophesied in your name, we have driven out demons in your name, we have performed numerous miracles in your name." "I never knew you; get away from me," he replies faced with their lack of humility (7:22–23). His extreme humility is the most beautiful of responses. This alone reveals that he was indeed the one that should come. Jesus didn't tell John's disciples who he was any more than he had the day of his baptism when he left it to his Father to speak from heaven; now he humbly left the word to the blind, the lame, the lepers and the poor; it was for them to tell John's disciples who Jesus was when they asked.

John's disciples then returned to pass on to their master what they had seen and heard. Hearing them witness to the extreme humility of Jesus, John the Baptist would have rejoiced to find that Jesus was as he had known him to be, as indeed the one that should come. He would then have been able to say that this extreme humility was enough to reveal Jesus as the one who had to come, and then tell them the story of Jesus' baptism; he would have told them that he was touched by this humility when he saw Jesus bow before him to be baptized, that he had seen this humility in his eyes, in his attitude, in the way he went down into the water and then walk back out; he would have said that he had never seen such great humility and that Jesus was humble like his Father and the Holy Spirit; and that even in the depths of the prison, he never ceased to wonder in contemplation of the inexpressible humility of the Father, the Son and the Holy Spirit.

After hearing this from their master, John's disciples would not feel they were left as orphans after his death; they could turn to the one whose way they had prepared, who would receive them with inexpressible humility.

11:16–24

Heavenly Father, from his youth you led John into the desert (Lk 1:80), and there you prepared a way in his heart to make him your prophet. He espoused the silence of the desert in order to listen to you and receive instruction. He opened his heart to you and you opened yours to him. In the secret of the desert, in the gentle breeze,[2] you spoke to him of the inexpressible, of the wound to you caused by our offences, and his heart was crushed and humbled.[3] You taught him the way of repentance and the unfathomable depths of your mercy, and in this way he was prepared to preach among us.

Then he arose to leave the desert and come where we are, crying out a lamentation that was full of his love for you and your mercy towards us; but none of us beat our breast or lamented, none of us shed tears of repentance, and we thought he had a demon. Faced with the hardness of our hearts, he returned to the desert and wept before you.

Father, your beloved Son also came to where we are, his heart overflowing with love for us. He had a flute

2. Philemon here picks up on the "gentle breeze" which was a sign to Elijah of God's presence (1 Kgs 19:12); this enables him to bring Elijah and John the Baptist together, in the same way that Jesus did (Matt 11:14).

3. "Crushed and humbled": here Philemon uses an expression from the Septuagint (Ps 51:19) to convey John the Baptist's repentance; Psalm 51 accompanies repentance. In Hebrew, the two words are slightly different: "broken and crushed."

and began to play. His music reverberated around us and revealed to us that you are our Father, not our judge, a Father whose love is so strong and luminous that no one can keep their heart closed in your presence and no one can hide their faults or hold back their tears of repentance. The song of his flute also announced that you have come still closer in order to draw near and wipe away our tears. His music became even more joyful, inviting us to dance in celebration of your pardon; but not one among us wanted to listen, no one wanted to share his joy and our hearts stayed shut in the presence of one we considered with disdain to be a glutton.

He laid down his flute and began to do miracles before us to touch our hearts. He opened the eyes of the blind so they would be ready to contemplate you on the day you come. He opened the ears of the deaf so they would be ready to hear the song of grace on the day you come. He cleansed the lepers so they would have turtle doves to offer you when you come (Lev 14:2–4). He spoke to the heart of the poor so they would be ready to dance before you when you come. But no one was touched by the signs of his grace; then, he fixed his gaze on Chorazin, Bethsaida and Capernaum and sat down to weep over your sorrow at their permanently closed hearts.

My Father, with my heart crushed and humbled, I quietly slipped away to withdraw into my cell and weep with repentance; I shut and locked my door and found myself immediately in your presence (6:6)! You had gone before me and were waiting. Then I fell to my knees; your heart is now open in silence before me and I open mine to you.

121

My Father, in your infinite wisdom,[4] you give us a time for everything, a time to mourn and a time to dance, but in our foolishness we don't know how to discern the times you give us to experience with you when you in your love want to enjoy them with us. When John the Baptist called us to repent, you were there to receive our tears and to wipe them away with the tenderness of your forgiveness, but we neglected this chance. When your Son invited us to dance, you were there for us to dance in your honor as David danced before you (2 Sam 6:16), but we neglected this opportunity too. You give us a time for everything, and each of these times is a time of your grace, but we neglect them and wound you by living out of all rhythm with you.

My Father, you are giving us now a time to weep (Eccl 3:4) and I welcome it with thanksgiving as I shed the tears of my repentance before you. In your mercy, please forgive us; and may the time come too when you enable us to enjoy with you the happy laughter of your grace when you cause us to enter into your eternal joy. I pray this of you, our Lord and our God to whom be all honor and glory with your Son and the Holy Spirit, now and throughout the ages. Amen.

11:25–30

The image of the yoke as Jesus uses it here is truly magnificent. In the Holy Scriptures, yes, it's always an image

---

4. Philemon notes that Jesus concluded this passage by talking about wisdom (11:19) and that he also referred to the contrast between "lament" and "dance" from the book of Ecclesiastes (3:4), which is considered a wisdom book. This is noteworthy because, while in this book the presence of God is not easily discerned, Philemon nicely emphasizes it in his meditation; he transforms "There is a time for everything" (Eccl 3:1) into "Father, you give us a time for everything."

of obedience, but at times even an image of a slave's forced obedience to a tyrant;[5] here, though, there is nothing of that aspect. Jesus makes it an image of the obedience to which he calls us with his own special gentleness: "Come to me . . . I am meek," he says. It belongs to each of us to respond to him in complete freedom and draw near to him without fear.

Obedience is a great school of humility. Here, Jesus is proposing that we learn humility with him; he is already perfectly humble to the fullest depth of his heart. We will certainly never find a better teacher than him; we have only to respond to his invitation.

The image of the yoke particularly suggests being joined to another in a way normally meant for, indeed, a pair. Jesus doesn't actually say with whom we will be yoked, but curiously he does speak about "my" yoke, which, very discreetly, gives us to understand that it is a yoke to which he is already bound. His invitation then becomes more precise: he proposes to each of us to join him and be yoked together with him! What generosity! He who is humble of heart is so humble as to put himself under the yoke together with me so that we will bear it together. What a wonderful example of humility!

5. The yoke is an image of obedience in submission to the yoke of Assyria (Isa 14:25) or, indeed, Babylon (27:12). Elsewhere, it is also a positive image of filial obedience: "It is good for a man to bear the yoke in his youth" (Lam 3:27).

The invitation is issued to all who are tired and worn down beneath their burden.[6] What love! Beneath the yoke he proposes to bear our burden with us; in compassion for us, he comes to lighten it by making it his, to the extent even of saying that our burden is henceforth his: "my burden," he says! What magnificent love, so full of compassion for us!

If the yoke is a school of obedience, who is it we are to obey? Not Jesus, who also obeys with us under the same yoke; so who then? Jesus doesn't say, and his silence leaves a sense of silence in the presence of the inexpressible divine. Who is that Jesus obeys? The master of the team, who yokes us together with him and guides us: his Father, for sure! What a surprise! Jesus is comparing his Father, albeit discreetly, to a farmer working with his beasts! A farmer's love for his animals is well known, but is nothing compared to the love of the Father for his beloved Son and for whoever who sets himself to humbly obey him beneath the yoke alongside the humble Jesus. What an extraordinary image, revealing the Father full of wonderful love for us and humble to the point of being compared with a simple peasant farmer. How marvelous!

Before giving us this image of the yoke, Jesus tells us, "No one knows the Father except the Son!" Who could have chosen such an image except the Son, and he adds with joy: "What I am saying here of the Father is hidden

---

6. "Tired and worn down," says Jesus. *Phortizô* ("worn down") is difficult to translate. It derives from the noun *phortion* ("burden") used by Jesus, so "to be worn down" means more precisely "to be worn down by a burden." The TOB French translation says the equivalent of "to suffer beneath the weight of a burden," which is very good. The term "burden" (*photion*) is found in a verse which shows sins as a real burden (Ps 38:5). It is good to know that Jesus comes to bear with us the burden of our sins.

from the wise and the learned, who are in great danger of not accepting such an astonishing God!" But the little ones rejoice with Jesus since, for them, there is nothing incongruous about this incredible image. Assuredly, the little ones will rejoice to contemplate this wonderful rural scene of gentleness and peace in which a simple farmer drives his team with inexpressible and humble love.

In the rest of the gospel, God is so far beyond words that he is merely suggested in the simple mention of inaccessible and indescribable terms such as a "voice coming from heaven" (3:17). Here, however, he is evoked as being very close, silently driving a team of oxen in which his beloved Son teaches us meekness and humility of heart in the concrete reality of obedience. How good it is to respond to the invitation given us so generously by Jesus. But before responding, it is good to take our time contemplating this image in which everything is meekness and humility of heart so that we will then allow ourselves to be led in silent obedience, listening to this teaching which brings a thirst to grow in this meekness and humility.

You are blessed, heavenly Father, you who also teach me with the same gentleness and humility of heart as your beloved Son, and who lead me in a life in your service. In your grace, please send your Holy Spirit so that, with the gentleness and humility of a dove, he may settle on me and fashion me into your image and the image of your Son. You are blessed for lightening our loads by placing us beside your Son, who bears them with us beneath the yoke of your love. You are blessed, you who gently remember our tiredness and cause it to disappear by your simple presence with us. You are blessed for your silence into which you cause us to enter, welcoming us alongside your beloved Son.

MATTHEW 12

12:1-8

JESUS DID NOT SAY, "THERE IS SOMEONE HERE WHO IS greater than the temple," but, "There is something greater." If he had said "someone," we would have understood that he was speaking of himself because he is indeed greater than the temple. However, he said, "something." What was this? Well, it's what he talks about next, "mercy."[1] He is not thinking here of the infinite mercy of God, who is incomparably greater that the temple, greater even than the heavens (Ps 108:5), but of the mercy God desires, which is to say, ours: "I desire mercy and not sacrifice," says God (Hos 6:6). This is what is greater than the temple in Jesus' eyes: our mercy. It's also the subject of my meditation today.

Human mercy, even the greatest, seems to me of less account than the Jerusalem temple, majestic and venerable as it was. That's in my eyes, but to Jesus things are different:

---

1. Here, "greater" is neuter (*meïzon*) rather than masculine or feminine (*meïzôn*), meaning that Jesus did not have a person in mind. In the continuation, "mercy" (*to* éléos) is also neuter, so clearly it is mercy that is greater than the temple. In classical Greek, "mercy" is masculine (*o* éléos), while in biblical Greek it is nearly always neuter, as is clearly the case here, where éléos is the verb complement and is accusative; it would be éléon if it was masculine as in Ps 4:1 and Hos 12:6. Unfortunately, many translations say or imply "someone" rather than "something," which seriously affects any interpretation.

according to him, human mercy is greater than the temple, which means that in his eyes, a person who spreads mercy around is much greater, more majestic and more venerable that the temple and all its sacrifices.

Nevertheless, all the sacrifices offered to God in the temple were a sweet smell that gave joy to God's heart (Exod 29:18, 25 . . .). True, no doubt, but surprising as it might seem, God prefers the fragrance of mercy to sacrifices because sacrifices are offered to him and him alone, while mercy is offered to others, above all to those who are suffering from having hurt a brother and who thirst for forgiveness and mercy; it also applies to those who fear the condemnation of others and so thirst for their kindness and mercy. Mercy is not vengeful and never speaks ill of anyone; it forgives and does not condemn. God does not want sacrifices when he knows that someone is suffering and longs for mercy. He prefers that we grant our mercy to others rather than offer him sacrifice. Jesus himself told us on the mount, "If you bring an offering to the altar and remember that your brother has something against you, leave your offering at the altar and go first to reconcile with your brother" (5:24). God prefers brothers reconciled and at peace to any and every sacrifice! How beautiful!

God's desire here overwhelms me because it shows the extent of his humility. He prefers to renounce our offerings, even those we bring with all our love; he prefers that we offer others a word of mercy, an act of mercy or simply a look of mercy because mercy is an offering of love for a brother who longs to be forgiven and lifted up, or else fears being condemned or repulsed in his quest for pardon. This humble God, in his wonderful discretion, steps back into the shadows to honor his children who draw close to each other on the way of mercy and become reconciled.

In the Holy Scriptures, there is no law and no prohibition concerning mercy. Mercy is beyond prohibition or permission. It flows from a loving heart in the way a spring flows from the heart of the earth. Springs flow even on Sabbath days; there is no law against them. They flow without counting the cost, day and night, freely, without looking for anything in return, without any instruction being given them, because their joy is to offer their water to the thirsty.

However, a heart which grants forgiveness without love is a heart with bitter waters from which the thirsty separate themselves. Happy is the person who forgives with love because the sweetness of their water brings joy to all. God himself is pleased to see a merciful heart whose water is truly sweet. It is enough for him to see such a thing for him to marvel; when he does, he draws near to this heart to contemplate with inexpressible blessing each drop of mercy offered in the gentle murmur of its flow. In his joy he comes to take up residence in such a heart with more joy than in the Jerusalem temple.

O my soul, the Jerusalem temple is now destroyed. The smell of sacrifices no longer rises towards God, but you know what he desires and what pleases him. If our mercy has no sweetness of love, may the Lord do us the grace of sweetening and purifying the water from our fountain! Then we can offer him our heart for him as a dwelling place.

Heavenly Father, you who are merciful and compassionate (Exod 34:6), the temple is no longer there, but the cross of your Son is always standing and will remain until the end of time; from the cross there flowed a spring of perfect sweetness when your Son forgave us and turned to you . . .

12:9–21

Here we are in Jesus' presence at a most important moment of his life. He has just learned that the Pharisees had met in counsel to decide how they would cause him to perish. The news was shocking because from this moment the profile of the cross was there on the horizon.[2] He had always known that he had come to earth to offer his life, but now the project to take his life had germinated in the hearts of certain men. He was no longer the only one to have the end of his life in view; others were thinking of it too, though in a different way: he saw himself as an offering made to humanity, they as just the victim of a plot hatched by men. He then looked to withdraw, wishing to distance himself from people to be alone, but he was unable to manage this since the crowds followed him; he served them by healing the sick, and then instructed them to be silent and say nothing about him. In the silence, he was then able to withdraw.

I don't know now how to talk about this retreat because it is very surprising. Jesus withdrew, but not to some habitual place; he withdrew, as it seems to me, into the Divine Scriptures![3] He immersed himself in the writ-

2. "The horizon": the idea is so good because beyond the horizon is the unseen, but we know it is not a void. This is the nature of the cross because beyond the horizon of death is the unseen, not a void but rather the inexpressible fact of the resurrection.

3. The verb for "withdraw" (*anachôréô*) used here is one Philemon would have been sensitive to; it is much used in the monastic literature, giving rise to our word "anchorite" (*anachôrètès*); it became prominent in Athanasius' Life of Anthony: "Everyone proclaims as blessed those who withdraw from this life" (87:1). Philemon, who withdrew every day to meditate the Scriptures would have noted the profound anachoresis of Jesus, who withdrew into the Divine Scriptures.

ings of the Holy Spirit, listened to the Father, and so with-drew into an inexpressible heart to heart with the Father and the Holy Spirit. Just as the Pharisees had held a council, now the Trinity was in council. This is the amazing retreat Jesus experienced: as he meditated a prophecy given by the Holy Spirit to Isaiah, he listened to the words of his Father; this is precisely what he was looking for when he retired from being among people, to hear his Father in order to be strengthened, encouraged, blessed before going through what men were going to inflict on him.

All the Father's love is revealed here in the inexpressible depths that human words, even those of a divinely inspired prophet, can only hint at. It is, however, a wonderful privilege that we can, if only a little, enter into the great Trinitarian council.

"This is my Son . . ." (Is 42:1–4): here, the Father is not speaking directly to his Son in the second person but to the Holy Spirit, using the third person. What wonderful delicacy at the heart of Trinitarian love! The Father speaks about the Son to the Holy Spirit, but with a different word to the one used at his baptism. "My Son," (*uios*), he had said then (3:17), but here it is "my Son," (*païs*).[4] To speak of this sonship in two different terms leads us to understand the divine sonship as beyond simple words, in the inexpressible reality that no human person can grasp at saying. Further, by saying "my Son" using *païs*, the Father

---

4. *Uios* was the official term for a son, the one we would find in a genealogy: thus, Isaac was the son of Abraham. *Païs* also means "son," but more humbly, including the idea of service to the father. In fact, the word came to take on the sense of "servant," which explains why many, indeed most, translations use that term here.

is applying to Jesus the great prophecy which begins with the same word and describes his way of suffering.[5]

The Father then designates the Son by an adjective that is reserved in the gospels for Jesus, "beloved" (*agapétos*).[6] With this word, the Father once again states the fullness of the love he has for his Son, and to underline its depth and strength he uses the adjective as a noun, "*the* beloved" and adds to this a possessive, "*my* beloved."[7] The Father had never spoken like this before . . .

"My beloved, who my soul loves," the Father specifies, using a phrase that completes what he said at the baptism: "He in whom I find affection." These two phrases wonderfully state the reciprocal affection: "He who my soul has affection for and in whom I find affection . . ."[8] This mutual love joins up with what Jesus himself says about his bond with his Father: "He in me and I in him" (Jn 14:10).

From its first words overflowing with love, this statement by the Father reveals to me a love so deep it is infinitely

5. The reference is to the great text known today as the "Song of the suffering servant." This begins with, "Behold my servant" (*pais*, Isa 52:13) and continues through chapter 53. *Païs* translates the Hebrew ('ébèd), correctly because both mean "servant." In the Greek, though, we can hear the two meanings, God saying both, "this is my servant" and "this is my Son."

6. The word spoken by the Father at the Baptism and the Transfiguration as an adjective complementing the noun Son (*uios*): "beloved Son." Here, though, the adjective becomes a substantive, "the beloved."

7. Literally, "the beloved of mine."

8. The verb here is *eudokéô*, which means "to judge as good," "to approve," "to be satisfied," "to be pleased with," "to have affection for," according to the construction. Here, in 12:18, "to have affection for" is followed by the accusative, expressing the affection the Father gives his Son; in 3:17 it is followed by "in" and a dative, denoting the affection the Father receives from his Son. These two passages when combined indicate the reciprocal affection between the Father and the Son.

beyond me. What follows leads us further into the inaccessible depths of Trinitarian love; alongside the Father and the Son we find the Holy Spirit in an expression which emphasizes him as the anointing grace of the Son's love for the Father: "I will place my Spirit upon him . . ."[9] The remainder of this passage points to the behavior of the Son, who, in his inexpressible union with the Spirit, is able to spread the divine love around him with infinite delicacy in such a way as not to break the bruised reed or quench the smouldering flax, extending this to distant pagan lands. I can go no further because my heart is already dazzled by so much light; I prefer to be silent and meditate again in silence all that is revealed to us here of the Trinitarian counsel.

On hearing the Father, the Son says nothing; he lets himself be invaded by and filled to overflowing with the love that gives him the strength he needs to pursue his path to the cross. I am unaware for how long Jesus read and re-read, recited, meditated and went over this lengthy passage, which, from the prophet Isaiah's time to Jesus and then on through the centuries, has enabled us to contemplate the eternal love that dwelt in and surrounded him . . .

12:22–32

The words of Jesus here were spoken following an exorcism similar to those he had previously performed with the same ease, the same goodness, but unlike this passage no commentary was added; the incident is so

9. From Old Testament times, anointing with oil was connected with the coming of the Holy Spirit (1 Sam 16:13; Isa 61:1). In the New Testament, "anointing" on its own stands for the Holy Spirit, and in the writings of the Fathers this is further reinforced. When speaking of the anointing of the Son by the Father, Philemon evokes the Trinity, as does Paul in 2 Cor 1:21.

enlightening that it is good for me to meditate it, and with all the closer attention since it allows me to relive my own baptism a little.

The world of the demons is a real kingdom of which Satan is the king; a kingdom which, since Adam's fall, has extended to include the human race, enabling the demons to dwell in each of us; the verb "cast out" used here shows that the demons are thrown out of us, from inside us, so that they were indeed in us.[10] Their presence in us is manifest in the sins they cause us to commit. Only a suprahuman force can free us from their grip; it has to be stronger than Satan, and Jesus is indeed revealed here as stronger (Lk 11:22). In fact, his power is such that it was enough for him to speak a single word: "Go!" he said to the demons, and they left without any resistance (8:32). Jesus speaks here about "binding" Satan, the term to be understood as an image: he binds him spiritually, thereby demonstrating his absolute supremacy.

We experience all this at our baptism. At the beginning of the baptismal liturgy, before being immersed in water, the baptized person is first rubbed all over with oil, a holy oil set apart for exorcism[11] which cleanses and purifies by driving out demons. It's through this oil that the exorcism takes places without resistance from the Adversary. For me, this moment was of great importance; I felt myself wonderfully delivered and cleansed of many impurities . . .

---

10. The verb *ekballô* consists of two parts, the verb *ballô* ("to throw") prefixed by the preposition *ek*, meaning "out of." Translations may not always do justice to the way demons are "thrown/cast out from within."

11. Fr. *Une huile exorcisée*, lit. exorcised oil, that is, oil that has been specially blessed [Trans.].

Before the exorcism takes place, there is another very important moment: the renunciation of Satan. This is spoken openly by the baptismal candidate, who thereby expresses his deep desire to be freed from Satan's grasp. No one is baptized against their will; it is always a freely undertaken step. Where Satan assails our liberty, God is fully respectful of it. When I myself experienced this renunciation, I was particularly moved to express it by three times pronouncing the word "renounce": "I renounce you, the crafty serpent so full of evil intent. I renounce you, the traitor, you who inspired our first parents to their infidelity. I renounce you, Satan, the author and companion of every evil."[12] I remember saying this forcefully and feeling very close to Peter who, after denying Jesus three times, later spoke out his love to Jesus three times . . .

In this present case it is hard to see free choice being exercised by the demoniac because he was mute and so couldn't be heard. The freedom of choice is also hard to see in the case of the two demoniacs of Gadara because there the demon had taken possession of their faculties of speech (8:29); but it is evident in the case of the man who came and prostrated himself before Jesus (Mk 5:6); his prostration demonstrates his voluntary submission to Jesus. Here, the demoniac was "brought" by those who knew him, but the verb clearly implies his agreement.

After exorcism, the baptized person is immersed in water, the water purified and sanctified by Jesus when he was immersed before us. The water we are immersed in

---

12. I don't know where Philemon was baptized, but what he says here is very close to baptism as practiced in Jerusalem in the 4th century (cf. Cyril of Jerusalem *Baptismal and Mystagogic Catacheses* 1:4). Everything he says about his baptism conforms to Cyril's teaching.

135

makes us beneficiaries of the purification and sanctification wrought by Jesus. The Holy Spirit can then come down upon us, even inside us, to take up residence in our heart which has been perfectly prepared to receive him. God then declares himself to be not only our Master and King but also our Father, so revealing the bond of deep love that wonderfully unites us with him. Indissolubly bound together as they are, the Father and the Son come to dwell in us with the Holy Spirit, making our heart the dwelling place of the Holy Trinity. Now fully divested of the presence of the Evil One, we can welcome the Holy Trinity inside us and put ourselves beneath his beneficent control. Here, Jesus continues wonderfully by telling us, "the kingdom of God has now become first for you."[13] The kingdom of Satan is completely supplanted by the kingdom of the Holy Trinity.

I learned recently that at Constantinople in the time of John Chrysostom, the baptismal formula was different to the one I knew at my own baptism. The priest didn't say, "I baptize you . . ." but "You are baptized in the Name of the Father, the Son and the Holy Spirit."[14] The use of the divine passive wonderfully says that it is God himself who baptizes us. It is he who comes to lay his hand on us; it is he, in his humble love, who immerses us three times in the holy waters; it is he who enables us to be in him and he in us in this bond of reciprocal interpenetration that he can alone can enable us to experience as he lives in and

13. The verb here is *phthanô*, and is variously translated as "come," "arrive," "overtake," "come near" (12:28). Bailly's dictionary, translated, gives "come first, take the lead," with the implication of a rival that has been displaced.

14. John Chrysostom, *Eight baptismal catacheses*, II:26.

envelops us in through his infinite love, pursuing his work in us of deification.[15] I am very . . .

12:33–42

Jesus' humility never ceases to amaze me, it is so great, so great indeed that none of the evangelists ever uses the word "humble" to describe him[16] or "humility" in connection with him; his humility is truly beyond everything, utterly inexpressible . . .

This inexpressible humility touches me in the deepest place of my heart and overwhelms me when I hear Jesus say not "there is some*one* here greater that Jonah: but "there is some*thing* here greater than Jonah."[17] Clearly, if there was someone more important than Jonah, it was Jesus. He could very well have pointed to himself, but this is not what he did; he is so humble that he carefully avoids speaking of himself and prefers to point to "something." The context leads us to understand that this "something" was precisely the "sign"[18] the scribes and Pharisees were demanding of

15. On this difficult theological question of deification, Philemon locates himself in the line of the great patristic affirmation evident from the time of Ireneus of Lyons (2nd cent.) As Athanasius of Alexandria puts it, "God became man so that man could become God" (*On the incarnation* 54).

16. Jesus himself said that he is "humble" (*tapeïnos*, 11:29), and he is alone in saying this. None of the evangelists or any other New Testament author dared employ this adjective for Jesus. The word "humility" (*tapeïnophrosunè*) is in the letters but not the gospels and is never applied to Jesus. Only the verb "to humble" (*tapeïnoô*) is used of Jesus in Phil 2:8, "Jesus humbled himself."

17. In fact, Jesus here uses a neuter rather than masculine form, to designate the one that is greater than Jonah, as in 12:6.

18. "Sign" in Greek (*to sèmeïon*) is a neuter noun; it is this that is greater than Jonah.

him. The meaning is that "there is a sign here that is more important than Jonah."

What was Jesus saying about this sign? He said that it "will be given," using a divine passive which lets it clearly be understood that the sign would not be given by himself, of whom it was being asked, but by God his Father. This is wonderful humility again: "It is not I who will give you the sign you ask for but my Father," he lets it be known.

Humbly again, when he states precisely what the sign is, Jesus does not point to himself, instead effacing self wonderfully; he doesn't say, "It is *I* who will be in the heart of the earth . . ," but rather, "*the Son of Man* will be in the heart of the earth for three days and three nights." What incomparable, overwhelming humility!

"Three days and three nights!" The scribes and Pharisees and even the disciples as they listened to Jesus at this moment could not understand what he was alluding to, but for we today who do understand, it is clear that Jesus is evoking the cross as the sign given by God, and this is certainly a much more important sign than Jonah. What does the cross lead us to contemplate?[19] The One who in his extreme humility came down from heaven, abasing himself to die the vilest death there could be, obedient in a way much greater that the humblest of God's servants. Jesus' extreme humility is so powerful that it overturns

---

19. From a strictly exegetical point of view, it would be more accurate to speak of the three days and nights as corresponding to the time spent by Jesus in the tomb and the place of the dead, but Philemon prefers to speak of the cross, which indicates he was more a contemplative than an exegete. It is difficult to contemplate Jesus in the tomb and among the dead; however, the cross is a wonderful aid to contemplation as it enables us to contemplate him as crucified, as conqueror of hell and as risen.

Satan, while so evident to us is the extreme weakness of the crucified one, exhaling as he dies his final breath.

And how humble is this love of Jesus as he points to his death and resurrection, knowing already that he would give his life for "an evil and adulterous generation," which, in our eyes, in no way deserved it, as well as for the Pharisees who were already plotting against him to take his life (12:14), some of whom were perhaps right now asking him for a sign . . . What infinite love!

Not only is Jesus humble but so is his Father, equally, giving such a sign to this evil generation that was plotting against his Son. This humble Father teaches us humility too, giving a sign that came not from above, from heaven (Mk 8:11), but from below, from the depths of the heart of the earth, as wonderfully stated by Ephraim.[20]

What humble love too from the Father, loving to the point of giving this evil generation that which was dearest to him, his beloved Son (21:37).

On the day of judgment, Jesus concludes, it won't be the kings, the prophets or even Jonah who will rise up to condemn this generation but the humble Ninevites who clothed themselves in sackcloth and ashes (Jon 3:6) to repent in the presence of God's infinite goodness.

O my soul! Overwhelmed by the humble and divine love of Jesus, I fall to my knees before the cross, which is the sign given to us all by his humble Father. In Jesus simple mention of Jonah, we see that, in the profundity of

20. Ephraim of Nisbe (Syria, 4th cent.) was so inspired that his writings, originally in Syriac, were translated into Greek before Philemon's time. Here, in his meditation on the Jonah text, he replaces the word for "sign" with "preaching": "to those who wanted to hear a preaching from above, our Lord offered preaching that came from the depths" (Commentary on the Diatesseron, XI–2).

the Holy Scriptures, the mystery of the cross had already been announced and offered to our contemplation. I can only bow down and worship.

Lord Jesus, Son of God, you who in your humble love became man to come and live among us, you lowered yourself from the very first day to be born in a cave[21] where shepherds and the magi came to adore you. You made yourself ready to descend still further, into the heart of the earth, to deliver us from the kingdom of darkness. The magi mysteriously understood and bowed before you, offering myrrh for your burial. I have no myrrh, but I do bow before you to offer you my life as a sign of worship, O you who . . .

12:43–50

This text is here to show us what can happen after our baptism; I take it as a follow up to the passage on Beelzebub (12:22–32), food for my meditation.

We know that through our baptism, Satan was driven out of our hearts, but we would be wrong to believe that we are once and for all rid of him; he is so jealous of God that he continues to consider us his property. "My house," he says, speaking of us. By every available means, he seeks to recover the grip he had over us prior to our baptism. He is outside now, certainly, but he feels dispossessed, frustrated and humiliated by our baptism, remaining jealous of God and the bond of love he has with us. We therefore need to watch constantly and pray not to fall into his hands, as the Lord instructs us (26:41). The Enemy knows our frailties, our weaknesses, and deploys every trick of

21. In the tradition of the Eastern Church, the stable Jesus was born in was more precisely a cave used as a stable, as still found today in the Middle East.

seduction and falsehood to trap us in his meshes. Happy are those who remain deeply attached to God in perfect humility because, with the Lord's help, humility enables us to escape the nets.[22]

Jesus isn't speaking about baptized people who stay faithful to the Lord, but about others, "this evil generation," as he says at the end of this short parable (12:45). This is how he speaks of those who maintain a bond with the Evil One,[23] so that when he comes back and approaches "his" house, he finds it "empty, swept and in order," which is to say, with a welcome sign for him. He finds it to be a sanctuary in which no one prays, is void of officiants who celebrate the Divine Liturgy, and without the slightest trace of a connection with God. He finds it to be a field stripped bare of weeds but not planted, with no hope of a harvest, which is a sign that the baptized whose sins have been taken away have done nothing to bear fruit. Such is the evil generation, a generation of the baptized who bear no fruit, having neglected the promises made at their baptism. Then Satan establishes himself, and the weeds whose roots remained alive completely take over the field; our heart, which remains an accomplice of the Evil One, gives all its strength to the weeds, not offering any resistance to their hold.

22. "To escape the nets" refers to a very beautiful apophthegm concerning Anthony the Great: "Abba Anthony said, 'I saw all the nets of the Enemy spread across the earth, and I said, bitterly, who can ever escape them?' And I heard a voice say to me, 'Humility'" (Apophthegm 7).

23. "This evil generation." Philemon noted that the adjective "evil" (ponéros) can also be a noun and then designates Satan, "the Evil One" (13:19); this is why in this meditation he also speaks of Satan as the Evil One. He thereby makes it clear that on one hand Satan remains attached to "his" house while, on the other, this generation remains attached to him.

Where, then, is God? He is always the master and Lord of our hearts. At our baptism, he completely cleaned out the field of the heart and prepared everything for us to set to work, putting full confidence in us and expecting the best, just like the master in the parable who entrusted his vineyard to the vinedressers (21:33); he awaits our prayers in the sanctuary of our heart, to welcome with joy our praise and to respond to our supplications when we need his help and his counsel. But we have left our sanctuary empty and our field abandoned. No word could be strong enough to tell the Father's pain before his children who have broken their bonds with him. Such is this evil generation!

But in his infinite love, God is still more attached to us than we could ever think; our heart in fact is "his" house. He it is who built it, he who created us and restored us at our baptism. Our faithful Father is more attached to us than is Satan, the imposter who covets what is God's and who seduces us to our loss. While Satan rolls out all his tricks of seduction and lies to ensnare us in his nets, God our Father deploys all the resources of his love and all the finesse of his teaching to lead us back to himself, in full respect for our freedom. He tirelessly watches for every favorable moment to touch our heart and reawaken our love for him, unfailingly hoping for our return. He knows how to raise up in our desert a John the Baptist to prepare a way into our heart and open it up to the humble love of God. He can prompt a brother to exhort us to repentance. He can set along the way a witness to his mercy and his compassion. He can whisper to our heart that on the cross, his beloved Son interceded for us with him that he forgive his children who don't know the extent to which they have wounded him (Lk 23:34), and he welcomes them with infinite mercy. In his humble love, God is waiting for our prayer.

Heavenly Father, I give thanks for your beloved Son and for the word that has come to me today and brought light to deep in my heart, and I sincerely ask forgiveness for everything in me that remains complicit with the Adversary and causes me so lamentably to fall into his nets . . .

MATTHEW 13

13:1-9

WHEN I MEDITATED THE SAME PARABLE IN MARK'S
Gospel, I paused over the different types of ground because
this was Jesus' emphasis, drawing attention to the way we
receive the word. Now I would like to spend time specifically on the sower himself since he has an essential role,
ever present as he goes to and fro across the various types
of land, generously sowing seed.

What strikes me at the outset is that Jesus doesn't speak
about just some sower or other but *the* sower.[1] Why be
so precise? Had the sower already appeared in the gospel?
Well, no, not at all. Could it be that Jesus is referring back
to a sower somewhere in the Scriptures? Again, this is not
the case. Rather, it's to tell us that this is the sower without
equal, the one and only. It therefore comes to mind that
Jesus must be speaking of himself. While this is surely the
case, Jesus merely suggests it since he is presenting himself
here in his divinity rather than his humanity, and he does so
in a veiled way, for three reasons. Firstly, because it was too
risky for him to speak openly to the crowd; he had tried this
before and it had turned out so badly that he had almost

---

1. Unfortunately, many translations, including the KJV, fail to
note the definite article.

been stoned (Jn 8:59). Then, because even the disciples were not really ready to understand the mystery of his divinity. And finally because he is so humble that he preferred to be as discreet as possible.

In the explanation of the parable that he gave to the disciples, Jesus never says anything about the sower (13:18); he explains plenty of things but is silent about the sower.[2] In the second parable where again there is a sower (13:24), he specifies that the sower is the Son of Man (13:37). This makes it clear that the sower is indeed Jesus in his divinity even though, for the disciples, this was still veiled because the Son of Man, though known to be a heavenly person, to them was somewhat enigmatic (Dan 7:13–14).

Jesus then says that the sower "went out," without stating where he went out from. However, on another day, Jesus had said to the crowd very clearly, "I came out from God" (Jn 8:42), and nearly got stoned (8:59). This is why on this occasion he was very careful. It was still too early to for him to talk about his heavenly origins, his divinity. For us, though, it's magnificent: sowing the word of the Kingdom on the earth is the mission of the Son of God. He is indeed the sower, but hidden behind the image. As he explained the parable to the disciples he said nothing about his own person, waiting instead until the evening before his death to do so; then, very clearly and repeatedly, he told them that he had "come from God" (Jn 16:27), in fact, "from the Father" (16:28). Jesus is humble, awaiting this final day, and even then, remains somewhat mysterious

---

2. Compared with Matt 13:18–23, in Luke's Gospel, Jesus is silent about the sower (8:11–15); likewise, in Mark's Gospel, Jesus does mention the sower in his explanation but without saying anything other than just "the sower" (4:14).

because his divine origin is beyond our understanding, beyond what human words can say. Sometimes he tells that he "came from *beside* God," and sometimes that he "came *from* the Father." Neither of these two phrases is enough to tell the mystery which lies beyond them both.[3]

We see, then, Jesus in front of the crowd, seated simply in a boat, just like any other man. He carried the secret of his coming to earth in his heart, offering to sight only his humanity, without saying anything of his divinity hidden in his humanity. He doesn't speak about it and just discreetly hints at it, but for we who have read all the gospels and know the mystery of his divinity, we understand that the sower is the Son of God who has humbly come from beside the Father to sow into our hearts the word of the Kingdom. He offers himself to our view here, seated silently. What grace is given us to be able to contemplate Jesus here in his humble divinity . . .

"The sower went out to sow": this is he, the Son, come among us from alongside the Father . . .

---

3. Translations are often not precise about this, but in the Greek the prepositions differ. Jesus said he "came from beside God" (*para*, Jn 16:27) and that he "came from the Father" (*ek*, 16:28, in some manuscripts, while others repeat *para*, which seems to me an attempt at harmonization with the preceding verse). In the prayer addressed to his Father, Jesus said, "Father, I came from beside you" (*para*, 17:8); this helps us understand that "God" and "Father" are synonyms because the preposition *para* is employed with both God (16:27) and Father (17:8). In the same way, *ek* is also used for both (8:42 and 16:28). The change in preposition produces such a mystery that the disciples didn't know which to use and settled on another in the following: "We believe you came from God," where "from" is *apo*. In all these passages, the verb "come/come out" is the same, *exerchomaï*, as in the parable. I note that in the continuation of his meditation, Philemon, obliged to choose, opts for the preposition that carries more of mystery, saying that Jesus came out "from beside" the Father.

At the close of time, on the day of the harvest, the angels and archangels will be there to share with him the joy of the gathering in, but here he is alone, here to sow, and we can take time to contemplate him magnificently seated with the hope of the harvest filling his heart . . .

Lord Jesus, I fall to my knees, and stay here before you: you came down from heaven from the Father's side to visit the earth; you present yourself to us humbly, as a simple sower, and you sow your word with love into our hearts, in the secret hope of a magnificent harvest. In your grace, I pray, don't forget me! I simply open my poor heart for you to sow your seed there and for it to produce the fruit you hope. You know how much . . .

13:10–23

Lord Jesus, divine sower, who came out from the Father to humbly sow into our hearts the holy word of your Kingdom, you are blessed for the infinite grace you do us by choosing our wretched hearts as a place to sow this word.

You are blessed for the diligence and infinite love with which you entrust it to our hearts for it to produce the fruit you desire.

You are blessed for the immense care with which you keep us attentive to anything that could compromise the harvest to come.

You are blessed for alerting us to the acts of the Adversary, who comes to pick over and steal what you have sown. Open our eyes so that we cry out to you the moment we see him coming because, while we are not able, you can drive him off simply by your presence. Help us to resist him so that we don't fall beneath his spell as he does everything he can to seduce us.

You are blessed for the care with which you also help us be aware of the stones, the thorns, everything that might impede your word from becoming deeply rooted in us and growing. Make us always more attentive, so that the word remains alive in our hearts and the blessing of meditation brings forth early fruit.

You are blessed for David as he declares happy those who meditate day and night in your holy word that becomes rooted in our hearts, who draw the best from your divine teaching to produce every fruit you hope for (Ps 1:2–3).[4]

You are blessed for my cell, this haven of peace and solitude, where you teach me to persevere in prayer and the meditation of your word.

You are blessed for showing us the importance of planting your word deep inside us, where it requires unceasing hidden meditation for it to produce it's hoped for fruit. You who are so humble, teach us to keep ourselves hidden away in solitude to meditate your word, far from the eyes of others, sheltered from the vainglory which spoils your harvest.

And you are blessed for those moments of grace in which you mysteriously join us as we store the word away, filling it with your tenderness.

Lord Jesus, divine sower, who came from the presence of the Father to entrust the word of your Kingdom to us, you are blessed for showing us the damage done to our hearts by the cares of the world and the deceitfulness of

---

4. Here, Philemon refers to the first psalm (v 2–3), inspired by Gregory of Nyssa (4th cent.), who interprets the "streams of water" as the "divine teachings" from which humanity draws in order to produce the fruit anticipated by God (*On the titles of the Psalms*, 5:12)

riches. They draw our attention to themselves so that we waste our energy on them, squandering our strength, and so reinforce in ourselves everything that stifles your word. By letting ourselves be seduced by the attractions of the world, we compromise the harvest of fruit you look for. I pray that you come in your grace to remove the rocks from our hearts so that they are softened by your Holy Spirit, and that you enable the roots of your word to make their way into the inaccessible depths of our souls. Have pity on us and come unceasingly in your mercy to renew our strength so that we can consecrate it to you, as we attach ourselves fully to your word alone so that it can produce in us the fruit you hope for.

And you are blessed for the good earth, for the mysterious corners of our hearts of which you take such magnificent care that they become in our eyes holy ground, places in your Kingdom which superabound with your grace.

O Lord, you who came from your Father, you are blessed too for those of your servants who have gone before us and who give us examples of the well-rooted word to which they applied themselves, and so, with love gave the best of themselves; we can see and contemplate in them abundant fruit ready for the harvest.

You are blessed for thus encouraging us to persevere in unceasing meditation in your word, applying ourselves to give, with love, of our best, O you, who lovingly prepare your harvest.

May the day come in which we share with you the joy of the harvest, you who share with us the work of bringing to germination the seed buried our hearts; I pray this of you to whom belongs all honor and all glory together with the Father and the Holy Spirit, now and throughout the ages. Amen.

13:24-30

Jesus first spoke this parable to the crowd and then later gave its explanation to just the disciples (13:36–43). I believed at first that I could meditate the parable and then the explanation, but very quickly I realized that this was almost impossible because I simply had to take into account the explanations given later by Jesus. I find then that the field is the world in which God sows the good seed and that the darnel is the work of the devil. This leaves me curious about the place in the parable of the master's servants, which Jesus doesn't discuss in his explanation; clearly it refers to us, God's servants.

What impresses me is to see that, for Jesus, the evil in the world is not the work of the servants and certainly not of God, but of the devil; this confutes the heretics who consider man to be an evil creature who does evil.[5] What a comfort it is to hear Jesus establishing the truth. Of course, people can be accomplices of the devil, as were Adam and Eve, but the origin of the evil lies in the work of the devil (Gen 3). This reassures me because I am astonished to see how many orthodox Christians continue to think that man is bad and guilty of evil's very existence.

The darnel was sown while the servants slept; it came as a trick of the Enemy, not through the servants' fault. The servants are not accused of having been asleep after their labors in the field. Their sleep is good for them, a time of rest, not some fault! It does good to hear this because it silences those who find us guilty in everything. Even of sleeping after heavy work.

---

5. Philemon is alluding to the Manicheans.

The remainder of the parable brings us something else: once the servants notice the presence of the darnel in the field, they offer their services to the master to pluck it up without delay and clean the field out. What a lovely intention! It's wonderful that they make themselves available. Praiseworthy though this is, God stops them. Why? Firstly, because we can confuse the darnel with the wheat. It's only later that they can be distinguished. Who is able to look into the hearts of people and discern what is bad and what is good, what is of God and what is of the Evil One? Only God can do this. Haven't we in the Church often pulled up wheat believing it to be darnel?

God calls his servants to patience here, requiring them to wait until the end of the growing season. Until both wheat and darnel are mature, God won't pull up anything! God himself is patient in the presence of evil because he is perfectly able to distinguish between wheat and weed. God thus teaches us patience in the presence of evil: "Let it grow together with the good." How difficult it is to hear this! Nevertheless, it is Jesus that is teaching us here to preserve the good grain from untimely, though well intentioned, human initiatives. It is beyond our ability to interfere in inter-connected root systems of the good and the evil.

Finally, God announces that the darnel will not be pulled up until the time the wheat is gathered in, at the harvest, which is to say, the end of time! It is for God and him alone to decide the day and the hour of the harvest. The question of evil is God's affair; the elimination of evil is his concern, not ours. What a lesson this is to shame all our human efforts to cleanse the Church! The darnel does not, in fact, compromise or delay the growth of the wheat; despite it, the wheat that was sown will bear the fruit hoped for by the master. I am told that darnel is harmful when ground together with wheat because, when mixed into the flour, it prevents the proper preparation of bread. It's at the moment of harvest that the wheat can be separated without any damage being done. God knows very well what he is doing when he calls on us to let him manage the issue of evil in the world, in the Church and even in our hearts. Our place is to trust him!

The most important thing for us in the teaching here is obedience. If the servants were to disobey their master and pull up the darnel before the right time, they would also pull up wheat, and in compromising the growth of the wheat, they would also compromise the harvest itself; despite their good intentions they would become accomplices of the Evil One, whose goal is to ransack the work of God and compromise his harvest.

O my soul, even when it has the best intentions, disobedience is still very serious because it compromises God's work. What a lesson this is for us!

13:31-43

When he told the parable of the bad seed, why did Jesus add to what he says about the enemy? Instead of just saying, "an enemy has done this," he says, "an enemy, a man, has done this" (13:28).[6] This extra word now attracts my attention. No word from Jesus' lips could be redundant. While to my eyes it seems a useless addition, it must certainly have had a real importance for the Lord. Perhaps it will become clear in the passage in which he explains the

6. Unfortunately, most translations in French [and English] leave out the word "man," just translating this as "an enemy has done this." There are some that do include "man," which is indeed there in the Greek.

parable to the disciples? What he says about the enemy is, "This is the devil." So this is clear: the word "devil" identifies the enemy. How then are we to tie these two pieces of information together, "a man" and "the devil"? Could the devil be simply a man? It would be truly astonishing if he thinks of the devil as a man since it contradicts the Scriptures which say nothing similar, instead seeing him as one of the unseen, evil powers. I believe that this becomes clearer if we understand Jesus to be revealing here that the devil in his trickery can pass himself off as a man. In the same way that he can disguise himself as an angel of light, as Paul tells us (2 Cor11:14), he can also disguise himself as a man, in the same way that he appears as a lion (1 Pet 5:8) or a serpent (Gen 3:1); all these ruses are strategies to pull us in. I give thanks to the Lord for the magnificent revelation he is offering us here, showing us the devil's dissimulation as a man. In his great love for us, Jesus is unveiling one of the Evil One's strategies so that we don't fall into the trap of falsely making a man out to be Satan.

This revelation about the devil is really wonderful, and it also brings me help when it comes to praying the psalms, in particular those that speak of certain men as our enemies and are full of hatred towards them. I remember that when I became a Christian, I was unable to pray the psalms that are full of hatred towards enemies, and now that I am the doorkeeper to the monastery[7] I find that many people have the same difficulty. How are we to hate men when Jesus calls on us to love our enemies (5:43)? How are we to address a prayer to God like this: "Reward evil to my

7. In his meditation on Mark (Mk 13:29–37), we learn that the higumen entrusted Philemon with the ministry of doorkeeper to the monastery; this was an important ministry because it brought him into contact with all the visitors so he had often to accompany them in their spiritual search.

enemies; in your truth, destroy them" (Ps 54:6)? But now, thanks to the Lord Jesus' revelation here, I begin to understand that I can address such a prayer to God if I see it as aimed not at people but at the devil hidden in them. Yes! May God reward evil to the devil and all his army, and may he destroy them! I can even say this with all my heart and all my passion!

I had understood that there are psalms in which the Evil One is hidden behind animals, for example, when it is said to God, "Save me from the maw of the lion and from the horns of the wild ox" (22:21).[8] Right now, I also understand that there are psalms in which the Evil One is hidden behind men and so I can fight against him before God with the same strength and conviction. "Reward evil to my enemies; in your truth, destroy them." I also understand that is good to add a further nuance with a further little precision: in Psalm 22, where David finds himself confronted by a lion and by wild oxen, he sees himself as a worm (v 6); obviously we are dealing here with images. However, when he is faced with men, they are real men, but men behind whom the devil is hiding, unknown to them. The violence of his prayer is therefore aimed only at the devil and not the men he's hiding behind. This helps me not to become confused: the violence of my prayer is aimed only at the devil and not the men he hides behind, who I should instead be seeking to love and lift up in my intercessions, as the Lord asks of us.

You are blessed, Lord Jesus, for this wonderful clarity you bring us, which helps me understand all that I experience so much better, holding me back from confusing the

8. According to the translators, the Hebrew re'em designates an aurochs, a buffalo or a bull. However, the Greek is monokérôs, "having just one horn," so, a unicorn.

devil with the men he hides behind as he tries to make me fall. You are blessed for the psalms which provide me the occasion to pour out all my violence or my anger against the devil and all his army. But I also pray that you fill my heart with love for those who seem in my eyes to be enemies, you who love them with infinite love; help me to be a peace-maker towards them, so that I don't . . .

13:44-52

A treasure does not hide itself! There has to be someone who has hidden it. Jesus doesn't specify here by whom the treasure he speaks of "was hidden," but the phrase he uses makes it clear; this is a divine passive, so we understand that the treasure "was hidden" by God.[9]

Naturally, God cannot have hidden a treasure that didn't belong to him, someone else's treasure. It would make no sense for him to do such a thing. So, if he hid a treasure, it could only be his. What, then, is God's trea-sure? Jesus tells us that it is "the Kingdom of heaven," but I believe that he is saying this out of humility, and that in reality God has something much more precious, that is, his own Son, his beloved Son. This is God's treasure, not a material treasure of precious stones, but Jesus himself, a treasure of love (Col 1:13), the one to whom his heart is most attached, inexpressibly bound.

Why hide this treasure? Well, to keep it away from the envious and covetous, more particularly, from the most envious and most covetous, Satan himself, who in his thirst and delirium of grandeur seeks to seize what is God's.

---

9. The treasure "was hidden" (*kékrumménô*), a past participle and therefore a divine passive.

Where, then, would he place this treasure to be safe? God knows Satan very well and knows perfectly where this prideful being would never go to seek treasure since it would repel him; he would even recoil because this place is particularly repugnant to him. This place is humility. There, God could hide his treasure with complete security. More precisely, the place Satan will never to go to search is in the humility of a human heart. He will search everywhere, but definitely not there! He wouldn't even dream that God's treasure could be hidden in such a place because his pride means he has a real disdain for the heart of the humble.

The field in which the Father hides his treasure, therefore, is the humble human heart. From the beginning of the gospel, from John the Baptist's preaching, followed by Jesus, we are given to understand that a humble heart is a heart that repents, a heart that does not seek to justify itself, a heart that is open to God and abases itself entirely in order to confess all its sins to him, including the most secret, those that other people are unaware of and that God alone knows. The further a person advances down the road of repentance, the deeper he descends into humility.

What does a person seek on the road of repentance? Not a treasure, because he is preoccupied with another matter; he thirsts for something else, God's forgiveness; he is searching for a word of mercy. He goes ahead with the pain of compunction, thirsting for a word of comfort, a word from God, who, in the tenderness of his mercy, will reconcile him to himself.

The way of repentance is undertaken in the light of the Holy Spirit since only the light of the Holy Spirit enables anyone to see their sins in depth. The more enlightened we are by the Holy Spirit, the more we discern our sins, down to those sins most deeply buried in the heart; the more we confess these to the Father, the deeper the immersion into humility.

Then suddenly, in the depths of the humble heart, the person finds, without having sought it,[10] the treasure of God revealed to him; he finds the beloved Son hidden by the Father, not a treasure of precious stones but one comparable to no other, a treasure before which the gold, incense and myrrh of the magi are nothing, a treasure that is indescribable and inexpressible, the supreme treasure above all others; he finds Jesus, the beloved Son, and he finds him after allowing himself to be led into repentance by the Holy Spirit. Then the Holy Spirit enables him to find deep in his repentant heart the Son hidden by the Father.

Joy inexpressible, joy beyond all other joy, joy springs up from the depths of the heart's humility, the joy of contemplating the Son in the light of the Holy Spirit, hidden by the Father, the joy of contemplating the Son in the depth of the mystery of the most holy Trinity.

The man then sells everything, lets go everything, quits everything, separates from everything and renounces everything since nothing has any value compared to such treasure. He sells everything for the treasure of treasures, for the true treasure, the only real treasure; he sells everything and, in the light of the Holy Spirit, opens his heart and marvels in the presence of such treasure.

O my soul, this man has no idea what to say about the beauty he sees and makes silence his dwelling place, but a glow of humble love shines in his eyes . . .

---

10. Unlike the parable of the pearl, where it is stated that the merchant "sought" pearls, the parable of the treasure doesn't have the verb "seek." The treasure was hidden but not sought; it was suddenly found unsought.

13:53-58

In his own country Jesus could no longer do what he had been doing. He gave some teaching and accomplished a few miracles, behaving as he had in many other towns (4:23; 9:35). No one could accuse him of having neglected his fellows. And of course none of his works went unnoticed; the wisdom of his teaching as well as the miracles escaped no one. Nonetheless, during his stay in Nazareth, Jesus didn't see an end to the people's unbelief. This unbelief challenges me and will be the subject of my meditation. What was going on? As we have seen, Jesus could not have done any better. It follows that it was on the Nazarenes' part that there was resistance or opposition to Jesus. It was not so much opposition because, despite everything, there was at least some welcome to his wisdom and the miracles; no, it was resistance. Exactly what was the nature of the unbelief?

Jesus' teaching was done in the synagogue, so it was among people who believed in God. Where there was unbelief, it wasn't unbelief towards God but towards Jesus in his divinity. The questions the people asked are very valuable as I seek to understand the situation, and we find that they all consider Jesus in his humanity and not his divinity. He was only seen as a man, as the listing of his family connections shows: his father, his mother, his brothers, his sisters. This list completely overlooks the question of his heavenly Father. Those who had been with John the Baptist knew who the heavenly Father of Jesus was, and those who had been on the mount also knew because they had heard Jesus speak of God as "my Father" (7:21). The demons knew as well (Mk 3:11), and many other too: Jesus was the Son of God. But in Nazareth no one raised this issue; for them it all resolved into the fact that Jesus was the son of Joseph, the carpenter.

The questions listed were asked in such a way as to exclude the divinity of Jesus: "Where does he come from . . . ?" is asked at the beginning and the end of the series of questions. "From where . . . ?" not "from whom . . . ?" This difference in the form of the questioning reveals a closed door that eliminates Jesus' relationship with God. To my mind, this closed door lies at the level of the heart: the Nazarenes had their hearts closed to the divinity of Jesus, shut off from the mystery of who he was. This makes everything clear to me: Jesus could not work in his quality of Son of God; his divinity could not be manifest to hearts that were closed to it. No more than his Father or the Holy Spirit does Jesus wish to force the door to the heart; he doesn't wish to do so out of respect for people. This is the way of the humble divine love, respecting human freedom.

The unbelief of the Nazarenes was to not believe in Jesus' divinity; they believed in God but not in the divinity of Jesus. I can see that in a way they were like the followers of Arius. They were confined to reason; they asked questions in the way of philosophers, sensitive only to human reason. Like them, the people of Nazareth listened to Jesus' wisdom[11] but were closed to divine revelation. If they had said, "Who do this wisdom and these miracles come from?" they would have been showing an openness to God and to revelation. But they were shut tight against it. What a lesson this is for me! Moving on from reason to revelation is the sign of a real humility, of a spirit that accepts not to

11. The Nazarenes were aware of Jesus' wisdom (*sophia*) and so seem to Philemon more like philosophers, those who love (*philô*) wisdom (*sophia*) and so were merely on the level of human wisdom, unaware of divine revelation.

understand by human reason and accepts being taught by God. This is important to me as I continue with my meditation of the Gospels: am I leaning only on my own understanding, just on human reasoning? Or do I really also accept that I need to trust the Holy Spirit to teach me, to lead me and to shed light for the understanding of the texts he himself inspired? He it is who led the evangelists in the editing of their gospels, and now my place is to open myself for him to lead me and reveal meaning in my meditation. Where the Nazarenes asked questions that were closed to revelation, I need to be careful about the questions I ask as I meditate; they might also be closed to the mystery of the Father, the Son , the Holy Spirit, of the Holy Trinity. Opening of the heart to the divine mystery is given by God, and, in his respect for my personal freedom, he will not force things. It's up to me not to be closed, to open myself up and to ask for this openness from the only one who can enable it in me. The key to meditation is unceasing prayer.

Lord Jesus, I open my heart to the deep mystery of yourself; don't leave me to fall back on my own understanding, but by your Holy Spirit, grant me the grace to be always opening up more and more . . .

MATTHEW 14

14:1-12

THIS HORRIBLE TEXT CAUSED ME A WORLD OF TROUBLE until the moment came when I was able to see it not as an abandoned field producing no edible fruit but as one in which a treasure is hidden, the magnificent treasure of God's mercy. What was my joy in discovering this treasure! The treasure of mercy is hidden in two divine passives which tell of God's secret work in Herod's heart. The king was abominable, but in God's eyes he was a lost sheep on whose behalf he worked with wonderful mercy.

"Herod was filled with fear" (14:5); this is the first divine passive,[1] and it refers to Herod's heart, where there was a real inner struggle between his desire to have John the Baptist killed and the fear of actually accomplishing

---

1. Matthew uses the verb *phobéô* in the passive ("he was filled with fear of the crowd"), which is indeed a divine passive, meaning "he was filled with fear of the crowd by God." Apart from the active and passive voices, Matthew also had the option of choosing the middle voice which exists in Greek with a reflexive sense; such a verb is found in Mk 9:32, "the disciples were afraid to ask Jesus," which means that their fear came from themselves, not God. However, Matthew deliberately chose the divine passive, a passive with might be considered doubtful since it is followed by an accusative, but the phrasing is correct according to Abel's grammar (*Grammaire du Grec biblique*, 54)

this murder. On one hand, his desire for murder was being encouraged by his wife Herodias, who was pushing him in this direction (Mk 6:19); on the other, the views of the crowd were holding him back. More deeply, we could say that Satan, who is a murderer himself (Jn 8:44), was also inciting him, and that God was restraining him through the fear he had awakened in him. Between these two camps, Herod had to choose which side he would please. It is our joy to note that at the beginning of this passage, he was in God's camp, wonderfully, because he resisted his own murderous desire. It is beautiful to see how this fear that came from God was a great help granted him, and also that it was a sign of astonishing mercy since God was helping a king who, to make it even more surprising, was adulterous and incestuous![2] God expressed neither disapproval nor, of course, approval, but in his immense grace, and despite Herod's incestuous adultery, helped him to resist murder. What extraordinary mercy! This is the magnificent treasure, hidden in this divine passive, at work in Herod's heart.

The second treasure is in the other divine passive: "He was saddened." Here we see sadness springing up in Herod's heart when he hears the young girl's request, and the sadness is surprising because the request met his own desire, the Baptist's death. He could have rejoiced over this convergence of wishes, but this was not the case; instead of joy he was saddened. The divine passive shows that the sadness didn't come from himself but from God, and it's a sadness whose fruit we know, thanks to Paul who tells us that it produces repentance (2 Cor 7:10), which is

---

2. Herod had a first wife who he had not divorced and was therefore in a state of adultery with Herodias; more, since Herodias was the wife of Herod's brother, Herod's adultery, according to Leviticus (18:16), was incestuous.

wonderful. This sadness was God's work in Herod's heart, a work of his merciful grace to lead him down the road of repentance. What a treasure. Herod's place now was to let himself be led by God down this road; then he would have repented of his vow and rejected the young girl's request. However, at this point, Herod shut God out, giving place instead to the work of pride and vainglory in his heart, in pride, despite everything, maintaining his vow in his wish to be admired by his guests. With this, as Paul again shows, sadness turns to produce another fruit, murder (2 Cor 7:10); the king became a murderer in the image of Satan (Jn 8:44). Where he had taken God's part by resisting the desire to murder, he now changed camp and went over to Satan, led on by pride and vainglory. In order to resist, he had to remain attached to God and, with his help, humbly go back on his oath.

Still more admirable in this account is that after the death ordered by Herod, God did not, so to speak, capitulate, as is discreetly revealed at the outset of the passage. Here we learn that Herod was aware of Jesus' fame, and that this seems to have awakened in him a certain sense of remorse. He confided in those close to him the sentiment that John the Baptist was reborn in Jesus, and that he might turn against him, perhaps in vengeance. Would this fear, which translated into a sense of remorse, lead him, in God's grace back to the path of repentance? Everything is possible to God's grace, but we don't know any more, learning elsewhere only that Herod sought to see Jesus (Lk 9:9), which does leave us with some hope. What, though, was his purpose in wishing to see him? Was it or was it not to ask forgiveness? Thank God he did later meet Jesus, but it finished badly for him because he was unable to open up to repentance and had nothing but disdain for him (Lk 23:11).

However, in his overflowing mercy (Rom 5:20), Jesus interceded for this lost sheep as he spoke to the Father from the cross: "Father, forgive him, because he doesn't know what he is doing" (Lk 23:24) . . .

14:13–21

John the Baptist's disciples came to announce the death of their master to Jesus (14:12). They wanted to tell him themselves because they knew how closely the two men were tied to each other. The death had been violent so they made sure to tell him gently, but the shock of the news was nevertheless important enough for Jesus to withdraw without delay and leave for a deserted place. He wanted to be alone to pray.

He climbed into a boat with his disciples, but, as though he was alone,[3] said not a word to anyone; he did nothing but pray throughout the crossing, sitting down in a corner of the boat unmoving, praying, just praying from the moment he was on board.

The crowd was making its way along the shore and would corner him the moment he arrived; he could not be alone, which is why it was so good for him to pray now in the boat, even in the midst of his disciples, who were accustomed to seeing him pray like this (Lk 9:18; 11:1). They

3. The disciples were certainly present with Jesus in the boat because immediately afterwards we find them with him for the miracle of the loaves (14:15). Curiously, though, in order to underline Jesus' desire for solitude, Matthew uses a singular, saying that "Jesus retired in a boat to a deserted place," as though he was alone. This singular cannot go unnoticed when compared with Mark who says the same thing but with a plural: "They left in a boat for a deserted place" (6:32).

were fully aware of John the Baptist's death; they knew why Jesus needed to pray and so left him alone.

The announcement of the Baptist's death was a turning point for Jesus, as had been the news of his imprisonment,[4] which had been the occasion for him to begin preaching. At that point he had not wanted to cast a shadow over the Baptist's ministry, preferring to support him in prayer. He limited himself to receiving John's baptism, an event which had profoundly united the two. For the Baptist, Jesus' baptism was so profound that he had not been able to discuss it with his disciples, simply telling them that from that moment his only task was to bear Jesus up in prayer. This is what he then did; he baptized almost no one else and withdrew once more into the desert; then, after being imprisoned, he did nothing but pray for Jesus. Jesus knew it and felt wonderfully supported in his ministry by his prayers. And now the Baptist's death overturned all that; truly, it marked an inflection point in Jesus' life.

To be upheld in one's life by another person's prayer is an inexpressible grace. I have noticed this since being here. Since my arrival in the monastery, I know that the Chief Elder has been praying for me, as he does for each of us.[5] I find from this that the bond of communion in

4. Matthew makes it apparent that Jesus waited until John's imprisonment to start preaching: "Having learned that John had been handed over, Jesus withdrew into Galilee . . . And from that moment, Jesus began to preach, saying 'repent'" (4:12,17). We note that where Matthew says John was "handed over," Luke is more specific and says he was imprisoned (3:20).

5. We have two letters from Barsanuphius to Philemon (Letters vol II, 359 and 360), and even if these remained unknown we would know that the two men were bound together in prayer. At the close of the Eucharist celebration, Abba Seridos would bring concerns to Barsanaphius, which reinforced the unseen spiritual bond between all parties.

prayer is very deep. United in prayer by the Holy Spirit, borne up by the prayers of the Son who intercedes for us (Rom 8:34), even when we are alone, each of us in our cell, our hearts are turned towards the Father together in prayer; this is very strong Trinitarian experience. Throughout the Baptist's time in prison, Jesus was already united with the Father and the Holy Spirit, but into this Trinitarian bond there insinuated the prayers of another man, which gave it an extraordinary supplementary depth and power. And now this death upset it all. This was the end of a great stage in Jesus' life, the end of a human fellowship at the heart of the Trinitarian love.

The death of the Baptist put an end to this stage but opened another, and it was also to enter this new stage that Jesus withdrew into solitude. What is new is that the Baptist would be present in a different way, present with the angels, the archangels and the multitude already near to the Father. The bond of love in the communion of prayer would now be strengthened by working still more in a communion in which the dead and the living take their place, all united in Trinitarian love. This sheds light on the fellowship I enjoy here, alone in my cell.

The Baptist was killed cruelly but from this time was in the divine light and peace. Jesus knew that he would soon be following him;[6] he knew that his turn was coming for the trial of death and that this would be a new baptism for him (Mk 10:38). He would be alone and abandoned on the cross, though that is not the whole truth; heaven would open anew and he would remit the Holy Spirit to the Father

6. Matthew has already told us that Jesus knew of the council the Pharisees had taken as to how to destroy him (12:14). On this news, Jesus evinced a wish to withdraw to pray (12:15).

(Lk 23:46). He knew that the Baptist was already with the Father and would be carrying him in his prayers.

Jesus needed solitude to prepare for his new baptism and so he retired into a deserted place and was already praying in the boat among the disciples.

You are blessed, Lord Jesus, for the grace you give us of praying for each other (Jas 5:16), in fellowship with each other, united by the Holy Spirit who bears us all up in his prayers to the Father (Rom 8:27), but also united by you who do the same for us alongside the Father (Rom 8:34), and by the Father whose gaze is fixed on us, opening his heart to us to unite us further. You are blessed for this communion which extends invisibly through heaven and on earth, across . . .

14:22-36

This is the first time for the disciples to bow before Jesus, not to ask him for anything in the manner of the lepers (8:2), Jairus and others (9:18), but simply to worship him without expecting anything in return, as had the magi (2:11). They were before him in an attitude of profound worship; there are no words to give further substance to their prayer and no words to complete this account,[7] as though their worship opened on to eternity. Their very short

---

7. This passage gives the impression of being unfinished. Nothing is said about the end of the crossing. For their part, Mark (6:45–52) and John (6:16–21) provide accounts that are constructed differently, but Matthew emphasizes the adoration of the disciples, in fact, eternal adoration; he had done the same with God's words at the baptism, underlining the way his words are eternal.

prayer echoes the very brief statement by God the day of Jesus' baptism, a divine word which was also followed by a silence that opened on to eternity (3:17). As they bowed, the disciples worshipped the Son of God.

What had happened for the disciples to reach this point of bowing before Jesus? I believe that their worship was a response to the revelation of Jesus' divinity given them by three wonderful signs: his inexpressible presence, his word of light and his act of salvation.

First, Jesus presented himself to them as only God can: he walked on the sea! This revealed him unequivocally as God because, in the Scriptures, only God can walk on the sea (Job 9:8). This event is so inexpressible that Matthew conveys it with an extraordinary paradox: in his eyes, Jesus was coming towards them while immobile, as though moving without moving.[8] Only an eye witness could express things like this, which is as it should be since Matthew was there

---

8. Philemon notes a turn of phrase which seems to be a grammatical mistake but in fact isn't. Matthew did this to point to the inexpressible by wonderfully twisting a rule of Greek grammar. According to this rule, the verb "walk" is a verb of movement which should normally be followed by a preposition and the accusative, and Matthew respects this when he writes that Jesus "walked on the sea" (14:25). In the following verse, however, he uses the same expression but with a genitive, which makes it a verb without movement; he does so to describe the inexpressible, as if Jesus was walking while staying still, moving without moving. Such grammatical anomalies are very exceptional in Matthew, showing the extent to which he had to go to express his feelings about this extraordinary theophany.

that night in the boat. What he reports to us is what he saw, his inexpressible, spiritual experience.[9]

Then, Jesus speaks words that only God could speak truthfully, "I am."[10] Since the time of Moses, no one had heard such words, and the disciples responded to it by bowing down: "In truth, you are . . ." They said this with such great emotion that they could only stumble out their words of worship: "In truth, Son of God, you are."[11]

Lastly, Jesus took Peter's hand and rescued him in response to his prayer, which, according to the Scriptures, could only be addressed to God, "Lord, save me."[12] This

9. In his parallel account, Mark also twice used the phrase "to walk on the sea" (6:48 and 49) and makes the same "mistake" as Matthew, not just in one verse but in both, less paradoxically; he therefore notes simply the lack of sense of movement, but he offsets this by saying that Jesus "made as if to pass by" (6:48), which, it seems to me, is much less surprising than Matthew's stark contrast. This paradox is tied to the Greek and doesn't correspond to anything in Hebrew, so if Matthew had at first written his gospel in Hebrew, we would have to admit that he translated it into Greek himself in order to express his experience that day in the boat; such a translation by Matthew is altogether likely and shows that he didn't wish to write only to Jews who had become Christians, but for all Christians.

10. "I am the One who is," God says to Moses in the Greek text (Exod 3:14). From then on, in Judaism, "I am" was not to be said by any man since only God can say "I am" in full truth. Were human lips to say this, they could only soil this "I am" which became the Name of God.

11. Philemon notes how the disciples were lost for words; articles and a pronoun are missing. Instead of *o uios tou théou su eï* ("The Son of God, you yourself are"), they say only *uios théou eï* (Son of God you are).

12. "Save me," is found sixteen times in the Old Testament Greek and is always addressed to God with one exception (2 Kgs 16:7), where it is spoken by king Ahaz to the king of Assyria, a great sin on the part of this king who "did nothing pleasing to God" (16:2).

action wonderfully attests to the truth of what the angel said to Joseph commenting on his name, "It is he who saves."[13]

In the presence of such a theophany,[14] the men bowed down in the boat are described somewhat strangely: there could be no confusion that they were the disciples, yet this word is not used and is replaced by the very vague phrase, "those who . . ." This is really very beautiful! The phrase shows us that all are included: "those who" are impelled to bow before Jesus' divinity are welcomed and can take for themselves these marvelous words of worship, the depth of which is Trinitarian. To say that Jesus is "the Son of God" is a discreet but clear way of naming at once both Father and Son. To say this while adding "in truth" is not possible unless we are being "led into all the truth" by the one who alone can do so , "the Spirit of Truth," as Jesus himself so wonderfully says (Jn 16:13).

"In truth, you are the Son of God": this wonderful prayer of worship immerses us in the mystery of the all holy Trinity. Only silence can follow such a prayer. It is not the fruit of human reasoning, that is, of intellectual reflection or the development of an argument, but a revelation that invites worship. After the calming of the storm, the disciples had been limited to a question that showed they were shut into their own reasoning;[15] here, their prayer is open

13. As the angel of God had said to Joseph using the same verb "to save" (*sôzô*), the name of Jesus means "the Lord saves" (1:21).

14. A theophany is a divine appearance; here it is used for Jesus' appearance in his divinity to the disciples.

15. "Who then is this," the disciples had said in Jesus' presence, not speaking to him, though they were speaking about him. Their neglect of prayer is evident here as they decline into mere human reflection (8:27). This is the sense in which their reasoning was limited.

to the one who is revealed to them. Their bowing down[16] joins with the action of the twenty-four elders and the four evangelists in heaven.[17] The men in the boat were celebrating Jesus as he is celebrated in heaven, bowing humbly before him in total self-abandon. Anyone bowed down or prostrate is abandoning their own life to the person they bow before; while their hands may hold no gold, no incense and no myrrh to offer him, they can offer their existence. "Those who" worship the Son in this way are opening their hearts and are silent as they enter into communion with all who in heaven and on earth are likewise prostrate before him . . .

O my soul, we are offered a place in the ship of the Church; we too are to bow, welcoming into our hearts these words of adoration: "In truth, you are the Son of God . . ."

O Jesus, you are in truth the Son of God, the living one who draws near yet without moving, presenting yourself at the heart of our doubts; you light up our night times with the inexpressible light that shone in the burning bush; you reduce the wind to silence; and you speak the word that reveals your divinity; you, who save from the waves that threaten to engulf us, and before whom heaven and earth prostrate themselves . . .

16. The French translated as "bow down" is always *se prosterner*, which could be translated as "to prostrate oneself." [Trans.]

17. The twenty four elders and the four creatures bow before God at the wedding feast of the Lamb (Rev 19:4). When Philemon speaks of the four evangelists, he is referring to an ancient exegetical tradition going back to Ireneus of Lyon (2nd cent.), who considered the four creatures already named in Rev 4:7 to be the four evangelists: Matthew the bull, Mark the lion, Luke the man and John the eagle.

MATTHEW 15

15:1–20

AT THE HEART OF THIS TEXT THERE IS A VERSE FROM THE Holy Scriptures (Isa 29:13) which Jesus quotes publicly and then comments on when alone with the disciples. It's a statement of great importance when we consider that it was spoken by the Father, passed on to the prophet by the Holy Spirit and then commented on here by the Son. Having come from the heart of the Trinity and reaching all the way to us, it needs to be listened to and received with the closest attention, and all the more since it touches into the depths of our hearts.

The words were spoken with pain by the Father, who is deploring the estrangement of our hearts: "Their heart is far from me," he says! We should listen to him because all too often we believe ourselves to be close to God because we praise and venerate him, without considering the extent to which our praise comes only from our lips, not from our heart, which is far from him. We are not aware because we are blind, as Jesus says here (15:14); because we are blind, we don't see that our heart is far from God, the only one who sees into it (1 Sam 16:7).

What is going on when our heart is far from God? It lacks vigilance and discernment. The Wicked one then approaches secretly and, from the outside, intrudes evil suggestions which depend on the memory we have of evil, and then, if we stay with these suggestions and make them our own, they produce evil thoughts; and in this way, out of our hearts come evil thoughts.[1]

Without the influence of the Wicked One, what are the thoughts of our hearts? Well, they are good, surely, because they stem from a heart that is good as God created it, and this is all the more true if the Holy Spirit has come to live there. In line with this, we are told that Zacharias was filled with the Holy Spirit (Lk 1:67), and so, flowing from his heart came the magnificent canticle we still chant, a holy canticle composed without the influence of the Wicked One. As long as our heart stays close to God, it is filled with thoughts that are agreeable to God, but if it moves away from him, evil thoughts flow from it, as Jesus says here, as he discreetly denounces the Wicked One's sly influence.

What is our place in this? The moment our heart is estranged from God, we have to return to him in repentance, as Jesus has been inviting us to do from the start of his ministry (4:17). If we take the road of repentance, we who are far from God, we will encounter the prophet Jeremiah, who preceded us along this road and who has an extraordinary word for us. Jeremiah received this word from God, who let himself be seen "from afar," as he specifies (31:2); this word is for everyone who turns to God on the road of repentance and are hoping to see him, even if

---

1. Philemon makes the connection here between Satan, "the Evil One," (*o ponéros*, 13:19) and "evil" thoughts (*ponéroï*). The evil thoughts which issue from our hearts are thoughts that have been rendered evil by our hearts' adherence to the suggestions of the Evil One. Philemon was closely following the Fathers, and particularly, here, Diadochus of Photice (5th cent. *Spiritual Works*).

"from afar." But this is what Jeremiah heard from God: "I love you with an everlasting love; therefore I have drawn you with compassion" (31:3).[2] What words these are! Not only do they touch our heart which is nevertheless far from God, but they also light our way towards him as they reveal that God himself "draws with compassion" the person who is headed towards him in repentance. To the feeble efforts of our repentance are added the infinite resources of the God who draws us "with the cords of love," as he says himself through the mouth of the prophet Hosea (11:4).

How beautiful it is to hear the prophets Hosea and Jeremiah speak of the love God has for us! We should also not forget that if Jesus does not speak so clearly here of God's love for us, it's simply because of how insufficient and poor the word "love" is, and how incapable it is of expressing the divine love which is truly inexpressible, so far above all we can say or think. It is good that we understand that in inviting us to repent, Jesus adds this simple statement, the unfathomable depth of which we can only guess, that "the Kingdom of heaven is drawing near" (4:17). Mysteriously hidden in the Kingdom that is drawing near, God is there, unseen.[3] Jesus tells us much more than the prophets: God doesn't just draw us to him with bonds of love, he draws near himself . . .

O my soul, you know how happy I am to sing with my lips the glory of God, but you also know how my heart can

2. Translators from the Hebrew divide between "drawn" or being "kept" (or cognates) by grace, with Israel being addressed as feminine, God's beloved. In the Greek, Israel is masculine and the verb is *elkuô*, which decidedly means "draw" rather than "keep"; Philemon follows the Greek.

3. By speaking of "the Kingdom of heaven," Jesus avoids naming God but suggests him, "heaven" being a discreet way of designating God.

unhappily be so far from him. You also know how attentive I am to our Lord's appeal, inviting us to repent. I am touched to the depths of my wretched heart by the word brought us by the prophet Jeremiah. How good God is! May he draw me to himself with the marvelous cords of his love and his compassion! But above all, may he draw near in his inexpressible love and in his compassion pursue his work in me . . .

15:21–28

O woman, the women of Gaza are Canaanites, as you were, and I give thanks that one day I heard one of them cry like you cried, as only a woman can cry when the child that came from her womb is suffering. They are strident cries that pierce the ears and rise up to touch and shake heaven; they are cries men don't know how to respond to because they don't know the suffering of a mother who sees the child she gave life to sinking into madness. In the presence of such unbearable cries, men are silent, hoping that heaven will respond.

O woman, you cried out with all your strength before Jesus to move his heart; you cried out, ready to cry until he answered you. You cried and he answered, but not to you but to his disciples! He answered, but not to send you away as the disciples had asked; yes, he answered. Then you fell to your knees, bowed before him and you cried no more because you knew in your heart that he had received your request. You knew because you knew that his ear was not like the men's who couldn't bear the cries of a mother; you knew that his ear is God's . . . O woman, who brought such faith to birth in you?

You bowed down as only the humble can. The proud don't bow, and if they do, it is only for appearance sake and in their hearts they stay standing. You bowed down with your whole being to let your faith open up entirely in the presence of your Lord. O woman, who taught you that Jesus is the Lord?[4] Who taught you, a pagan Gentile who hadn't read the Scriptures and had received no teaching from a man of God? Only the Holy Spirit, in his infinite grace, could have given birth to the faith that was in you now.[5] This is why I marvel. I am silent to contemplate the work of the Holy Spirit who caused you to receive faith into your heart as only the humble can receive it and then allow it to grow in their heart so that they live by it; this faith is inseparable from humility because faith and humility have need of each other to be tightly knit into unity and then grow together.

Jesus didn't send you away because he wanted to demonstrate to the disciples what he had seen in your heart: your wonderful faith together with your humility that was just as great, the two virtues united inseparably in the secret of your heart. O woman, I am now silent with the disciples in order to receive the lesson Jesus wants to give us.

It was to lead us and establish on our spiritual journey that Jesus brought you so low, because only the humble

4. Philemon notes that each time this woman spoke to Jesus, she addressed him as "Lord" (15:22,25,27). This title might be used for an ordinary man but the woman also calls him "Son of David," which makes Jesus at least the greatest of men. By repeatedly called him "Lord," she indicated that she saw Jesus as not less and surely more than the "Son of David"; in speaking of him as greater than king David, she indicated that she was speaking to God.

5. Philemon is doubtless referring to verses from Paul which set out the work of the Holy Spirit in the heart, giving faith (1 Cor 12:9) and attributing to Jesus the title "Lord" (1 Cor 12:3). The woman addressed Jesus as "Lord" each time she spoke to him (15:22,25,27).

can receive such humiliation without defending themselves. And when the humiliation comes from God, only faith can receive it peaceably. But here, faced with the humiliating words that Jesus spoke to you, you didn't rebel, didn't defend yourself, but responded in total peace.

He humiliated you first by not responding to your initial prayer, beautiful and true though it was; you had even honored him by calling him "Son of David," a Canaanite woman thus submissive to this royal family from a foreign land. He humiliated you by not deigning to answer you, but you received his humiliating silence without being troubled.

Then he humiliated you again but making you understand that you, a pagan outsider, had no place among the children of Israel; you received his words not as an offence but as an honor from one who had no need to answer a pagan but had nonetheless acceded to speaking to her.

And again he humiliated you, treating you as a "little dog"; and you rejoiced to receive this insult as an invitation to share in the children's bread.

O woman, as Jesus said to you, great is your faith which enabled you to receive so many humiliations so that now you could welcome, without growing prideful, his wonderful response: "Woman, your faith is great, let it be to you as you wish!"

You are blessed, receiving from the Lord a miracle equal to your faith, a miracle that fed you more than just a few crumbs from beneath the King's table.

O woman, may God our Father bless you and enable you to walk through the Holy Spirit the way of humble faith until the day you contemplate the Lord Jesus, the Lord of the children of Israel and the children of Canaan, Jesus, the Son of God who will have you participate in the great feast and give you infinitely more than crumbs in the blessed eternal light of the Kingdom . . .

15:29–39

"I am moved to the guts, the entrails": nowhere else does Jesus speak like this,[6] which is not too surprising since it is a very personal and intimate way of speaking. If he had never spoken in this way, we would have readily understood. He does say it though, not to the crowd gathered around him but just to the disciples, which preserves the proprieties and his modesty. So this is something he said, and it is a great gift to us because it opens a door onto a profound divine mystery. It follows that I meditate this text with close attention and great thankfulness because the revelation Jesus is offering here brings him closer to us and causes our love for him to grow.

According to the Scriptures, it is in the guts that mercy and compassion are born;[7] from these two virtues emerge the two great divine attributes that God puts up front when he reveals himself: "The Lord, the compassionate and

6. "To be moved to the guts" (Fr. *entrailles*; KJV "bowels). This attempts to translates the Greek *splanchnizomaï* (15:32), as it derives from the word for the entrails (*spanchna*). However, it is not readily understandable that Philemon should say that this was the only time Jesus spoke in this way; in fact, Jesus says the same thing in Mark 8:2, but since this is the parallel account, it is possible to say that this was just one occasion; however, again, the verb is found elsewhere in the gospels, though admittedly not in the first person as it is here (Matt 9:36; 14:14; 18:27; 20:34; Mk 1:41; 6:34; 9:22; Lk 7:13; 10:33; 15:20); it is never used outside the gospels.

7. This is evident in the phrases "guts (bowels) of mercy" (*splanchna* éléous, Lk 1:78) and "guts (bowels) of compassion" (*spanchna* ôktirmou, Col 3:12), which show clearly the seat of these two virtues.

merciful God . . ." (Exod 34:6).[8] It's beautiful to see that God just reveals himself in this form once, and that to just one intimate friend, Moses. It's also beautiful to find the same reserve and modesty in Jesus as in his Father.

The two virtues reveal the way God acts towards human suffering in his love: mercy towards those who suffer from their sins and who look for forgiveness, and compassion towards those who suffer innocently and who look for comfort. These virtues are manifestations of his infinite love; in order to respond to our sufferings God draws on the deeps, his entrails, as on treasures of love of unfathomable depth.

"I am moved to the guts towards the crowd": here Jesus is engaging more with compassion than mercy because the crowd is not described as having committed sins but as suffering innocently. More precisely, the issue is not the suffering of the sick seeking healing, as at the time of the first multiplication of loaves (14:14), or of suffering through a lack of teaching, as found in another text (Mk 6:34), but a suffering yet to be felt and still to come. It is wonderful to sense the degree to which Jesus cared for people who risked fainting on the return journey and to see him bring to pass a miracle to keep the crowd from what they might suffer

---

8. The list of attributes given by God in his self-revelation reads: "The Lord, the Lord, the compassionate and merciful God, slow to anger, of great pity, observing justice and showing mercy . . ." (Exod 34:6–7). The list is lengthy and goes on, but "compassionate" and "merciful" lead the way. In the Old Testament, these two attributes are always cited together, but only the once in God's mouth as a description of himself.

later after they left. So he does this miracle in anticipation! O my soul, this wonderful prevenient grace from Jesus in his compassionate love makes my love grow for this one who does such miracles for us.

As he has compassion on those who might faint along the way, Jesus is particularly concerned for the weakest, the children and the elderly . . . O my soul, this marvelous attention from Jesus to the smallest staggers me and makes my love for him grow still more.

The miracle of the multiplication of the loaves is a miracle that no one asked for, neither the disciples nor the crowd. Jesus did it on his own initiative, in pure grace. Wonderful Jesus, who cares for us before we ask! Not only did no one ask him, but neither did anyone testify of their thankfulness to him! He accepted this ingratitude without saying anything, with extreme humility. O my soul, Jesus' humility in his compassionate love overwhelms me and causes my love for him to grow still more.

He gave out the bread and the fish he had received from the disciples and indeed from his Father, to whom he gave thanks. There was nothing of himself in what he gave, but nonetheless, with the bread he was giving his compassion which came neither from his disciples or his Father but from the depths within, from his entrails, from his divine nature. The Son of God didn't receive compassion from his Father because they had this compassion in common, both also being of the same compassionate nature with the Holy Spirit; it is from divine compassion that Jesus draws to give us the bread that means we don't faint along the way.

In the first multiplication of loaves, we are told that Jesus "was moved to the guts on the crowd's behalf (14:14), and now Jesus tells us that he is "moved to the guts towards the crowd"; this is a wonderful difference![9] In the first account, his compassion is described with a verb of state which reveals Jesus' nature; and here, Jesus reveals his compassion with the same verb but as a verb of motion, which makes his compassion a dynamic reality, a movement of love towards the hungry and the little ones. Jesus thereby reveals that his divine nature is a dynamic reality. The divine being is a dynamic being, a movement of love towards us! O my soul, I can only fall to my knees before Jesus, before the bottomless depth of the mystery of his compassionate love, given by pure grace to all, even to the very least . . .

9. On the first occasion, "being moved to the guts" was used as a verb of state; this is a problem because it would normally be a verb of movement. As a verb of state, it is followed by a preposition with the dative case (14:14). Here, on the second occasion, the same verb is followed by the same preposition but now an accusative, making it a verb of movement. It is difficult to translate this nuance of Greek because we don't have cases; I have tried to do so by changing the preposition; "towards" rather than "on behalf of" seems to me to convey movement.

MATTHEW 16

16:1-12

THIS ENCOUNTER BETWEEN JESUS AND THE PHARISEES
and Sadducees ended in a most surprising way: "Jesus left
them and went away"! He had never behaved in such a way
with people he was talking with, had never finished a discussion so abruptly. It wasn't the Pharisees and Sadducees who
left, but Jesus! What had happened for things to conclude
like this?

Always a good teacher, Matthew carefully helps us
understand by presenting Jesus' interlocutors meaning-
fully as "tempters."[1] So much is clear; Matthew could
hardly have done better in his choice of words, using the
same word he had chosen to present Satan at the start of

---

1. In the account of Jesus' temptation in the wilderness, the devil
is called "the Tempter" (4:3), with a present participle used as a
substantive (*o peïrazôn*). Here, Jesus' interlocutors have the same
word applied to them in the plural (*peïrazontes*), which, to be used
properly, should be preceded by the article to make it a noun, but that
is not the case here; nevertheless, from the point of view of meaning,
Philemon considers it to be used as a noun, which seems right; so we
can translate it here as "tempters" (word for word, "the Pharisees
and Sadducees tempters"). This is particularly relevant because the
verb "to tempt" is not used in either passage. It is also helpful to note
that the Greek verb *peïrazô* means both "to tempt" and "to put to
trial/test," which explains the different translations.

his account of Jesus' temptation in the wilderness (4:1). To emphasize this, he opens this account by saying that the tempters "drew near," just as he had said that the Tempter drew near to Jesus in the temptation account.[2] This is very well done! Matthew couldn't have been clearer as he invites us to make the connection: the Pharisees and Sadducees would act just like Satan when it comes to Jesus and should even be considered as representatives of Satan.

Jesus knew very well what he had to deal with, and just as in the wilderness with Satan, he replies by proffering Scripture without adding any commentary: "'It will be given no sign other than the sign of Jonah.' Then he left them and went away."[3]

In the wilderness, with Satan, it wasn't Jesus who left; it is important that we realize that he is perfectly able to face the Tempter and make it so that it was Satan who departed. Here, things are not the same. Now, he was not alone with his tempters but was there with the disciples; this is why, taking their presence into account and in order to build them up, he left, thereby teaching them the correct attitude to adopt when their turn came to deal with tempters. Additionally, immediately afterwards he said to them, "Watch out."[4] This warning is very important for us, who are not capable of facing the Tempter in the same way as

---

2. In fact, the first word of the account is the verb "to draw near," (*proserchomaï*), used here as a present participle, exactly as in the account of the temptation in the wilderness (4:3).

3. In the wilderness temptation, Jesus always replied by citing the Scriptures, without any commentary, emphasizing the power of the word of God on its own.

4. The verb "watch out/be on your guard" is so important that it used here three times (16:6,11,12).

Jesus. The end of the passage shows us that the disciples thoroughly understood that it was not a matter of guarding against the Pharisees and Sadducees themselves but against their teaching. They were human, God's creatures who he loved; but their teaching was bad. The best way to protect against the leaven which would spoil the dough is to get away from it: "Jesus left." Jesus did the very best thing to help the disciples grasp the lesson. He quoted the Holy Scriptures, without commentary, leaving his opponents faced with the Word of God; and then he left.

O my soul, what a beautiful lesson we are given by Jesus here, teaching us how to behave with heretics, those whose teaching is not orthodox, whose speech is evil yeast that spoils the bread. Our Fathers in the faith grasped the lesson wonderfully, calling on us not to dispute with heretics[5] since we are not fully able. We are not Jesus; we are more like Adam and Eve who didn't have the wherewithal to face the serpent and respond properly. They too had

5. "Guard against disputing with heretics in your desire to defend the faith, fearing lest the poison of their shameful words wound you. If you come across a book reputed to be heretical, do not desire to read it lest it fill your heart with deadly poison; instead hold fast to the faith of your baptism without adding or subtracting anything. Guard against pretended science/knowledge which is opposed to 'sound doctrine,' as the apostle says (1 Tim 1:10; 2 Tim 4:3)," says Abba Isaiah of Scetis (*The Asceticon*, 4:67–69.) Today, we don't really know who Abba Isaiah was; he may be Abba Isaiah of Scetis or indeed Abba Isaiah of Gaza (5th cent.). The question has not been resolved by the specialists, though this matters little to us. We can note that where Philemon refers to him elsewhere he doesn't give a location for this Father, either in Scetis or Gaza. Likewise, Barsanuphius, also referred to here, mentions him in a few letters (240, 252 and 311) without placing him geographically. It may however be, according to Jacques Touraille in a note about him (*Philocalie des Pères neptiques*, Desclée de Brouwer, 1995, p.66) that the same person, after living at Scetis left for Gaza, where he died.

only to recall the word of God which forbade them to eat the fruit, but they didn't do so. As Jesus taught both in the wilderness and here, we are to guard our hearts with the Word of God alone; we are not to enter into a debate with those whose teaching is not orthodox, above all, we who are monks. We should leave this task to those who are equipped for theological discussion and content ourselves with meditating the Holy Scriptures which are pure leaven to us; such leaven is good, working within us to make us into good bread.

"Watch and pray so that you don't enter temptation," Jesus says elsewhere (26:41); this, above all, is our place. O my soul, wasn't it in order to watch and pray that I was shown the monastic way?

"Watch out," Jesus tells us. I hold on to this warning when I receive visitors, above all with those who want to discuss questions of dogma; I make sure it's clear that I am not there to debate but to open the door of prayer to them and indeed to pray for them.

16:13–20

O my soul, have you properly understood what Jesus is saying to us? He has asked us not to say that he is the Christ. Why this prohibition? It's because it is a revelation given by the Father, one that is so important that it is a beatitude, a blessing, to those who, with Peter, welcome the revelation into the depths of their hearts. A revelation from the Father is a word of unfathomable depth, an eternal word. Jesus asks us not to talk about it so that we first have time to listen to it in its infinite depth; only after this can we talk about it. But who can understand this word from the Father of such depth? Its depth is as great as the depth of his heart. O my soul, have you measured the depths of the Father's heart? It would require an eternity to even catch a glimpse of something unending. But Jesus is exactly offering us the necessary time, offering it to us in his grace.

O my soul, have you understood what the Father said? I ask you this question because I believe that Peter himself had not fully understood. Nevertheless, the Father did make a full statement; but Peter didn't understand properly because the human heart is too narrow, too small or too hard, I don't know which, but too limited to truly understand the Father's words. This is why Jesus asks us not to talk just yet but take time to listen truly, and he asks quite simply because Peter hadn't understood. He hadn't understood a statement which was really extremely important that the Father had spoken at the Jordan (3:17) and that he would repeat on Tabor (17:5). The Father had said that Jesus is his "beloved" Son, but Peter didn't confess this because he didn't understand it. The word itself is surprising, and Peter failed to understand because it's something of such unfathomable depth, conveying the depth of the Father's love for his Son. O my soul, let us take time to understand not only this love, but also, and perhaps above all, to see it; the love of the Father can certainly be seen, but with difficulty because it is extremely humble and so greatly self-effacing. No doubt this is why the Father here brings it as a revelation, lifting the veil that covers it so that our hearts can see clearly. O my soul, have you seen the love with which the Father went along with his Son into the wilderness to be confronted with the Tempter? In his infinite love, he was there, unseen behind the visible angels who he sent to serve (Mk 1:13). He was there to serve him with the humility of a servant, the heavenly Father, the Father of infinite majesty. O my soul, have you seen the humble love with which the Father raised his Son on the indescribable Paschal night, the love with which he went to bring him up from the bottomless depths of the place of the dead? O my soul, the love of the Father for his Son is indescribable, inexpressible, beyond anything we can think or understand; this love never failed to be manifest throughout the time of the Son's presence among us, from his baptism to his resurrection, though it escapes our notice, humble as it is. Have you taken time to consider this?[6] Jesus invites us to take this time, and he was right. Only after this, after contemplating this love, can we speak about it truthfully.

O my soul, Jesus asked us not to say that he is "the Christ"! Why forbid using this one word and not the others of this revelation? Because it is a word particularly in need of the closest attention if it is to be understood in depth. It is a word as deep as the Trinity, containing in itself the mystery of the Trinity. Jesus himself explained it centuries before; like the others it comes from deep in the past. It is Jesus who said, "He has anointed me," which makes him the anointed one of the Father (Is 61:1).[7] But how did the Father anoint the Son. By causing the Holy Spirit to descend upon him.[8] The anointing of the Son by the Father was

6. [Translator's note: an invaluable source here is DB's *The Silence of God during the Passion*.]

7. The verb "to anoint" (*chriô*) gives us the noun "Christ" (*christos*); "the Christ of the Father" means "the anointed of the Father/the Father's anointed." This is the verse from Isaiah that Jesus commented on at Nazareth (Lk 4:18). While the verse comes to us from Isaiah, it was spoken not of him, since he was not the one anointed, but of Jesus. Jesus is telling us what had already taken place by the prophet's time, deep in the past, "He has anointed me." This is why Philemon says that "Jesus himself explained it centuries before." Jesus' explanation of events deep in the past had been greatly enriched by Philemon's time and still more so today.

8. As stated in the same verse from Isaiah, "The Spirit of the Lord is upon me because he has anointed me" (61:1).

manifest in the descent of the Holy Spirit onto him; thus the word "Christ" is full of the mystery of the Trinity. Neither at the baptism nor on Tabor did the Father say that the Son is the Christ; he didn't say this because he demonstrated it by causing the descent of the Spirit either like a dove or a cloud.[9] At both the baptism and at Tabor, the Son was silent in order to listen to the unfathomable words of his Father and to see the descent of the Holy Spirit, whose love is also unfathomable.

O my soul, I need to be quiet now! Let us take time to listen to all the Father is giving us to understand, coming from the depths of his heart; let us take time to look at what he sets before us to see. Jesus is offering us the time to listen to and contemplate the unfathomable and inexpressible mystery in which there is the depth of the Trinity and of the ages, and which nevertheless . . .

16:21-28

"If anyone wishes to come after me": Jesus is not here recruiting new disciples, far from it. He is not speaking to the crowd in which there might be eventual candidates but to his disciples, those who had already been following him for a long time. He was therefore not recruiting but rather giving his disciples complete liberty to stay or to go, a sign of Jesus' immense love, which absolutely respects the freedom of those he loves. Why was he speaking to them in this way?

9. Among the Fathers, the cloud at the Transfiguration designates the Holy Spirit because the cloud "covered with its shadow" (épiskiazô, 17:5) Jesus and the disciples just as the Holy Spirit "covered with his shadow" Mary on the day of the annunciation (Lk 1:35). Also, for the Fathers, the high mountain of the Transfiguration was Tabor.

Jesus was leaving the disciples free to stop following him because the situation had changed to a point where everything had still to be decided. Until then, the disciples had been following a master, but this was no longer the case since, through Peter's lips, the Father had revealed Jesus' divinity. If they continued to follow him, they would be disciples of the Son of God. With such a change, it was right to free them to either continue to follow him or not.

To follow the Son of God is exhilarating. How could you not wish to follow him when, moreover, walking behind was to take the place of Moses, who saw God from behind. This connection with Moses is suggested by Jesus himself because when he says, "If anyone wishes to come after me," he was picking up the expression spoken by God to Moses, "You will see my back" (Exod 33:29).[10] Nothing could be more uplifting than to be able to contemplate God from behind. What an extraordinary grace God was allowing Moses, and now this same grace is proposed to the disciples. It is true that Moses didn't reveal any of what took place after this moment of contemplating God. God passed in front of him; he certainly saw his back, but did he then follow? We are not told. We will discover what comes next with the disciples after Jesus invites them to follow him.

Jesus doesn't ask the disciples about the motivations that impelled them to follow him, and, in fact, we could follow him desiring all kinds of benefits: riches, favors, privileges, glory, power . . . Jesus doesn't ask but does state the decisive factor: anyone who wishes to come after me

10. In the extraordinary text in which God grants Moses the immense grace of seeing him from behind, God says more precisely, "You will see what is behind me" (*opisô mou*, Exod 33:23), and this is found again when Jesus calls us to "come after me" (*opisô mou*).

must "renounce himself." Then all the above mentioned motivations fall away because, in renouncing self, I have to renounce all of that. To follow Jesus is to step out along a road which will be his, and he has just described this as a way of suffering and death, his cross!

What motivation can I have to follow him? Just one: love for him, in compassion for what he would experience. For me, it means abandoning my life in order to give it back to him, to give it to him as he gave his for me. We are called to quit the shelter of the cleft in the rock and the protection of God's hand to march behind him bearing our own cross.[11]

Am I able to love Jesus to this degree? Whatever the case, at every moment Jesus is repeating his invitation to me, "If you wish to come after me"; he says this to me with his infinite love, which at every moment leaves me free not to follow. Jesus never forced the least of his disciples to follow him. In his immense love, he doesn't engage in any blackmail, puts no pressure on anyone. In fact when the time came that many left him, he said to his disciples, "And you, don't you also wish to leave?" (Jn 6:66), using the same verb, "wish," that gives full liberty. What respectful love for our freedom! Will I be able to love him enough to follow him along his way of suffering all the way to Golgotha? They all abandoned him, I know, (Matt 26:56), and my love for him is no greater than theirs. All I can do, therefore, is to count on God's help, listening to Jesus himself as he says to the disciples at the same moment when many left: "No one can come to me unless it is given to him by my Father" (Jn 6:65). He too renounced his own

11. Philemon continues to refer here to Moses; before he saw God from behind, he was placed in a cleft of the rock, protected by his hand (Exod 33:22).

life and the desire to save it in order to give it to each of us in his infinite love. It is this same love that we can ask of the Father so that we can follow the crucified one. When Moses saw God's back, he didn't know what it meant to follow behind him as he looked. Now, we know: it means to march on with our cross on our back, following the one who was crucified, no longer even capable of seeing his back because of our all too heavy cross, seeing only his heels, and perhaps not even them because our pace is slower than his. Happy are we if we see only the traces of his footsteps.

The path of the Passion begins here, but it passes extraordinarily through Tabor where we are able to contemplate not the back of the Transfigured one but his face: "His face shone like the sun" (Matt 17:2). But will the strength received there be enough?

MATTHEW 17

17:1–13

ELIJAH WAS PRESENT BUT SAID NOTHING TO THE disciples, though his mere presence was enough to evidence the grace that was granted him. One day, full of fear, he had lain down deeply discouraged. The angel of the Lord then touched him and said, "Rise up!"[1] Here there is one who is more than the angel of the Lord, the Lord himself, and it is he who touches the disciples and says, "Rise up and don't be afraid."[2] What immense grace this is: the one who touched them had just been revealed by God himself as his beloved Son!

In the same way, Moses was present and said nothing to the disciples, but his presence was likewise sufficient to witness to the gifts of grace granted to him. When Moses spoke with God on the mountain, the people stood at a

---

1. We are told that one day Elijah was "overcome with fear" (1 Kgs 19:3), a detail that is in the Greek but not the Hebrew. The same day, the angel of the Lord touched him and said, "Rise up" (v 7)

2. The instruction to get up is not conveyed by the same verb. With Elijah, the verb was *anistémi*, but with the disciples, égeïrô; both, however, suggest the resurrection, beautifully so because Elijah and the disciples all had good reason to feel overcome because of their experiences. On the other hand, the same verb for "to touch" (*aptô*) is used both here and in 1 Kgs 19:5.

distance so they wouldn't hear God, fearful of dying; only Moses spoke with God.[3] Here, the disciples, like Moses, were able to go up the mountain and hear God speak to them without dying. But one day Moses saw the cloud cover the tent of witness with its shadow and he couldn't go in because the glory of God had filled the tent.[4] But here, there was one greater than Moses and the disciples were able to enter the cloud that covered not the tent of witness but the Father and the Son, both present with them. This is incomparable grace because the cloud was none other than the Holy Spirit himself.[5] Beneath the cloud of the Holy Spirit, the disciples were together with the Father and the Son, enveloped in the infinite mystery of the Holy Trinity, and they were not dead: what extraordinary grace! They were not even at a distance from the Trinity but at the Trinity's very heart like no one had ever been . . . "Don't be afraid," Jesus said to them. They were then able to rise and go back down the mountain accompanied by Jesus himself. They needed such grace to give them the necessary strength to now carry their crosses and follow Jesus on his way to his cross; for six days they had been thinking over Jesus' most recent pronouncement, which had the potential to profoundly discourage them (16:21,24).

Moses had been granted the grace of seeing God without dying; it was an immense grace because really no

3. We are told this many times: Exod 20:19; Deut 5:25.

4. The verb épiskiazô ("to cover with one's shadow") and the noun néphélè ("cloud") are only found in one other place in the Bible, where we are told, "the cloud covered with its shadow" (Exod 40:35).

5. Philemon can say this because in the account of the annunciation the angel tells Mary that the Holy Spirit will "cover/overshadow [her] with his shadow." Unfortunately, translations don't always enable us to see this link, but it is certainly the same verb used here and in both Lk 1:35 and Exod 40:35.

one could see God and live (Exod 33:20). Here there was one greater than Moses, and the disciples were granted to see not God's back but his face, and, we are told, "His face shone like the sun." Again, this is immense grace because the disciples, far from being dead, were not even blinded (Acts 9:8). They were allowed to be face to face with Jesus in his divine splendor and to contemplate him to the degree they were enabled to bear. What extraordinary grace!

As they came back down the mountain, the disciples might have remembered a prophecy Jesus had announced to them. The sun-like splendor of Jesus face would have awakened in their hearts the memory of this prophecy because it spoke of the same splendor being granted to the righteous in the Kingdom of God. Jesus had told them, "The righteous shall shine like the sun in the Kingdom of their Father" (13:43). Such a prophecy is unforgettable, and the disciples had felt in their hearts that it was meant for them too. What a wonder. We see that the transfiguration of Jesus announced a similar transfiguration of the disciples in the Kingdom to come.[6] It announces this by speaking of the Father as "their" Father, their own Father, with this bond of infinite love that the Father himself had just proclaimed while speaking to Jesus. This same love

6. See e.g. the account of Seraphim of Sarov in Little Russian Philokalia Vol 1 pp 98–107, St Herman of Alaska Brotherhood, 1996. "Then Fr Seraphim took me by the shoulders and said, 'We are both in the Spirit of God now, my dear. Why don't you look at me?' I replied, 'I cannot look, Batiushka, because lightning is flashing from your eyes. Your face has become brighter than the sun, and my eyes ache with pain.' Fr Seraphim replied, 'Don't be alarmed, your Godliness! Now you yourself have become as bright as I am. You are now in the fullness of the Spirit of God yourself; otherwise you would not be able to see me as I am' . . . . After these words I glanced at his face and there came over me an even greater reverent awe. Imagine in the center of the sun, in the dazzling light of its midday rays, the face of a man talking to you . . ." [Trans.]

was also for them. They too were the Father's beloved sons. What grace! They had been told this when they were in the luminous cloud of the Holy Spirit with the Father and the Son, all together in an inexpressible communion of love. Words fail me to express the inexpressible . . .

This transfiguration of the disciples to come was prophesied by Jesus with a nuance it's good to review. Here, the face of Jesus shone like the sun, and Jesus had announced that the splendor of the disciples would derive from his own splendor,[7] like a light flowing from another light, a sun issuing from the sun. It was being proclaimed that from the divinity of Jesus would come the divinity of the disciples, who would thereby be participants in his divine nature, as Peter puts it (2 Pet 1:4). This infinite grace plunges me now into a deep state of wonderment because the communion of love of the Father, the Son and the disciples in the cloud of the Holy Spirit is the sign of an unspeakable divine communion which will transfigure the disciples and is promised to us too if we are given to be counted among the righteous. O my soul, to bear your cross with such a promise in the heart is an indescribable grace which encourages me beyond all other encouragement . . .

---

7. The verb "to shine" (*lampô*) which is used to describe the face of Jesus transfigured is not the same as that used to describe the righteous. Jesus said that the righteous would shine using *eklampô*, a very rare verb derived from the first, suggesting that the splendor of the righteous would issue from (*ek*) the splendor of Jesus. The preposition *ek* meaning "out of," "coming from," "issuing from," "drawn from," says that the transfiguration of the righteous will proceed, flow, from the transfiguration of Jesus. In this way, the righteous will participate in the divine nature of Christ. I give thanks that Philemon enables me to understand something I previously had not grasped. I hadn't understood how the Fathers in commenting on the transfiguration could also speak about our transfiguration. I didn't see what basis they had for saying this, Now, though, I give thanks that I know.

17:14-27

Coming down from the mountain top is always difficult; Moses found this when he discovered the golden calf at the foot of Mount Sinai (Exod 32). Here, Jesus finds himself confronted by men's unbelief: "O you unbelieving and perverse generation," he cries when he discovers that the disciples had been unable to heal a child. This cry of pain is not particularly aimed at them but at the whole generation, and this must surely include all future generations as well, down to ours today. When once again alone with the disciples, Jesus does soften his approach by talking about their "little faith"; but this was doubtless a way to look after them because the rest of his statement shows that their little faith was smaller than the tiny mustard seed, and there is nothing smaller than that! This is as much as to say that the disciples' faith was infinitely small, perhaps even non-existent! I ask myself, what about my faith? In Jesus' eyes, perhaps it is nothing?

What is faith then? Paul states clearly that the greatest faith, the faith that moves mountains, is nothing without love (1 Cor 13:2). Not only is it nothing, but, says Paul, "I am nothing." What then of my love for God? Jesus doesn't talk about the connection between love and faith since it was so obvious to him. For him the number one commandment was to love God (22:37). So everything begins with love; it is love that comes first because God made the heart of man to love him. It follows that if my faith is still nothing, it can begin with love and in love it will grow. How true this is: without my love for God, my faith in him will be nothing.

The summit of love lies in humility, as we find in Jesus when he washes his disciples' feet (Jn 13:1).[8] The more humble my love for God, the more it will grow and the more my faith will grow. Faith and humility are insepa-rable, as Jesus demonstrated with the Canaanite woman, whose great faith he saluted along with her great humility (Matt 15:28). Paul tells us that love is not proud (1 Cor 13:4); therefore, it is humble. Everything thus points to the basis of faith being found in humble love, and that the two grow together. This is just what God is looking for and hopes for in each of us: our faith, intimately bound to our humble love.

So, how are we to begin? With prayer, Jesus says (17:21)! This is why he calls me to return to my cell (6:6) because that is where faith, love and humility can come to birth if my heart is lacking. At its beginning, may my prayer be the prayer of a beggar who opens his hands before God and looks to him for everything. May it be with the perse-verance of the beggar who will stay entire days in the same place. Then the smallest crumb[9] of faith received from God will call me into continued prayer, and the slightest crumb of love or humility will cause my faith to grow. And

8. "Jesus loved them to the fullest extent/to the utmost/ completely" (*eïs telos*, Jn 13:1): this expression speaks of the very summit of love, The episode of the foot-washing is surely one of extreme humility, even though John doesn't use words such as "humble" or "humility" in his account or indeed anywhere in his gospel. Jesus' humility is far beyond any other humility; it's God's. Further, when it comes to the phrase "love to the utmost" there are not many translations that put it this way, many of them having "to the very end" or similar; this is not wrong because *eïs telos* can mean this. At all events, in Philemon's meditation, the meaning of "love to the utmost" is preferable.

9. Here, Philemon picks up the word from the passage on the Canaanite woman (15:27), whose humility is as remarkable as her faith; he compares himself at least a little to her.

if there is love in the gift, my thirst to give will grow, to give God my time, then my heart, then my entire life. As he has given his life for us (20:28), I will offer him mine. My stretched out hands will offer him my life, an offering of repentance, since in the presence of his luminous love the darkness in my life will be apparent. Then I will give back to him my diseased love with tears of compunction. My prayer will not demand a thing but will beg for God's care, for his forgiveness, because God binds up our wounds.[10] As I discover his humble love for me, my gratitude will grow as well as the sense of wonderment in prayer. My trust will grow too as I discover that he knows better than me what is good for me, what I need. In the presence of his humble love which cares for the birds and the young ravens (Ps 147:9), I will discover his provision and his love for all others, my friends and enemies alike. Then I will give them space humbly with love and trust in my intercessions; and if I don't know what is best for them, I will open my hands and place them confidently into his heart, with the humble love of the Samaritan who entrusted the wounded man to the hotel keeper (Lk 10:35).

And if I still don't know how to pray, I have only to turn humbly to Jesus and say, "Lord, teach me to pray" (Lk 11:1), and I believe that in a gentle whisper he will say, "I will come with you to pray in your cell." So I will go to my cell, and I know that the Father, with his infinite

---

10. "Binding up wounds": in the Bible this expression is not used in this form other than in Lk 10:34, which is most interesting in that it shows Philemon comparing God, Jesus, with the good Samaritan; this is altogether in line with the Fathers, who interpret the parable like this to underline the humble love of Christ, who bends over the dying beings that we are. As he continues his meditation, in the manner of a disciple endeavoring to imitate his Master, Philemon likens himself to the Samaritan.

humble love for Jesus and for me, will be there to welcome our prayers. Then I shall be silent to listen to Jesus' prayer, and I believe that he will say, "Father . . ." (Lk 11:2). With him beside me, my faith will begin to grow, along with my humble love for the Father.

O my soul, now I shall begin;[11] I am going to my cell . . .

11. "Now I shall begin" is taken from the Greek translation of Ps 77:10, where the Hebrew which is the basis for most of our translations is completely different. See above, note 14 on Matt 6:25–34.

MATTHEW 18

18:1–9

BROUGHT LOW AND HUMBLED ONE DAY BY THE ENEMY, David turned to God to tell him about his suffering and ask for help (Ps 143:3); there is great pain in being subject to humiliation at the hands of another person because the humiliation can be full of hatred and violence, a spirit of vengeance or domination. Being humbled by others is not the case here though; Jesus does not talk about being humbled by others but by self: "Whoever humbles himself," he says to describe not so much a situation we undergo as a freely undertaken, voluntary process. No one, not even Jesus, can impose on another voluntary self-humbling. Jesus, however, calls us to this and vigorously counsels it because in it he sees a path that leads to the Kingdom of God.

He takes as an example a small child, but there is another, still more beautiful exemplar, Jesus himself, on the day when during the supper he got up to wash the feet of his disciples. He did this freely, on his own initiative, without being asked by anyone; he, the master, stooped to perform the task of a slave! He humbled himself. What grandeur!

And what a lesson! After washing their feet, Jesus called on the disciples to do the same (Jn 13:14–15). Truly, the perfect example for us is not the little child who Jesus called for but Jesus himself.

So many disciples, saints, monks, laymen, bishops have committed themselves to following Jesus, forming the most humble cortege as they pursue the way to the Kingdom. It's wonderful! However, the Evil One gets involved, jealous and always on the lookout; he gets involved and is still meddling, sowing the seed of vainglory into hearts. Then, though we humble ourselves by washing others' feet, it is with the thought that we will be admired by men, and so we are snared; the appearance is one of humility, but vainglory reigns in the heart.

We can also wash the feet of others and seem humble while holding in our heart a desire to be honored by God, rewarded by him, and we do so the more readily because Jesus announced that if we humble ourselves we will be great in the Kingdom of God. Here is another of the traps of the Evil One, who sows into the heart the thought of humbling oneself in appearance, but with self-interest involved, the prideful pretention of being rewarded by God. This is not how Jesus washed the feet of his disciples. He did so without a trace of pride but in pure love, even "extreme love" as we are told (Jn 13:1). There was no way he could hope that at some following meal one of his disciples would wash his feet because there would be no following meal; it was his last! Jesus is full of profound, humble love.

In order not to fall into the trap of pride or vainglory, no doubt it is best to do as the Fathers did,[1] to humble oneself far from the eyes of others and before God alone, not in the manner of a mercenary looking for pay, but as a child of God who loves his Father freely, without expecting any recompense. That is what Jesus is asking here. He takes the example of a little child who obeys him without delay, without looking for any profit, without calculation; there is no hypocrisy in this child, who obeys humbly, not for appearance sake, but from the depths of his heart.

A very beautiful example of humility of heart is given us in David, who presented himself to God in repentance, with a heart that was not humbled by others but by himself.[2] He humbled himself voluntarily, impelled from within by the Holy Spirit who was helping him.[3] Certainly, he suffered compunction, but this was not a lengthy process because God's forgiveness was given to him immediately

1. The Fathers endeavored to humble themselves, not in the eyes of others, and not only with humble deeds and words but with humble, lowly thoughts, in humility of heart, as stated particularly by Abba Moses: "Be humble not only in your words but in your thoughts because it is not possible to be raised up without humility in one's works according to God" (Apophthegm XV–45). This does away with hypocrisy.

2. Philemon must be thinking here of Psalm 51 with its reference to a "humbled heart." The Greek text says literally, "God does not despise a heart that is crushed and humbled" (v 19). This psalm of repentance speaks not of a heart that is humbled by others but a heart humbled by self, in repentance.

3. Philemon mentions the Holy Spirit here because in Psalm 51, David is very conscious that his repentance takes place with the help of the Holy Spirit since he asks God, "Don't take your Holy Spirit from me" (v 13). Philemon doesn't develop this in his meditation but it is important to emphasize that humbling of self is impossible without the Holy Spirit's help; perhaps he took this further in the part of the text that is missing because of the manuscript's poor condition.

(2 Sam 12:13), a liberating forgiveness given long before the coming of the future Kingdom.[4] What grace! Anyone who humbles self can head with full confidence towards the Kingdom.

Whoever steps out along the way Jesus proposes will humble self with all their heart, and in order to humble self in this way will do so more and more spontaneously, naturally and without forcing self because God will enable their humility. It is to those who humble themselves that God gives humility, not as a recompense but by pure grace, a grace he deposits in a child-like heart. This humble child of God will then even accept being humbled by others and make such humiliations their own; they will receive humbling from God as a benefit and say with David: "It is good for me that you have brought me low" (Ps 119:71).[5] In this way, humbling is received with thanksgiving, as is every benefit received from God.

18:10–14

Here, Jesus offers the wonderful parable of the sheep that went astray. If we are to understand this parable, we need to identify the sheep. What does it represent? Is it a person or a group of people? Since commentators are divided on this,

4. Lying behind Psalm 51, as indicated in its title, is the passage in 2 Samuel where David confesses his sin to Nathan. Nathan announces God's forgiveness to him, given without delay (2 Sam 12:13). David was granted relief and freedom from his error without having to wait for the end of time, anticipating Jesus statement in verse 4 here: "Whoever humbles himself like this little child will be the greatest in the Kingdom of heaven."

5. The Hebrew text says, "It is good for me to be humbled," without specifying by whom the writer was humbled. The Greek translation understood that there was a divine passive here, "to be humbled by you," where in the Hebrew the humbling could have any source.

at first I hesitated. However, the issue became clear to me when I found in the book of Jeremiah a similar parable to which Jesus must have been referring; it compares the sheep not to a person but to an entire people, Israel, a sheep astray and ravaged by lions but saved by God (Jer 50:17–20).[6] I was confirmed in reading by Cyril of Jerusalem,[7] who interprets Jesus' parable on a still larger scale, including the whole of humanity along with Israel; Jesus didn't come just to save the people of Israel but the entirety of Adam's children. This seems to me to be the correct understanding of the parable, and it becomes clearer still in Peter's epistle where we find that the lion which seeks to seize and devour the sheep is the devil (1 Pet 5:8).

A sheep that has really gone astray is incapable of rejoining its flock; the shepherd has to go off to look for it, find it and bring it back. This is just what Jesus did as his greatest joy and for the joy of the Father; he leads lost humanity back to the Father after seeking it in the very den of the lion which had seized it to devour it. The whole of Jesus' life is there, wonderfully summarized.

Hoping to be found, the sheep begins to bleat, calling out to its savior, and we hear this call in one of the psalms:

---

6. Both "sheep" (*brebis*) and "[go] astray" (*planaô*) are exactly the same in Jeremiah and here.

7. Cyril of Jerusalem (4th cent.) interprets the parable in this way in his *Baptismal Catacheses* (XV–24). The same interpretation is found in many of the Fathers, including Ambrose of Milan (4th cent.) in his *Treatise on the Gospel of Luke* (VII–209). Those who follow this line generally make a connection with Zacchaeus and Jesus' statement that "the Son of Man has come to seek and save that which was lost" (Lk 19:10). In his commentary on Matthew's Gospel, John Chrysostom doesn't spend much time on this parable, but the little he does say sees the sheep as the individual (*Sermons on Saint Matthew*, 59:5), as does Gregory of Nyssa (4th cent.) in his commentary on the Song of Songs.

"I have gone astray like a lost sheep; come and seek your servant" (119:176). This wonderful appeal was uttered by David, not in his name alone but on behalf of his people as a whole. The love of this king for his people was so great that he saw them as one with him. We can understand it in the same way when he says, "I will keep your law forever, in eternity and through the ages" (v 44). No single person can speak like this because no one can live that long; if David says this it's because he was praying in the name of the entirety of his people, to which he saw himself belonging. He could say both, "I have not strayed" (v 110) and "I have gone astray" (v 176), a contradiction which can only be understood if he was speaking on behalf of everyone, those who had strayed and those who had not. This wonderful teaching shows me that an intercessor full of deep and humble love will manage to take all for whom he prays into himself. Indeed, an immense love and immense humility is needed to pray in this way, effacing oneself completely but without losing a sense of solidarity with those we pray for. Such humble love is found in the Canaanite who interceded for her daughter with Jesus when she said, "Have pity on me" and "Come and help me" (15:22, 25). What she was saying was not her own prayer but her daughter's. She was so humble that she didn't express her own distress but only her daughter's, who she loved to the point of taking her into herself.

The same applies to Jesus as he prayed on the cross, "My God, my God, why have you forsaken me?" (27:46; Ps 22:1). This wasn't his own way of praying since when he prayed he always said, "Father," never, "my God." In his infinite humility, he was effacing himself in favor of all the abandoned and forsaken who he loved to the point of assimilating himself to them and making their prayer his own. How beautiful this is! O my soul, may God fill my heart with humble love to intercede like this.

"I have gone astray like a lost sheep; come and seek your servant," David says at the end of his Psalm, making this appeal his final cry to God. Jesus heard this prayer spoken on behalf of us all. Then he composed his parable, using every one of David's words, showing that he understood his cry. Not only had he heard but he responded by setting out to seek his sheep in the depths of hell, where, after going astray, it was being devoured by lions. What humble and immense love our good shepherd has for us! This is also how he obeyed his Father, whose will is that not one of his children be lost, not even the smallest or least important. He became a man to save men and women and went to the place of the dead to seek all who were lost and bring them back to his Father. Jesus concludes the parable by speaking of his joy, and I marvel at the extreme sobriety with which he speaks; but how could it be otherwise when this joy is beyond words and beyond every other joy? This joy is Jesus' joy, for sure, but it is also his Father's, the joy of the sheep that is restored, and the joy of the rest of the flock, the angels, the archangels and the heavenly host.[8] This joy is ours, a joy that overflows our thankful hearts in the presence of the one who saves from death and leads us back from the place of the dead.

18:15–20

For these words of Jesus to be fulfilled, it is not necessary to have a large number present such as the Fathers at

8. The mention of angels again shows Philemon being consistent with Cyril of Jerusalem, for whom the ninety nine other sheep were the angels and the heavenly host left by Jesus with the Father when he came to accomplish his mission among us.

an ecumenical council; it's not necessary to gather twelve, like the disciples in the upper room on the day of Pentecost (Acts 2:1),[9] and not even four, such as Mary, Joseph, the infant Jesus and Simeon in the Jerusalem temple for the Holy Encounter (Lk 2:22).[10] It is enough to be just three or even two, and to pray together somewhere on earth. Then the heavenly Father will answer the prayer; such prayer has all the beauty of a symphony, is cosmic in its scope and Trinitarian in depth.

Such prayer really does have Trinitarian depth because when the two or three pray together, Jesus says he is there in the midst and that the heavenly Father is listening, ready to answer their prayers; and the Holy Spirit is there too, of course, because it is he who brought them together, as Jesus specifies with a divine passive: "They are gathered together."[11] This is how such prayer is Trinitarian in depth. It is also cosmic in scope because those who pray are firstly "on the earth," as Jesus says, and then there is the Father, who is "in heaven." Finally, this prayer has musical beauty because Jesus uses a term for a symphony[12] to describe the sound of two or three human voices harmoniously filling the

9. The place where the Twelve met is not specified but Philemon supposes, correctly no doubt, that it was the same upper room where they had previously gathered to pray (Acts 1:13).

10. The "Holy Encounter" (*Hypapante*) is the eastern term for the feast known in the west as the Feast of the Presentation or Candlemas.

11. "They are gathered together," or more precisely, "having been gathered together." *Sunègménoï* is a perfect passive participle from *sunagô* suggesting that they are gathered by God, which is to say by the Holy Spirit; the Father has already been said to be in heaven and the Son is present in the room and so cannot be considered the one who brought the believers together.

12. "If two agree," uses the verb *sumphônéô* which gives us the word "symphony"; it is indeed a musical term meaning "to sound together" and "perform a symphony."

silence of the Father, the Son and the Holy Spirit, who listen to their melody, which for them has a wonderful musical beauty. Further to all this, such prayer crosses time and fills it since the Spirit "had drawn" (past) the brothers together, the Son "is there," (present), and the Father will answer in a future that will overtake us.[13] The specific content of the prayer matters little, so long as it is in agreement with the Holy Spirit, who prompted it, and the Son who promotes it; then the Father receives it in profound communion with them. No doubt it's also enough if the prayer is full of deep, humble love, even when it's the prayer of two or three beggars or two or three children.

This is the inexpressible beauty of these words from Jesus: it is enough that two or three pray together. What are we to say, then, of the prayers of one person alone in their solitude or out in the bleakness of the desert? Will the Father hear such prayer?

O my soul, the Lord is blessed for giving Abba Isaiah an answer to this question,[14] revealing to him a further depth to this saying. He said that it is enough if, rather than two brothers being joined in prayer, the spirit and soul of just one person are united in prayer. It is a miracle of the Holy Spirit to unify a human person in prayer, to unite their soul and spirit, their lips and heart,[15] their whole being.

13. As in note 11 above, the verb for "unite/gather together" (*sunagô*) is in a perfect tense which, in Greek, means a present situation with a beginning in the past. Philemon continues by underlining the way Jesus says, concerning himself, "I am" in the present tense, and then "he will come" (*génèsétaï*) in the future tense pointing to the Father fulfilling his word.

14. Philemon is referring to Abba Isaiah's *The Asceticon* (25:2).

15. God's complaint is reported by the prophet Isaiah and quoted in Matthew 15:8: "This people honor me with their lips but their heart is far from me." This clearly states the disunity of the human person, even when praying.

Where there is this profound unity, Jesus will join in and the Father will receive their prayer. While it is difficult to be perfectly unified in one's being in prayer, the Holy Spirit will perform this miracle; the Son then joins in and so does the Father. The most holy Trinity is there in perfect silence to receive the prayer of one individual united in their being. The Trinity is there, unseen, in humble, profound love to accompany this prayer wherever it takes place on earth, whether in the oratory of the patriarch in Constantinople, in the cave of a hermit in the desert of Scetis, on a street in Gaza or beside the road that leads out of Jericho (Mk 10:46). O my soul, the Trinity is also here by grace in my cell, already present in the silence that precedes my prayer in that blessed moment when the Holy Spirit comes to unify my being before helping me pronounce the first word of prayer addressed to the Father in the presence of the Son. O my soul, this is an indescribable moment that fills me with emotion and, I believe, brings joy to God. Don't forget that in his Trinitarian mystery, God created the heavens and earth and on the seventh day was silent to welcome from the lips of Adam and Eve the first words of the symphony of their prayer. God is silent, now . . . It is a blessed moment when the Father, the Son and the Holy Spirit along with the whole celestial host are listening for the simple words of human prayer.

Heavenly Father, you are here, attentive, silent, filling my cell with love. With overwhelming humility you await the first words of my prayer; I am here, grateful but a little hesitant since it is hard for me to break the silence I have prolonged so I can taste its beauty. You are here in silence, as is Jesus, also silent, as well as the Holy Spirit; your silence alone has a beauty that overwhelms me, a symphony of silence that envelops me in your love. And I am here, just pronouncing the name, Father, this name that is so sweet to the ears of my heart . . . .

18:21-35

With his question, Peter draws Jesus' attention to the issue of forgiveness and how it is to be granted to a brother who has sinned against him; he first proposes to forgive up to seven times, which seemed to him to be quite generous, indeed the limit of what could be thought reasonable. In his immediate answer, Jesus pushes any limit out to the illimitable, way beyond what is reasonable: "I say to you, seventy times seven," which more or less means it's incalculable. Then he adds a parable which makes his response explicit while setting Peter's question aside.

When he proposed a number, Peter was making this a matter for accountants, not an issue of sin and forgiveness; he was mixing together two areas which simply shouldn't be confused. We can tally up a debt, but not sins or forgiveness; these are beyond counting. Further, to talk in terms of numbers puts us on the professional basis of relationship between a master and a servant, not the family or ecclesiastic relationship that Peter envisages here when speaking about a brother.

The parable sets the question as it stands aside by involving God; this was not Peter's concern, which was limited to issues between brothers, having to do with solely human generosity, independent of God. Jesus, however, talks about "the Kingdom of heaven," discreetly introducing the inexpressible divine element, it being well understood that the word "heaven" meant God; the king of the parable could only be God. With this, everything changes: while Jesus continues with Peter's terminology of accounts, now it is accounts with God; this sets us before the illimit-able and even unimaginable because a servant could never pay God ten thousand talents![16] Before God, our faults are innumerable and incalculable, all the more because they are renewed every day. No one could ever count up or tell their faults when it comes to God, nor the forgiveness received from him.

More than this, Jesus introduces terms which have nothing to do with accounts and only take on their full meaning when connected with God; he speaks of "compas-sion" and "mercy," in reference to the two great attributes of God, the merciful and compassionate (Exod 34:6). It's certainly the case that these two concepts are part of the human reality as stated by Peter in his question; God is not alone in being merciful and compassionate since we too can extend these two attributes to a brother, and Jesus calls us to be merciful in his conclusion (v 33). The issue then is mercy towards a brother, but this has really to do with the heart and not with reason; mercy and compassion know nothing of accounting; a heart that loves with mercy and compassion gives and forgives without keeping score.

Compassion makes us aware of a brother's suffering in order to relieve it and even take away the source of his suffering by forgiveness. When we are merciful to a brother, we free him from the slavery of a debt. Compassionate and merciful forgiveness restore the brotherly relationship which had been downgraded and damaged by sin.

The parable also shows that we ourselves live on the basis of the compassion and mercy of God, who forgives

---

16. "Ten thousand talents" is a considerable sum, perhaps as much as sixty million dollars, so a situation with no way out for the indebted servant.

every day in a way that is unlimited, infinitely more than we can forgive a brother who sins against us. In forgiving, we are not drawing on the reserves of our mercy but on the endless mercy received from God. More, our debt towards God, which is being forever augmented, makes us aware that we are much worse sinners than is the brother who sins against us; this calls us to be humble and not to measure our forgiveness. While Peter might have thought himself generous in forgiving his brother up to seven times, Jesus invites us to be humble towards a brother who is less of a sinner than we are.

Finally, Jesus makes himself part of the new relationship described in the parable, but not at all in the way Peter expected. In his question, Peter wanted Jesus to act as a sort of arbiter, but in the parable, Jesus puts himself in a quite different role insofar as the king in the parable turns out in the end to be his Father (v 35), which makes Jesus our brother. As a brother, he is adding his prayer to ours to touch the Father's heart, as he did on the cross: "Father, forgive them, they don't know what they are doing" (Lk 23:34). If my brother comes to me to ask forgiveness, Jesus also comes with him and intercedes on his behalf to touch my heart, saying, "In the same way that with mercy and compassion I have forgiven you without ever keeping an account, you also should be merciful and compassionate towards your brother, who is also my brother, as are you . . ."

MATTHEW 19

19:1–12

"THERE ARE EUNUCHS WHO HAVE MADE THEMSELVES eunuchs for the sake of the Kingdom of him; let whoever can understand, understand!" If our higumen hadn't entrusted the formation of novices in the monastery to me, I wouldn't have written down my mediation on this verse but would have kept it in my heart and in my prayers for God alone; it really touches the depths of my soul.

Very few Fathers have written on this verse; to my knowledge Abba Isaiah is the only one to have done so, no doubt for the benefit of Abba Peter, his spiritual son, and for the novices in his monastery. He wrote very humbly, without mentioning himself; I take him as my example, and I pray the Lord will help me prepare for the day when I will stand before the novices who will all be voluntary eunuchs in the way the Lord discusses here.

Jesus was very succinct and discreet on this subject, knowing full well that it's a matter that goes deep into the soul and that only the light of the Holy Spirit enables an understanding of such mystery.

What I can certainly say is that since creation, the condition of man has not been to be alone but to marry (Gen 2:18). Jesus fully assumed the human condition, yet without marrying, which is a great surprise, though he did see himself as a spouse (Matt 9:15; 25:1) without saying who his partner was. Paul informs us that Christ's spouse is the Church (Eph 5:25), so this is a spiritual and collective reality rather than being personal. He speaks collectively like this, without however rejecting the idea that a person could appropriate this spiritual connection with Christ since everything that concerns the Church concerns us personally.

In the Scriptures, God himself is seen as a spouse (Is 61:10; 62:5) and reveals that his spouse is his people; this certainly helped Paul understand that for Jesus too the spouse was collective. A cause for wonder here is to see that Jesus fully assumed the human reality by calling himself a spouse while remaining at the same time within the divine reality, again with the term spouse. How beautiful this is! Jesus is fully God and fully man as the spouse of his people, the Church, and this never excludes the same personal connection with each of us as a member of the Church.

Curiously, Jesus uses the image of the yoke to speak of the espoused couple, and this is something new; he does this here, in this very text,[1] before discussing the eunuchs who are not married. Earlier, he had used the image of the yoke[2] to describe himself as the bearer of a yoke, inviting us to join him under the same yoke. On that occasion, the invitation was personal and not collective, addressed not to the Church in general but to each of us, whether married or not. The image is used as an invitation to join him person-ally, not physically but spiritually, and it is this that the Holy

1. "Let man not separate what God has joined together," Jesus says (19:6) using the verb *sunzeugnumi* ("unite") which literally means "to place under the same yoke." We have our word "conju-gal" from the Latin. In the Old Testament, this image of the yoke is never used with respect to marriage, so Jesus is innovating here.

2. "My yoke is easy" (11:30).

Spirit is setting before us here in our verse, that is, the voluntary eunuch as one who consecrates his entire life to walking beneath the yoke together with Jesus, united with him by a spiritual bond. In the grace of the Holy Spirit, all monks have understood it this way and so live out Jesus' words. The famous apophthegm that shows us that a voluntary eunuch does not emasculate self is there to spell this out for we monks.[3] A eunuch for the Kingdom, as Abba John the Prophet[4] and Abba Isaiah say, is a spiritual eunuch who offers his whole being to the Lord in response to the invitation to put self under the yoke with him as one who is affianced.[5] This image of the yoke is a wonderful invitation to a life totally consecrated to the Lord in total obedience, a complete trust and love that surpasses any other since the love offered by Jesus is the divine love that surpasses all others. In the same way that, in the Scriptures, God offers

3. Apophthegm 1334. In the 4th century, two monks emasculated themselves as a way to put Jesus' words into practice; as a result they were excommunicated by the patriarch of Alexandria. Not understanding this, they went to see other patriarchs, who had the same reaction; finally, it was Epiphanius of Salamis who helped them understand where they were mistaken. After repenting, they were able to take up the monastic life once more. The apophthegm helped other monks avoid the same error.

4. Abba John, or John the Prophet, was a disciple of Abba Barsanuphius, the Chief Elder. He spent the last eighteen years of his life in a hermitage alongside his mentor and died in 540. I don't know whether he was still alive when Philemon wrote his meditations. In a letter addressed to a monk, John the Prophet cited a part of this verse from the gospel but adding the word "spiritually," which makes things clear; "There are eunuchs who makes themselves spiritually eunuchs for the sake of the Kingdom of heaven" (Letter 169 in the *Correspondence* vol 1 of Barsanuphius and John of Gaza.

5. On many occasions, Abba Isaiah speaks of the soul as affianced to Jesus (The Asceticon, 19:4–5; 25:22–25; 28:35). [As a translator's note, the term *affianced* and cognates have to do primarily with trust and confidence and only secondarily with marriage; this seems a suitable note of caution.]

his love collectively to his people but this can also be interpreted personally, Jesus offers his love to each of us personally as a total gift to which we can respond with a like total gift, putting ourselves with him under the yoke, as a voluntary eunuch, in God's grace. The mystery of this reality of life enables us to receive with joy the wonderful words God entrusted to the prophet Isaiah: "As a bridegroom rejoices with his bride, so the Lord will rejoice with you" (62:5).

O my soul, in his infinite love, God does not wish to leave man on his own; he carefully prepares a helper to walk beside him. To one he gives a woman as his spouse to help him, to the other he humbly proposes himself as a help, and he is welcomed in wonderment: "My help and protector, it is you . . ." (Ps 119:114).[6]

19:13–15

The first verb in this text shows what an excellent teacher Matthew was, more so than Mark or Luke, who use the same verb but less clearly. Mark (10:13) and Luke (18:15) both say, "They brought children," using an impersonal construction that gives us to understand that behind this activity were the parents, though it might equally be understood, discreetly, that God was at work through the parents.[7] To avoid any such misunderstanding with

6. The first Hebrew noun here (sétèr) is usually translated today as "shelter," "hiding place," "shield," "refuge," but in the Greek of the Septuagint we find boèton ("help/helper"), the word used in Genesis (2:18,20) to designate the spouse who would be a helper to the man.

7. An impersonal construction is another way of evoking God without naming him so as to respect the commandment in the Decalogue requiring that the name of God not be taken in vain (Exod 20:7).

respect to the name of God, which was not to be spoken, Matthew says, "Children were brought,"[8] using a divine passive which doesn't rule out the parents' role but does make very clear God's role working through them. How lovely! The parents' actions are very beautiful because they desired Jesus' benevolent intervention in their children's lives; even more beautiful, though, is to see God, through the parents, also caring for the children and bringing them to Jesus. Did the parents understand what God was doing through them? So much the better if this was the case, since it would show that the parents here knew to trust themselves and the lives of their children to God's care. If not, it is to be regretted but is not so serious because God was no less attentive to the lives of the children and was working despite other factors, still more discreetly. As for Jesus, who never missed what his Father was doing, he knew very well what was going on behind the parents' activities, as he says elsewhere so clearly: "No one can come to me unless the Father draws him" (Jn 6:44). This is why he corrected the disciples so that they wouldn't prevent obedience to and the performance of what was being asked of him by the parents as well as by his Father.

It's important for us to understand this because it applies to the baptism of children. Whether they know it or not, parents are led by God in what they do. I am happy every time I assist at the baptism of a child; through the parents, God himself is asking for the child's baptism. It is truly beautiful to contemplate this! This humble God, in his infinite love, hides himself reservedly in this process!

8. In the French, unlike many English versions, translators mostly pay little attention to this divine passive. One translator, Osty, does note it and translates clearly; it's unfortunate that inexact translation can prevent a reader who doesn't know Greek from meditating in a way that sees the humble, discreet work of God in our lives.

God knows how to work wonderfully through us, always perfectly respecting our freedom. What magnificent love!

"Leave the children alone and don't stop them coming to me; the Kingdom of heaven is for those who are like them": O my soul, how good it is for us to meditate these great words; it is Jesus who is speaking to us! How good it is to open our hearts to the Holy Spirit for him to lead us in our meditation. And how good to know that it is the Father who cares for the children and those who are like them, leading them to his Son. O my soul, let the children come to Jesus; it is God who is leading them; it is the Father who leads them to his Son. Let them come because of themselves they don't resist but allow themselves to be easily led by the Father to his Son, abandoning themselves to him, as should each of us. We resist the Father who wishes to lead us to Jesus, while children don't resist at all, and in this they are truly models for us, which is why Jesus presents them in that way. Our place is to listen to Jesus and allow ourselves to be led to him by his Father without resisting and without disobeying him. A child obeys God naturally and spontaneously; he or she also mysteriously obeys the Holy Spirit, who works within them and causes them to obey God. Naturally, children resist neither the Father, nor the Son nor the Holy Spirit; they abandon themselves to the Trinity without pausing to think or look for objections; they abandon themselves whole-heartedly, with their whole beings because they feel the infinite love of God leading them; they are naturally reassured by this love and are open to it; they believe in God naturally since they see in him only his love. Unbelief is a spiritual sickness that may trap a person, but later; it is a sickness that only affects adults. As for an unbelieving child, such a thing does not exist; a child that is closed off to the love of God does not exist.

Therefore, we need to be like children, open to the infinite love of God. It wasn't the children who somehow declined to be taken up in Jesus' arms; they went there without any resistance, drawn by his infinite love. It was the disciples who wanted to stop them, but the children abandoned themselves to this love which surpasses all love; the children were abandoned to the love of the Son, to the work of his Father who was leading them to him and to the work of the Holy Spirit who prodded them from within. What an infinite mystery of love this is, begging to be deeply meditated, immersing us in the mystery of the thrice holy God. O my soul, like a child, let us allow the love of God to invade our heart and soul in full strength so that we love him in return with our whole heart, our whole soul and with all our strength, according to his deep desire. It is this . . .

19:16–22

"What good thing must I do to have eternal life?" This was the young man's question, which Jesus immediately corrected before continuing the conversation. He corrected him on two fronts, firstly by changing the article in front of the word "good," because for him "good" is not a thing but a person: "Only one is good," he says.[9] To avoid any doubt, Mark and Luke specify that the person here is God (Mk 10:18; Lk 18:19), but Matthew doesn't do this because Jesus didn't, having perceived that this young man was a pious Jew who respected the commandments and knew that he should not take the name of God in vain (Exod 20:7).

9. In Greek, there are masculine, feminine and neuter articles. The rich young man used the neuter to indicate a thing, but Jesus replaced it with a masculine, indicating a person.

On Jesus' part, there was doubtless more than respect for the holy name; it stood for the inexpressible divine mystery.

The second correction had to do with life; this man spoke of it as an asset he could "have," revealing in him a rich man's thirst for possession. For Jesus, life is not something one "has," but is something to "enter," which puts us at one end of a process, on a path.

With these two corrections in place, Jesus continues the conversation, seemingly ready to take this man with him: "Come," he says, as an invitation to him. Come and follow me along the road we will take "to enter into life" and which leads to "the one who alone is good." Alongside his invitation, Jesus has this preface: before following me, sell everything and give it away; then, when you are rid of it all, you can set off towards the one who is good. However, the man declined to follow Jesus. He had, though, already taken a very important step that disposed him to take the journey, obedience to the Law. "All this I have observed," he had said to Jesus, who, Mark tells us, was full of love for him (10:21).

So, we see this man declining to follow Jesus, but that doesn't mean that the way was closed; it remains open to those have sold everything to follow Jesus. What is the nature of the path to be run in voluntary poverty towards him who Jesus doesn't name?

When Jesus talks about the commandments, he lists them and stops at the one to do with love of neighbor (v 19), thereby showing that the way of obedience includes love; he stops before citing the great commandment which calls us to a much greater love, love to be given with the whole heart, the whole soul and with all one's strength.[10] This is love for the one Jesus doesn't name, the one who alone is good, whose infinite and eternal love for us we know (Jer 31:3). "Come and follow me," says Jesus, inviting us to follow him along the way of an immense love for the one who alone is good and whose love is indescribable.

Why, then, sell everything and give it away? To lighten the burden, to free oneself from the all that has no value in the face of the only good, in order not to be attached to anyone other than him, the one who loves us beyond all else, infinitely and eternally. If the young man had understood this, he would have sold everything. Jesus had even sign-posted the way with a promise: "You will have treasure in heaven." The promise was given to help the young man be engaged; the word "treasure" was very much part of his vocabulary and would surely motivate him. This was decidedly a sign-post, not a goal to be attained because Jesus specified that entering into life did not mean acquiring something but joining with someone in a relationship of love; the goal remained well and truly a person, the only good, not the treasure of good but the good himself, in a relationship of indescribable love.

"Come and follow me": Jesus says nothing else here, but says enough to make us want to follow. Later, on the evening before his death, he would say a little more to the disciples and those who were accompanying him. He spoke of the life into which they were to enter, saying, "I am the life"; and with respect to the one good who he hadn't named here, he said, "He is in me and I in him" (Jn 14:10), and we understand that this is he whose name alone is filled with

---

10. In 19:19, Jesus says, "Honor your father and mother; and love your neighbor as yourself," and stops there. [Trans.]

infinite love: his Father. Then he specifies, "I am the way, the truth and the life; no one comes to the Father except by me" (14:6).

O my soul, this is the goal of the path: the Father, whose love is inexpressible and beyond all other loves; the Father, whose name itself is beyond words, his fatherhood being beyond all other fatherhood. "Come and follow me," Jesus says to us; so it is not for us to head towards the Father in the manner of mercenaries who thirst for possessions, even heavenly treasures, precious though they may be, but like beloved children, who, after giving everything away, have nothing more to give than their poor love and their lives, walking behind the beloved Son who has given us his life and unfailingly gives us his infinite love, as inexpressible as his Father's, who is our Father and who . . .

19:23–30

"Who can be saved?" Jesus' answer is very surprising because he doesn't answer the question itself but another, modifying what he had been asked. He replies, "For men, this is impossible, but for God, everything is possible." When asked, "Who can be saved?" he replies by saying that it is God who saves, as if he had been asked, "Who can save?" His answer doesn't discuss those who are saved but the one who saves. What a surprise! Jesus is so surprising that it's best that we be silent before him and allow him to speak further without rushing in after the manner of Peter.

We should be quiet and fix our attention on the one who has replied so strangely; we should look to him while keeping our questions in our hearts; we look to him to take in the fact that the one who saves, this God who saves, is him, Jesus! It is he whose name was explained at the outset of the gospel when the angel said to Joseph, "You will call him Jesus, because it is he who saves" (1:21). The disciples hadn't heard the angel, but they were Jews and they knew all the same that "Jesus" means "God saves." They know that Jesus wasn't so much giving an answer to the question as he was the answer, he incarnated the answer. With this, there is nothing more to be said: he is the answer. It's not a matter of simply listening to him but above all of looking at, contemplating him; if our heart is full of questioning, it can return to peace by contemplating the one who incarnates our salvation.

Before answering them, we are told that Jesus looked at his disciples. We are to look at the one who is looking at us; his gaze attracts ours and invites us into a wonderful face to face encounter. Why go any further? He answered, and that is enough; we can stop right here without listening to the rest of the conversation. And stopping is just what I do; I am not a theoretician and neither am I an empty talker; I am just a monk. To contemplate Jesus as the one who saves is enough for me. When novices ask me about salvation, I invite them to contemplate Jesus, who is the answer; he incarnates salvation, life with God, heart to heart loving of God. Nothing is more important than this . . .

"He looked at them." What a look. This is not a simple rapid glance, but a deep look, penetrating into the depths of the heart,[11] a look of love which saw into the heart in the way only God can see (1 Sam 16:7). This is not a look that judges but one that sheds light into my heart's depths.

---

11. The verb "to look" that Matthew uses here is not the simple form *blépô*, which he uses eighteen times, but *emblépô*, which is a composite verb meaning more precisely "look within," which he only uses twice (6:26 and here). With this rare verb, Matthew seeks to draw our attention to the profound gaze of Jesus.

It invites me to look at him, to be sure, but also to look at him while letting him look into me, allowing him to see in my heart anything that causes him shame or wounds him, anything sick and that needs precisely to be saved. That is what he is here to do. His look cares for me and invites me to tell him what needs to be tended, healed, saved. He invites me, but not to pursue some theological discussion about salvation but to confess to him what needs to be saved. He invites me to open my heart to him. If Jesus incarnates the answer to the question about salvation, he is also salvation at work, the physician who tends and brings life.

In his answer, Jesus responds in a general way: "For men, this is impossible." He says, "for men," not "for you." This is great delicacy! He looks at us, but without curiosity, without staring, without forcing us, but gently, leaving us free to show him whatever is good for him to see. He doesn't only see the things that are sick; he is not only a physician but is also a brother who sees the creature of God, the child of God, the brother that we are to him. He sees the sick child, yes, but also the child the Father loves and who he, Jesus, loves just as much. He already sees someone who will have a throne with him in heaven; he looks at us in the way he looked at and loved the rich young man (Mk 10:21).[12] The one who looks contemplatively at us is the one who loves us, who loves us with such love that our desire is to unveil everything to him with infinite trust.

O my soul, don't look elsewhere when he looks at you, don't close your heart but allow him to fix his loving gaze on the depths that are invisible to you, knowing that he is

---

12. Mark also uses the verb *emblépô* for the gaze fixed on the rich young man, but adds "to love" (*agapô*), which shows that his gaze came with love.

able to see even those things you don't know to confess (Ps 19:12), and that his gaze will tend, heal, restore and bring to rest whatever needs it, making you into a new creature . . .

O Jesus, my Savior and my God, your gaze when fixed on me is one of infinite love that doesn't judge, a gaze that sees in the depths of my soul a child of God, that alights gently on anything sick in order to tend to it, a gaze that does good, that meets with mine to invite me to contemplate you with a love that responds to yours, a gaze that wishes to save me from that everything that . . .

MATTHEW 20

20:1–16

THIS PARABLE STARTS WITH THE ESTABLISHMENT OF A contract which is perfectly legal and just. One penny a day was the right amount;[1] in fact, so right that the agreement is concluded with a musical term.[2] Justice is harmonious. The workers set off to work with a song in their hearts. However, the working day finished on a discordant note of murmuring[3] because the first workers thought that the master was being unfair to them. He replied to one of them, "I have not been unjust towards you."[4] This was true because the contract had been fully respected; nevertheless, in his generosity, the master had effectively given extra to those employed last, and it was this generosity which the first comers saw as an injustice. Instead of dwelling on the

1. In Jesus' days, one penny was the average wage for a worker for a day's work.

2. "Conclude an agreement" here is *sumphônéô*.

3. The Greek *gogguzô* (v 11) means "to murmur" or "grumble." Translators are uncertain; it all depends on the intensity supposed of the workers' reproaches! Whichever is right, Philemon was correct to think that they were not very melodious.

4. Some translate *adikéô* as "I have done nothing wrong" (v 13), but it seems better to me to say, "I have not been unjust" because injustice (*adikia*) is precisely the problem presented in this parable (also, *dikaïos*, "that which is just," v 4).

murmuring, the master asks a question: "Isn't it the case that your eye is evil?" which comes to saying, "Is it I who am unjust or you whose eye is evil? It's for you to decide between the two. If you take my generosity for injustice, this must come from your evil eye."

It's true that the master was just towards the first and generous towards the last, and this generosity does have an unjust aspect to it when seen with an evil eye. In the Scriptures, the expression "an evil eye" designates either jealousy or envy, according to the context.[5] It is clear here that those who thought the master unjust were jealous and that their jealousy stemmed from their selfishness; selfishness or egoism makes you think more of yourself than of others. The first workers believed they had been injured when they had not; injured, because they thought they should have received more because of their hard work and the great heat. However, they weren't thinking of the latecomers who had spent long hours without work, hard as that would have been, with the inner frustration of waiting for work which didn't come, faced with the anguish of going home, ashamed of having nothing to feed their families with. The latecomers might also have been jealous of the first, who would be able feed their families; they might even have murmured against a God who had abandoned them to misery.[6] We don't know if they had jealous

5. The "evil eye" is found in both the Septuagint (Deut 15:9; 28:54,56) and the New Testament (Mk 7:22; Lk11:34). Some translators are literal while others replace the term with "jealousy" or "envy."

6. The verb "to murmur" (*gogguzô*) is commonly found in the Exodus account where the hungry people murmured against Moses and Aaron (16:7), who retorted by saying that the murmuring was in fact against God, and was unjust because God had heard their murmuring and was about to respond by giving the people quail and bread (16:12); he then gave them manna every day for forty years (16:35) until they entered the promised land (Josh 5:12), an expression of his extraordinary goodness. All this lies behind the word "murmur" used in the parable.

thoughts, but the first comers certainly murmured and gave expression to their jealousy. Jealousy is serious because it sees injustice where there is generosity and is then unable to rejoice with the person on the receiving end of generosity. It knows only to murmur against others and against God instead of rejoicing with those who receive a sign from God of his generosity. It makes the eye so bad that it can no longer see God's goodness, so sick that it is becomes unable to contemplate God in his generosity. Jealousy cannot be a contemplative. Jealousy destroys love in relationships with others and with God. It is a real blight on communal life; this is why Gregory of Nyssa (4th cent.) had good reason to see jealousy as the principle malady.[7]

Jealousy is certainly a malady and not some congenital malformation of the eye. God didn't create the eye evil or man jealous. It's the malady that makes the eye evil, and it comes from the Evil One, who is jealous himself.[8] Evidence of the seriousness of this malady is that it was the Evil One who introduced it into the human heart at the beginning, making Adam and Eve jealous of God with the thought that he was keeping for himself the privilege of knowing

---

7. "Jealousy, the passion that is the first cause of evil, that gave birth to death, sin's first entrance, the root of evil, the source of sadness, the mother of evils, the cause of disobedience, the beginning of shame. Jealousy, having become a serpent to seduce Eve, drove us out of Paradise (Gen 3:5); jealousy separated us from the tree of life and, having stripped us of our garments of holiness, clothed us with the laughable leaves of the fig tree (3:7); jealousy armed Cain against his brother (4:5) and inaugurated the death of sevenfold punishment (4:15); jealousy made Joseph a slave (37:11) [. . .]; jealousy is the *sickness* of our nature [. . .]; it sees as evil not its own evil but the good of others [. . .]" (Gregory of Nyssa, *The Life of Moses*, HCSC p111–112). I have emphasized the word "sickness," as noted by Philemon.

8. The eye that is "evil" (*ponéros*) is a product of the "Evil One" (*ponéros*), another term for Satan (Matt 13:19).

both good and evil (Gen 3:5). It was the same malady that assailed Cain's heart, making him so seriously jealous of Abel that he finally killed him (Gen 4:3–8) when he might have rejoiced for him that God had generously received his offering; Abel was the weak one, while Cain had the privileges of being the older brother and also the security of a settled life, not the insecurity of the nomadic life. Jealous is so serious that it can destroy communal life because it destroys the love between brothers. It also destroys life with God because it replaces love for him with suspicion, and thanksgiving with murmuring.

It is good to think of jealousy as a malady because this means it can be treated and healed. It can be healed by God, the doctor of souls, who, according to the Fathers, prescribed the best of remedies by inviting humble repentance. Repentance is needed by anyone who has accused God of being unjust because he is good and indeed the only good, as Jesus had just been saying to the disciples (19:17). A person who repents can be forgiven and will then discover the merciful generosity of God in the forgiveness. Isn't the grace of forgiveness a sign of generosity towards someone who accuses God unjustly. The unjust person is one who accuses God of being unjust when he isn't.

O my soul, may the sick person who has been forgiven stop murmuring and instead give thanks to God for his mercy in which his immense generosity towards us is revealed.

20:17–28

"The Son of Man will be handed over . . . they will crucify him . . . he will be raised." These few words spoken by Jesus have been in my thoughts for many days, calling me to a contemplation which is beyond anything I am able to say. I now earnestly ask the Holy Spirit to give me words that enable the best possible account of my meditation before I return to silent contemplation.

It is extraordinary to see the way these few words spoken by Jesus are enough to sum up the message of the Christian faith: the death and resurrection of our Lord Jesus Christ. Their concision and density are part of why it is so difficult for me to discuss them.

"They will crucify him": this is the work of the nations together with the chief priests and the scribes, which is to say it is the work of the whole of mankind, of us all. This work is inserted between two divine passives, "he will be handed over" and "he will be raised"; these passives say that it is God who hands the Son of Man over to men, and who raises him. The crucifixion was the work of men, and the resurrection, the work of God; it is the same person who is crucified and resurrected, Jesus.

I want to examine the concision of this summary. It was certainly God who handed over the Son (Rom 8:2) to the chief priests and scribes, but it wasn't his plan for them to crucify him. He handed him over for them to be led by him into life, in the way a flock is led by its shepherd. They, however, the chief priests and scribes, handed him over to the nations for them to crucify him.

Crucified people died upright, in a vertical position; this was a particular feature of crucifixion. To my knowledge, only the crucified can be said to die like this. It's wonderful to know that when Jesus was raised, he always appeared upright, standing in front of the people who saw him,[9] and

9. None of the accounts of the resurrection state that Jesus was standing upright, but many times we find the verb for "stand" (*istèmi* in Lk 24:36; Jn 20:14,19,26); in other passages it is implicit because Jesus "came to meet them" (*upantaô*), "came forward" (*proser-chomaï*, Matt 28:18) or "drew near" (*eggizô*, Lk 24:15).

so true is this that it is even possible to superimpose the two moments and contemplate Jesus as risen behind the image of him crucified. A simple cross is enough for me to be led into contemplation of both the Crucified and the Resurrected Jesus; such contemplation for me has unfathomable depth.

On the cross, death was victorious over life, but this victory was so fleeting that the life of the Resurrected One rapidly and sovereignly supplanted it; this life is so definitively victorious over death that it can no longer touch Him (Rom 6:9). As painful as it can be to contemplate the Crucified One and be brought to repentance, this pain cannot resist the joy given by contemplation of the Resurrected One and the attendant thanksgiving.

Life is not only for the Resurrected Jesus but is offered by him to the multitude. This was Jesus' only commentary after the disruption of the request from James and John's mother (Matt 20:20–23). "The Son of Man came to give his life as a ransom for the multitude" (20:28), and it's in this light that we are to consider him who gives us his life.

The two divine passives are so profound that they express the inexpressible. While it is the Father who hands over the Son, the Son also hands over himself (Gal 2:20). Similarly, it is surely the Father who raised his Son, but the Son also raised himself.[10] This is an endless mystery! It is so mysterious that Jesus has to breathe the Holy Spirit upon us (Jn 20:22) if we are to contemplate the mystery of the mutual work of the Father and the Son. By means of these two divine passives, the work of the Holy Spirit is apparent, lighting up my meditation with inexpressible light.

10. The verb "raise/bring back to life" here is a divine passive, expressing the work of the Father, but elsewhere Jesus resurrection is expressed by *anistémi* in an active form, meaning that Jesus raised/resuscitated himself (Mk 9:8,31 . . .).

The work of the Holy Spirit operates in our hearts to enable us to move from the painful contemplation of Jesus crucified to the blessed contemplation of him raised; it is he who, in a sense, tips us over from one form of contemplation into another by transforming our inner focus.

This transformation of focus will be very discreetly revealed to us later in the gospel when we are told about the women who stood at a distance at Golgotha and contemplated the Crucified One in deep silence (27:55).[11] Three days later, the same women were there, always silent, contemplating him risen.[12] They are always there, welcoming us to join them: I am there with them today, in silence contemplating him as Crucified and Resurrected.

You are blessed, Holy Spirit, for having led me in this meditation; you are blessed, you who have enabled me to fix my gaze on the Crucified One and have led me in repentance, who has enabled me to contemplate the Resurrected One, who graces me with his forgiveness and leads me on in wonderment . . .

20:29–34

In this beautiful text, it is Jesus' compassion that holds my attention and feeds my meditation. It is rarely mentioned in the gospels and when it is, it is usually compassion for a

---

11. Matthew specifies that the women "contemplated" (*théôréô*, 27:55), a verb which states that there was a look (*oraô*) given by God (*théos*).

12. In their encounter with the Risen One (28:9–10), it is not positively said that the women saw Jesus; at the beginning of the account, however, it is said that the women came to the tomb to "contemplate" (*théôréô*, 28:1). They would be enabled to contemplate in a way that is inexpressible, beyond anything Matthew manages to say.

whole crowd (Matt 9:36; 14:14; 15:32; Mk 6:34; 8:2) and is rarely connected with an individual. In Matthew, it only comes up here; in Mark, only with the leper (1:41), and in Luke, only with the widow at Nain (7:13). In John, it isn't found. What is revealed here about Jesus' compassion on which to meditate?

Jesus healed two other blind men (Matt 9:27–31) without his compassion for them being mentioned. Why, then, is there the issue of compassion for these two new blind men? It seems to me it's because as well as being blind, they were also beggars. Their begging isn't mentioned, certainly, but it is discreetly suggested by the fact that they were seated beside the road; that is precisely where beggars were to sit.[13] Matthew, then, only suggests that they were begging, out of delicacy, but also so that Jesus' attentiveness to such things would be apparent. The first two blind men had not been reduced to such a degree of poverty; they came and went but were not seated. Not all the blind were beggars; here, though, they were, and they knew the pain and the shame of being beggars in addition to being blind.[14] Beggary is really the most painful form of poverty. Blindness and beggary; this is what awakened Jesus' compassion.

The two blind men began to cry out and, unlike the other two, the crowd wanted to silence them. It is humiliating to be reduced to silence, but so far as the crowd were concerned, these fellows had no right to speak; if they were going to beg, they should be quiet. Jesus was moved by their

13. This is clearly stated when it comes to Bartimaeus: "A beggar, he was sitting beside the road" (Mk 16:46), and the same with the man born blind: "He sat and begged" (Jn 9:8).

14. Begging was in fact shameful, as recognized by the unfaithful steward (Lk 16:3).

humiliation and called them to get up and come to him. A man's honor is to stand up tall; this is why we pray standing before God, like men whom he welcomes in their dignity. Then Jesus asked them a question so they would have to speak, giving them the right to do so and so restoring them to their humanity. Here we see the active compassion of Jesus: he was aware of the suffering of these men who had been humiliated, and he healed them by giving them back their human dignity.

The blind men's response also touched him deeply because their request was one that could only be made of God, and to us this request and its answer must surely appear as the fulfilment of a prophecy that said God would save the blind by opening their eyes.[15] When they were seated, the blind men had addressed Jesus as the Son of David, the Messiah; now that they were standing upright before God, they prayed to Jesus in his divinity, as Lord.[16] The men's faith moved him to the core;[17] then he touched their eyes. His compassion for a person was always expressed by some action of his hands; he touched a leper (Mk 1:41) and the bier carrying the widow's son (Lk 7:14). These actions were full of the gentleness of compassion.

Jesus touched their eyes with such emotion that he was unable to speak. When he healed the other two blind men, he had spoken as well but didn't here. Nothing else was said, such was the depth of his compassion.

15. No doubt Philemon is alluding to Isaiah 35:4–5, which says, "Your God will come and will save you; then the eyes of the blind will be opened." This was a miracle of God, not the Messiah.

16. Philemon notes that once in Jesus' presence, the blind men no longer say "Son of David," but just "Lord," in the way God is to be addressed when before him in prayer.

17. Philemon here says literally "guts" (*splanchna*).

This beautiful silence seems to me to have another depth. The crowd wanted to impose silence on the two beggars, and Jesus was now taking on their supposed role; he was silent, taking on himself the suffering of men who had themselves been reduced to silence. This is how he shows compassion, as stated by the prophet Isaiah: "It is he who has taken our infirmities and borne our diseases" (Is 53:4; Matt 8:17). In his immense compassion, Jesus took upon himself the suffering and shame of these beggars.

Compassion for a person always impelled Jesus to perform a miracle: he healed the leper and raised the widow of Nain's son; here he gave back both sight and dignity to blind beggars. This double miracle comes from his compassion for them.

O my soul, "he who was rich made himself poor" as the apostle says (2 Cor 8:9); he made himself poor to the point, in his immense compassion, of joining the beggars in their pain and shame, and in his grace, he gave these humbled beggars back their dignity as men. This is the merciful and compassionate God (Exod 34:6) presented before us to contemplate.

You are blessed, Lord Jesus, you who abased yourself to the point of restoring to these two humbled beggars their human dignity. You are blessed too for giving them back their sight so that they . . .

MATTHEW 21

21:1–11

JESUS IS HEADING ALONG THE ROAD THAT LED TO HIS
Passion, and it was good that the crowd know this; they
would be present all the way, right up to the moment he
breathed his last on the cross. He was actively involved in
preparing the way, choosing for himself the mount on which
he would ride in a way suggestive to all of the fulfilment
of prophecy. God himself had given this prophecy in which
he announced that the one who came on this humble beast
was a king: "Behold your king," he said by the mouth of
the prophet Zachariah (Zac 9:9); and it was a king that the
crowd acclaimed: "Hosanna, Son of David . . ." The crowd
recognized the Messiah who came in the name of the Lord.

The disciples were strangely mute. One of them, John,
would say that they didn't understand what was happening
(Jn 12:16). If they didn't understand, it's clear that the crowd
would understand still less, and this is seen to be so because
we sense some real confusion. The crowd was acclaiming
the Messiah at the same time as asking, "Who is this?" and
then affirming that he was a prophet. It wasn't really possible to confuse the Messiah with a prophet, particularly
when David's (Messianic) family had no link with Galilee
and even less with the unknown town of Nazareth.

So we see Jesus surrounded by disciples and a crowd that understood nothing of what was taking place. He was alone, and more, silent in his solitude. For him this was the beginning of the way of the Passion, along which his solitude would continually grow. The crowd would turn against him and shout for his crucifixion, and the disciples would abandon him and flee. It was a solitude from the abyss, and it shocks me deeply. Nevertheless, as he would say to his disciples, "You will leave me alone, but I am not alone because the Father is with me" (Jn 16:32).

Jesus was acclaimed as king but there was certainly confusion about his royalty; he was effectively king, but not in the way the people believed. The confusion was real and quickly explains the reversal of the crowd which thought in terms of a king for Israel who would drive out the Romans. Doubtless, Judas thought this too, and this is why he betrayed him. Perhaps there was even some confusion in the hearts of the disciples.

In spite of everything, the Father was there and had not left Jesus alone. In fact, the Father was acting to make sure that the prophecy "be fulfilled," as clearly indicated by the divine passive here.[1] The Father, in communion with the Son, carefully chose the kingly mount. When Jesus said to his disciples, "The Lord needs it," this communion finds expression because "the Lord" is the Father, but is Jesus too. For the first time, Jesus was designating himself by this title, which reveals that his royalty was really divine.

Not only was the Father there, but so was the Holy Spirit, who inspired Matthew in his recounting of events. Thus we are told that Jesus "was seated" on his mount,

---

1. "That it might be fulfilled," is stated with the passive of the verb for "fulfill." The prophecy was fulfilled by God, and more precisely by the Father, the Son and the Holy Spirit, as Philemon shows.

using a very rare verb which makes things very clear: the verb is used elsewhere to say that God "is seated" upon the Cherubim (2 Sam 22:11).[2] We therefore have it revealed here that in sitting "upon an ass and a colt the foal of an ass," Jesus was, more accurately stated, seated, invisibly, on the Cherubim; this explains the strange plural, "He was seated on them."[3] Seated upon the Cherubim in the way only God is seated, Jesus is revealed by the Holy Spirit in his divinity. Furthermore, it is beautiful to see that God is seated like this in order to come to the rescue of his servant,[4] which Jesus is doing too, accomplishing a salvation other than that expected by the crowd.

The Holy Spirit was not only at work in the production of this text but also on the day itself, adding to and completing the crowd's acclamation. The crowd was acclaiming a king, but amazingly their acclamation includes "in the highest": "Hosanna in the highest." The psalm the crowd

2. The verb for "to be seated" (épikathizô) is not found elsewhere in the New Testament. In the parallel accounts, Mark (11:7) and John (12:14) use the ordinary verb (kathizô), which is found fifty times in the New Testament. In the Old Testament épikathizô is similarly rare (just eight usages) but is there in 2 Sam 22:11 for God seated on the cherubim. In the Hebrew here, "cherubim" is singular, but in the Greek text it's plural as in the plural found elsewhere (2 Sam 6:2; 2 Kgs19:15; Ps 99:1 . . .).

3. It is said that "He sat upon them," which poses some problems to exegetes. In the parallel accounts in the other gospels, the question doesn't arise because there is only one donkey. What exactly was Jesus seated on according to Matthew's Gospel? On the donkey and the colt at the same time? This seems improbable and somewhat acrobatic! Was he seated on the clothing? This is possible, but I find it very lovely to see that Philemon sees Matthew as alluding to the cherubim thanks to the verb that suggests them. God alone is seated on the cherubim, and in doing so was seated on both at the same time (2 Sam 6:2; 2 Kgs19:15; Ps 99:1 . . .).

4. The psalm of David recorded in 2 Sam 22 describes at length the salvation brought by God to his servant David.

is quoting doesn't say this (118:26), but the Holy Spirit was instigating the crowd so as to implicate the armies of heaven, in line with reality. Jesus was progressing along the way of his Passion in increasing solitude but surrounded by the acclamations of the armies of heaven which would never fail him and always be there, all the way to the cross.

O my soul, I didn't understand why the liturgy for Palm Sunday acclaims Jesus as seated in heaven on the cherubim[5] when he was passing through the streets of Jerusalem on his strange, humble mount. Blessed be the Holy Spirit who sheds light on the real depth of this festival day, helping us to hear the heavenly host acclaim the Son who comes in the name of the Father. How good it is to enter like this into communion with the Church of both heaven and earth to unceasingly acclaim the King heading in his humble glory for Golgotha.

21:12–17

Since the temple in Jerusalem has now been destroyed, this episode might have lost some of its interest for us today; nevertheless, there is another temple to which the holy apostle Paul draws our attention, and this brings the present passage in the gospel home to us now. "You are the

5. I don't have the texts for this feast from Philemon's time; however, the best known Kontakion is Romanos the Melodist's (6th cent.), from which the following verse: "On the back of a donkey, we contemplate the one who the Cherubim bear on their shoulders" (Hymn XXXII.2). The editor of this Kontakion indicates that a sermon by Proclus of Constantinople (5th cent.) says something similar (Romanos, *Hymnes*, SC 128, p.33). In modern day liturgy, the mention of the Cherubim is frequent; "He who sits on the throne of the Cherubim, who for us is seated today on an ass . . ." (*Triode de Carême*, Office du matin, Cathisme, Editions de Chevetogne, 2007, p.449).

temple of God," we are told (1 Cor 3:16),[6] and further on, "Your body is the temple of the Holy Spirit" (6:19). What good news and what immense grace!

This being so, I believe that Abba Isaiah was right to call us to care for our bodies.[7] However, these words or Abba Isaiah's can be misunderstood; this is not a matter of managing the passions that govern our bodies but to respect the body as belonging to God and to which he comes to take up residence (Jn 14:23).

To our great shame, though, there are merchants present, buying and selling within the precincts of our inner temple, making this text in the gospel very up to date and challenging. Who are these buyers and sellers? Might it not be ourselves because of the way we behave with God? The temple is a house of prayer, Jesus tells us, but our prayers are often sullied by a spirit of commerce. Often we engage in trading with God. We try to buy his grace, his love, his forgiveness or some answer to prayer with what we give him as if we were giving him money. We do good works in the hope of buying him and putting him in our debt so that he will concede at a fair price whatever it is we are asking. We sell our works to God so that he will provide benefits in exchange. This is the mercenary spirit which makes us buyers and sellers. It is scandalous and even blasphemous towards God! The love of God, his grace and his forgiveness are not sold and not bought. His love is absolutely free, otherwise we denature it; and if we think of loving

6. In this text from Matthew, the temple is designated by *iéron*. In his letter, Paul uses a different word (*naos*), but it is agreed today that the two words were synonyms, which is what Philemon must have thought.

7. Here is Abba Isaiah: "Take care of your body as the temple of God; take care of it because it must rise and give account to God" (*The Ascetikon*, 15:87).

God in this way, our love is merely a false copy of love and it becomes essential, indeed urgent, to drive out such a mercenary spirit from the inner temple.

Jesus drove out the buyers and sellers from the Jerusalem temple, but when it comes to the temple of our hearts it's specifically up to us to throw them out, without waiting for him to come and do it. It is our place to expel the mercenary spirit from our hearts. We can do this by repenting and changing our behavior. It's true, though, that this is very difficult because this spirit is part of our habitual way and has almost become second nature. We have real need of help, and this help can only come from Jesus. For this reason, O my soul, let us pray and ask him to come and drive out all the buyers and sellers from our holy inner temple; let us ask him in profound repentance because we have soiled the holy temple of God. It is important that we repent if we are to be able to pray in such a way that it is not the request of a business person but of a son or daughter because our real relationship with God is as a child with its father. If no love can be bought, this is still more true of the love of our Father who is totally gratuitous love, an infinite love which calls us to love him in return, freely, to honor him and give him thanks, for his glory alone. O my soul, may our prayer be truly what it should be, prayer that is pure and free, the prayer of true love, totally free like that of children who love their father.

Jesus' attitude in the temple gives expression to great suffering, the suffering he felt to see these people offend God and hurt him deeply with their buying and selling. The only words Jesus spoke were a quotation from the words of his Father in the mouth of the prophets. What his Father had said was full of deep pain as he saw his temple made into a den of thieves! The pain Jesus shared with his Father was so deep that it is inexpressible, beyond any other pain. It is the same pain felt by God when he drove Adam out of Paradise, as so wonderfully understood by Abba Macarius: he didn't drive him out with a stick but with tears.[8] Jesus drove the merchants out of the temple in tears. These divine tears invite us to deep repentance with our human tears, tears of compunction, not like mercenaries who want to buy their pardon, but like children who suffer to have wounded God.

Have pity on me, O God, according to your great mercy, and in your immense . . .[9]

21:18–22

"He was hungry." In the opening pages of Matthew's Gospel we are told that Satan didn't understand the true nature of Jesus' hunger (4:3), and the disciples made a similar mistake soon after (Jn 4:31). On this occasion, it would have helped if they hadn't repeated the mistake: Jesus was not looking to the fig tree for nourishment; he was

8. The tears of which Macarius (4th cent.) speaks are not God's tears when he drove Adam out but of the moment his sin was revealed and the moment he died: "On the day Adam fell, God came to Paradise to walk around. He wept, so to speak, to see Adam and said, 'What good have you left to choose such evil! What glory have you lost to be clothed with such shame! How dark, vile and foul! What light you have lost and what darkness now covers you!' When Adam fell and died far from God, the Creator wept over him . . ." (*Spiritual Homilies*, XXX.7) This passage is so beautiful that we can understand Philemon also thinking of the tears God shed God when he expelled Adam.

9. Philemon quotes the great psalm of repentance, Psalm 51. Since the psalm was inspired, Philemon relies on the Holy Spirit to bring the psalm as prayer to both Jesus and his Father, seeking forgiveness from both, and indeed from the threefold holy God because the temple is also the temple of the Holy Spirit and he too is hurt by our attitudes (1 Cor 3;17).

hungry for something else. Relying on the Holy Scriptures, he had told Satan that he was hungry for "every word that comes out of the mouth of God" (Matt 4:4; Deut 8:3). To the disciples He had responded in the same way but still more specifically: "My food is to do the will of the one who sent me and to fulfill his works" (Jn 4:34). Here is what, with the disciples, we need to understand: Jesus' hunger was always the same; he wasn't hungry for figs but to fulfill the will of his Father; this will is that all men be saved, as the apostle declares (1 Tim 2:4). It was for this that Jesus had gone up to Jerusalem: to save men, to drink the cup, be put to death, crucified, hung on the tree (Gal 3:13). His hunger was to do the will of his Father by giving his life on the cross for the salvation of the world.

The way Jesus was following was one of obedience; what did he meet with along the way? A fig tree which offered to view just one thing, not figs, but leaves. It wasn't just that the leaves were not sheltering fruit, though there were none; they revealed, rather than mere hidden fruit, human disobedience. Why so? In Jesus' eyes, the fig leaves spoke of Adam's shame; after disobeying God, he wanted to hide his disobedience by making a belt of fig leaves (Gen 3:7). So Jesus, on his way of obedience, encountered the manifest sign of Adam's disobedience; it wasn't just Israel's disobedience but the whole of humanity's, a disobedience which seeks to hide itself from God's eyes but cannot do so despite all its efforts to care for appearances. In the presence of God this is nothing but hypocrisy, vain hypocrisy which can't fool him.

Jesus' reaction is the same as God's in the garden of Paradise; there, it was a strong reaction which lead to the cursing of the earth (not Adam), and above all the cursing of the serpent (3:14) concealed in the fig tree. This violent reaction hid the immense pain in the depths of God's heart, as Abba Macarius was given to understand. God spoke to Adam in tears. This indescribable pain, hidden in the tears, was Jesus' pain as he stood before the fig tree; he wept over the disobedience of men as one who hungered for obedience and was advancing along the way of obedience: "You will never bear fruit again," he said weeping. It was another tree that would yield the fruit God was looking for.

The disciples didn't understand, but Jesus wasn't about to tell them what he was feeling. God didn't explain his sorrow to Adam; Jesus wouldn't do so to his disciples. An obedient person does not explain his obedience but simply lives it out, which is enough to bring joy to God's heart. Jesus therefore simply continued along his way, the way of obedience.

His way would lead him to Golgotha where the cross loomed before him. He went from one tree to another, from the fig tree to the cross. The tree of the cross would yield its fruit, the fruit neither the fig tree nor Adam could give, the fruit of obedience, which feeds all who are hungry.[10] On this tree, Jesus himself would be hung like ripe fruit, given as nourishment to all who hunger for it and eat it; it was his body and blood that he would give as food.

O my soul, Jesus advanced towards Golgotha bearing on his heart all who hunger and thirst for the righteousness of God (Matt 5:6). No fig tree could satisfy them; but

---

10. In Greek, the word *xulon* means both "tree" and "wood," and the same word is often used for the cross (Acts 5:30; 10:39; 13:29; Gal 3:13; 1 Pet 2:24). This helps us understand Philemon here. When he uses *xulon*, we can translate by "tree," "wood" and even by "cross," making rather clearer the connection he is making between the fig tree and the cross. *Xulon* also is used for the tree of life in Paradise (Gen 2:9), so that the Fathers could compare the tree of life with the life-giving cross. Philemon seems to be making the same connection.

happy are those who are satisfied by Jesus himself, the one who became righteousness for them (1 Cor 1:30). In order to fulfill this beatitude, Jesus now hungered to offer himself as food for the hungry; he hastened towards one thing alone, that this hour should pass so that without delay the beatitude be fulfilled, prefiguring what would be fully accomplished at the end of time.[11] Jesus now hungered to break the bread and give it to the disciples so that they could then give it to all the hungry throughout the earth so that we would all be filled (Matt 14:20). His body and blood could then be given to each person; this is why he came to earth, the bread come down from heaven (Jn 6:35). In his obedience, Jesus brought consolation to the Father who shed tears over our disobedience.

21:23–32

This is not the first occasion that Matthew is alone in relating one of Jesus' teachings; but here the transmission of the parable has especially touched me, because, it seems to me, I have the sense of finding in Matthew the son who initially refused but who finished up doing the will of his father by performing the work asked of him. I really wonder at this because it is the first time that Matthew, who is ordinarily so humble, opens up a bit about himself, though he does remain wonderfully discreet. Once this parable became clear to me, I could no longer meditate it without having my eyes fixed on Matthew.

11. "They will be filled," says the beatitude, using a future which can be understood as an announcement of what will be given to the hungry at the end of time, but also as announcing all that is already given on the cross. The cross takes in all time, unifying the present, the near future and the future of the end times, in the same way that the bread and wine of the Holy Supper already provide all that will be given in the Kingdom (Matt 26:29).

What must have touched Matthew is Jesus' wonderful statement about the tax collectors. As a tax collector himself (10:3) he had good reason to be deeply impressed when he heard Jesus talk about the tax collectors entering the Kingdom of God. What a revolution and what grace for him to hear this as one who had at first said "no" to God and lived far from him, as his profession demanded.[12] Nevertheless, despite his dishonest life, like other tax collectors (Lk 3:12), he had gone to hear John the Baptist, whose message had awakened his conscience and produced remorse: "Don't demand more than the prescribed amount," he heard the Baptist say (Lk 3:13). To quieten his conscience he had made an effort to exercise his profession differently. Sometime later, he had gone out to the mountain on that blessed day when Jesus had given his wonderful teaching (Matt 5–7), and had understood that God was his Father and so, as in the parable, he was a son and not a servant. He had begun to pray to the Father in his closet (Matt 6:6),[13] and his remorse had been transformed into repentance;[14] and then the day came when Jesus passed his desk and told him to follow him (9:9). This call was decisive; he got up and followed Jesus to go to work with him in the Father's vineyard. No doubt this is all guesswork on my part, but it's how I see Matthew.

12. Tax-collectors were accused of extorting more from the people than their due and keeping the extra for themselves.

13. *Taméion*, as above in the note on Matt 6:1–6.

14. Matthew twice uses the verb for "seized by remorse" (*métaméléô*), which is all too often translated as "repent" (*métanoéô*), which impedes a proper understanding of this parable. Remorse is a fruit of a conscience purified of the passions by the Holy Spirit, the consideration of sins in one's spirit, but without yet being open to God; it is the first step along the way of repentance, which does open us up to God

The fact that this touches me is also undoubtedly because I recognize myself a bit in Matthew; at first I said "no" to God, without having understood that he is my Father and that work in his vineyard is not for some salary based payment but is the work of a son laboring out of love for his Father who he knows he is loved by. After I said no to him, God put in my path a John the Baptist who awakened my conscience and my remorse; I was then a little more open to God. Reading the Fathers then taught me and brought me light, particularly about the nature of the conscience, because I understood that it is placed in us by God,[15] and that the Holy Spirit then comes to work with it to touch the heart and awaken in us remorse at being far from God. Thanks again to the Fathers, I also understood that this remorse can lead to repentance and to prayer. I then had a growing sense that I needed to change my way of life in order to obey God; with this there came an inner sorrow that I was out of line with his will until the day came when Jesus wonderfully revealed the Father to me and his infinite love. Then I got up and followed him with as much love as possible to go with him to work in the vineyard, and my repentance opened onto the grace of God's forgiveness which cleanses and purifies.

15. Based on, among others, John Chrysostom, Dorotheus of Gaza, a contemporary of Philemon, says this: "When God created mankind, he placed within him a divine seed, alive and luminous, a spark to lighten the spirit and enable him to discern good from evil; this is termed the conscience." (Spiritual Works, Instruction III, 40:1). The word "spark" is well chosen, making the connection with the fire of the Holy Spirit from which it is taken.

I never finish saying "yes" to the Lord. Each morning and many times a day, whenever I hear the simantron[16] I hear in its call the Lord's call, and each time I respond in my heart, "Here I am."[17] However, it's not enough just to say this, I have to live it. Thanks again to the Lord, I get up, take my work tools and follow him into his vineyard. What joy and what encouragement too to join the brothers and chant the liturgy with them![18]

O my soul, I give infinite thanks for this parable and for Matthew, who took pains to pass it on to us, having received it deep in his heart and then transmitting it with all his love.

You are blessed, Lord Jesus, for the holy apostle Matthew, whose heart you touched and who followed you to work in your holy vineyard. You are blessed too for the wonderful work you entrust to us by giving us the liturgy which unites us with you in communion with the heavenly host and . . .

21:33–46

This is the first occasion on which Jesus questioned his hearers about a parable he hadn't yet finished; it is beautiful

16. In eastern monasteries, the offices are not announced by bells ringing but by a board, the "simantron," being struck (Apophthegm 1596.7). According to a beautiful tradition, this practice goes back to Noah; when he had finished building the ark, he found a leftover plank and struck it to call the animals into the ark of their salvation!

17. Note that here Philemon changes from "yes" (*nai*) to "Here I am" (*idou égô*). "Yes" is the simplest affirmative (Matt 9:28; 21:16), where "Here I am" is more solemn, demonstrating Philemon's great respect for the Lord (Gen 22:1; I Sam 3:4).

18. "Liturgy" is from *leïtourgia*, a Greek word derived from *ergon*, meaning "work." Liturgy was a part of monks' work in the Lord's vineyard.

to see him here questioning the chief priests and the elders of the people and then to hear their answer.

The parable is so transparent that the listeners recognized themselves as the tenants; they also easily recognized that the owner of the vineyard is God because, with their excellent knowledge of the Scriptures, they knew that the parable was picking up a prophecy from Isaiah in which God is the proprietor of the vineyard Jesus talks about (Is 5:2–7).

The response was clear: God, the owner of the vineyard, would destroy the tenants, showing that the God they laid claim to was a God of revenge who punishes without mercy. Their point of view is based on texts from the Scriptures which, on a first reading, carry that meaning, but they were forgetting a fundamental factor that Jesus hadn't mentioned in order to see if these connoisseurs of the Scriptures really knew God. Their response shows it clearly: they didn't.

Jesus' hearers knew this prophecy well, but they seemed to have forgotten that it was a song of love, an unforgettable song of love sung by God himself. Here is its beginning: "I will sing to my well-beloved the song of my beloved for my vineyard."[19] I am unaware if it was the Father or the Son who was singing for the vineyard because their bond of love is so deep and they are so much at one in their love for the vineyard that I am unable to tell. The heart of Jesus was full of this love, but his hearers didn't know.

---

19. Philemon reproduces the opening of the song in the Greek translation. The Hebrew text is a little different: "I will sing to my well-beloved the song of my well-beloved for his vineyard." In the Hebrew, the prophet sings of the vineyard as God's ("his vineyard"), while in the Greek it is God himself who sings of the vineyard as his ("my vineyard").

Their response has two points: that the tenants be killed and the vineyard given to others. Jesus accepts the second point but doesn't join them in the first, which would make God a vengeful God of justice alone. His way of seeing God was really not the same as theirs.

Jesus was also relying on the Scriptures but to emphasize the love of God and his mercy. God can certainly be severe and envisage serious punishment; however, when this is the case, he always counts on the intervention of an intercessor. We have a very beautiful example of this when the people stood against God in the wilderness to the point that God considered their destruction (Exod 32:9–10); Moses then turned to him in a wonderful prayer appealing to his grace and asking him to forgive (32:11), and God granted his request (32:14).

The leaders of the people knew all this, but would they remember God's mercy? This would be the very moment to cry out for themselves, the tenants. But there was none of that! They continued in their intention to destroy Jesus. Nevertheless, they had here a wonderful occasion to repent of their criminal project and not bring it to pass. When Jesus told this parable, it was certainly to touch them and invite them to repent and appeal to God's grace. But in vain! They closed themselves off to the merciful love of God and instead demonstrated their lack of respect and proper fear of God. They thought only of themselves and their own illusory gain.

The chief priest and the elders of the people then left; Jesus made no effort to keep them. They would execute their plan and do as Jesus had said in the parable: "They seized him, threw him out of the vineyard and killed him" (v 39).

They left without knowing that there was an intercessor for them who, like Moses, would implore God's merciful love. They didn't know that the crucified Jesus would not look for justice or vengeance but would intercede on their behalf: "Father, forgive them, they don't know what they are doing" (Lk 23:34). What infinite mercy!

O my soul, whose disciples are we? Are we disciples of the leaders, for whom God was an inflexible god who condemns people's sins without a trace of merciful love? You know very well that we are not! We are disciples of Jesus who teaches us that God exercises justice with infinite love and infinite mercy, to such a degree that his judgments are shocking; he judges while granting pardon. As we follow Jesus, have we not also to intercede for the guilty, crying out for the merciful love of God?

O my soul, Jesus' hearers didn't keep a hold on his conclusion, in which he suggests that resurrection would follow crucifixion. This too is God's judgement, a genuine song of love which led him to raise the stone rejected by the builders and make it the chief cornerstone of the Church. Heaven and earth unite to take their turn in song: "This is marvelous in our eyes . . ."

MATTHEW 22

22:1–14

IT'S THE KING'S ANGER THAT HOLDS MY ATTENTION HERE
(v 7), especially since it is Jesus speaking and giving us to
understand that this is God's anger. What overwhelms me is
that he speaks of it so straightforwardly. A few years ago, I
would have been shocked and would have put this verse to
one side, but, after a meeting with Abba Ireneus, I am able
to make it the subject of my meditation.

Last month, I heard talk of a communal letter addressed
to the Chief Elder by many Fathers in the monastery, among
whom was Abba Ireneus, concerning the plague which had
struck us and which came from God.[1] The Chief Elder
replied, and I chose to go and see Abba Ireneus to learn a
little more, without wishing to be indiscreet.

The anger of God has always scared me. It is a subject
which undermined my faith until one day a brother
reassured me by explaining that this anger has to do with

1. This is letter 569 from vol II of the Correspondence. The
plague mentioned may have been the epidemic that raged throughout the empire in 542–543; it affected the emperor Justinian. It may
also have been a previous, unknown epidemic. Alternatively, it was a
spiritual plague caused by some evil generated by the human heart at
large; it seems to have touched the whole of the empire, mobilizing
intercessors everywhere, from Rome to Corinth and Gaza.

human sin and is not a cause for us to flee; on the contrary, it ought to turn us towards God in profound repentance because God listens to repentance and his anger dissipates. I blessed this brother who had explained that our repentance comforts God to such a degree that, when he is angry, he longs for and even seeks someone able to stand before him in the breach like Moses in order to pray to him and repent on behalf of all.[2] With this in mind, I went to see Abba Ireneus to listen to him.

Abba Ireneus welcomed me warmly, as is his custom, and confirmed that the plague afflicting the world today is indeed an expression of God's anger. The Chief Elder had replied that three intercessors were praying that day to appease God and that we could be sure that their prayers would be heard. Abba Ireneus told me that these were John in Rome, Elias in Corinth and the Chief Elder himself, all three sufficiently holy for God to listen to them as he had listened to Moses.[3] Then Abba Ireneus made things a little clearer to me about God's anger.

"You know," he said to me, "what a wonderful blessing it is for us to be protected by the prayers of holy intercessors, and, even better, to be able to count on intercessors who are even more holy, given that Jesus himself and the

2. From Philemon's meditation on Mark 1:14–15, concerning this brother: "As a brother taught me, the Hebrew word for 'repent' (*nâham*) has a second meaning which is inseparable from the first, which is to say, to 'console.' It follows that anyone who repents also consoles the person who was offended. What a revelation! When I repent, I console God whom I offended. To console God — what a mystery! Discreetly, Jesus indicates here that God can be wounded by my sins and consoled by my repentance . . ."

3. Barsanuphius gives the name of John and Elias in his reply. I know nothing further about these two men. The third is "another in the patriarchy of Jerusalem," which no doubt was Barsanuphius himself, humbly not naming himself.

Holy Spirit also intercede for us with the Father (Rom 8:26, 34). We can be truly confident, but this is not enough. The most important thing is not that we turn away God's anger but that we not provoke it in the first place. Our repentance appeases God, certainly, but the best thing is not to give his anger cause. What gives rise to his anger? Well, it's our all too numerous sins, our excessive sins. It's because our sins are beyond measure and no one repents that he becomes angry. When God strikes us with anger, it is to draw our attention to the gravity of our sins. But God then looks for an intercessor, as he himself said to Ezekiel;[4] he seeks someone who is aware of the seriousness of our sins, a person who desires to reestablish contact with him, a person who is sufficiently humble to seek forgiveness on behalf of us all in the way Jesus himself asked forgiveness for us all on the cross (Lk 23:34). But what do we do? Jesus bearing the sins of the world (Jn 1:29) does not authorize us to continue to sin and to abstain from repentance. You see, brother, we are not serious! We ought to truly repent, to truly understand that we are not worthy of God's immense love for us. When Jesus calls on us to repent as his first message (Matt 4:17), it was to call us to be serious before God, conscious of and responsible for our disordered lives, and to be true in our love for God. To love God means not offending and wounding him by our acts of disobedience to his will and our lives estranged from him. To love God means not provoking his anger by living without thought of him as if he was a stranger that we just walk straight by! In his reply, the Chief Elder called on us to pray too, to stand

4. In Ezek 22:30, God was seeking an intercessor to stand before him. Moses "stood in the gap" (Ps 106:23) to intercede for the people after they had made the golden calf (Exod 32:7). Barsanuphius refers to this in his reply to the Gazan Fathers.

courageously in the breach with true love for God and in real repentance. Then, yes, God will be appeased because he loves us. Before we repent for the world and for others, first of all we need to repent of our own faults from the bottom of our hearts."

O my soul, in the time of emperor Theodosus the Younger, the sins of men reached such a pitch that God in his anger struck the capital, but his love for men was still greater. In his grace, he drew to himself a young boy to enable him with the prayer of repentance he longed to hear from everyone, and the people recovered the favor of God, singing with one voice the magnificent Trisagion[5] which Abba Ireneus has been singing non-stop today and which I am adopting as my own: Holy God, Holy in strength, Holy and immortal, have pity on us! Holy God, Holy . . .

22:15–22

"Give to God that which is God's," Jesus tells us, but without specifying what he is asking us to give. However, the context is clear: if we ought to give back to Caesar his own image, so too we should return to God his own image. His image! This word sends us back, of course, to Genesis, which speaks of us, we humans, as being in the image of God (1:26–27). What, then, is this image? If God is unseen, then his image must be too. So that is it: the unseen image

5. In 437 during the reign of Theodosius the Younger, a great earthquake struck Constantinople. The emperor himself, the patriarch Proclus and all the people gathered together on the field of Mars in the Hebdomen. A young boy was caught up among the angelic choir who were chanting the Trisagion, "Holy God, Holy in power, Holy and immortal, have pity upon us" (Isa 6:3). He declared that God had ordered this supplication be made to him. The tremors ceased and Proclus decreed that thenceforth the Trisagion be sung as part of the liturgy.

of the unseen God is to be found in us. There is no doubt that Saint Macarius was right to say that this image is our soul, which is precisely unseen.[6]

"Let us make man in our image," said God in order to create us (Gen 1:26). He didn't say "in my image" but "our image," speaking to the Son and the Holy Spirit. What mystery is here! We are therefore in the image of the Holy Trinity, and this underlines the degree to which this has to do with the unseen. However, the image is invisible only to our eyes; we are told that after creating everything, God considered all his creatures, including his own image, and while we don't see this, God does, contemplating it as his most beautiful creation, the last to be created, after all the others, the one of which he said it was "very beautiful."[7] After each other creation, he said merely that it was beautiful, but after creating his own image, he said it was very beautiful. He waited until the final day to create what was most precious to him: the image of the Holy Trinity. We see God marveling as he contemplated his image in the secret of the Trinitarian council with the infinite love that is his.

This is the image that God contemplates in us, his image, created before the fall. But what became of this image after

6. "In very truth, the soul is a great work, divine and wonderful! When God created it, there was nothing of malice introduced into its nature, but he made it in the image of the Spirit's virtues" (Macarius, *Spiritual Homilies* 46:7). The Fathers are not in fact unanimous in their understanding of man as created in the image of God; Philemon stays close to Abba Macarius, faithful, no doubt, to the desert Fathers with whom he was associated.

7. In the Hebrew text, when God looked at his creatures, he saw that they were "good," but after creating the man and the woman, he saw that the creation was "very good" (Gen 1:31). In Greek, God's appreciation was not so much of "good" but of "beauty," which fits better with the context of contemplation: "God saw all that he had made and saw that it was very beautiful." This beauty goes beyond the aesthetic to include spiritual beauty.

the fall? Did it disappear? Certainly not, since Jesus is asking us here to give it back to God; it must therefore remain in us, but no doubt damaged, disfigured by our sins. What shame this is to us! And what sadness for God, who today contemplates his own image disfigured. I have difficulty saying this, but it is a disfigured image that Jesus invites us to give back to God. May the Lord have pity on us!

Why are we to return it to him? First of all because it is his; it his image, his most precious good, even if it has been brought low. We are in error if we think we belong to ourselves! What prideful folly. These words of Jesus make me realize that we belong to God, not to ourselves! And when we are told that we are his temple (1 Cor 3:16), it is so that his image may be placed there. His image in his temple . . . ! What care we should take over this!

What does it mean to "give back" or "return" to God his image? Might this be a way of speaking of our death in the way Jesus spoke to the avaricious man? "You fool, this very night your soul will be required of you" (Lk 12:20). The day we die, this will be the case, but first, Jesus is asking us to return to God the very thing he will entrust to us anew. God is not mean with his goods in the way we are. He entrusts his image to us, and when we give it back to him, he entrusts it to us again in the hope that this reciprocal movement will be perpetuated without end. It is with love that he entrusts his image to us, and the love is infinite since his image is so very precious to him; his love invites us to return his image with love. This exchange is part of prayer, part of an unending dialogue of love. If the image has been damaged, then we can return it to him with compunction, in deep repentance, as well as with thanksgiving for the confidence he reposes in us by entrusting us with this precious good that he loves infinitely. His love is so great that when he entrusts us with it anew, this is after he has tended it and restored it a little more. Paul says even more than this, that we are not merely restored but "transfigured in our image from glory to glory" (2 Cor 3:18).[8] In this unceasing exchange of prayer between God and us, we see that God transforms us little by little, from glory to glory! What grace! What infinite love!

O my soul, after creating man, God didn't speak of his image again until Jesus spoke of it here.[9] He never spoke of it because his image remains for him a good to which he is so attached that he contemplates it in the silence of wonderment; equally, it's because his now deteriorated image causes him to suffer, and in his reserve he prefers not to speak about his suffering in front of us. It's not something he talks about because, again in silence, he puts all his love into the transfiguration of this image which he is restoring with infinite care, tenderly preparing it for the day when we see him face to face in the eternity of love he has for us (Jer 31:3).

22:23-33

O my soul, the Sadducees were focusing on a saying of Moses. Great as he was, Moses was only a man, and his sayings will last only as long as our earthly lives because, in the eternity of heaven, there will be no question of marriage, of widows and a man's descendants; such questions will no longer be asked, and Moses' word will be obsolete, as will the Sadducees' arguments.

8. Paul uses the same verb as in the Transfiguration. Few translations pay attention to this.

9. This is correct with the exception of one passage (Gen 9:6), after which God says nothing more about his image.

To answer them, Jesus takes a word from God himself (Exod 3:6), the God of the Sadducees, a word the Sadducees could not contest because it is in the Holy Scriptures to which they were so attached. It wasn't Moses himself who said this; he only heard it when he stood before the burning bush where God revealed himself to him. Before speaking to him, God required Moses to take off his sandals because the place where he was standing was holy. In fact, it was so holy that as he listened, Moses turned away his face[10] and bowed[11] before the Lord who had spoken to him. These words, O my soul, are the most important there could be because they begin with something no mere man had any right to pronounce, not even Moses, words of extraordinary holiness: "I am."[12] No one apart from God could say such a thing without offending God. After such holy words, God continued to present himself to Moses, joining the names of Abraham, Isaac and Jacob to his: "I am the God of Abraham, the God of Isaac and the God of Jacob."

This holy statement is eternal in the same way God is holy and eternal. Just as God is alive, Abraham, Isaac and Jacob are alive, just as eternally as God because the living God made them partakers of his life. There is nothing to add to this and, moreover, Jesus didn't. The crowd was silent, marveling at what they had heard. The Sadducees were silent too. If they never believed in the resurrection,

10. We mustn't forget that Philemon read and meditated the Greek translation of the Old Testament. The Greek says that Moses "turned away" (apostréphô) his face, while the Hebrew says that he "hid" it (sâtar).

11. It is not clear where Philemon found this since it is not in Exodus 3 or 4. [Trans.]

12. Matthew was well aware that these words of God began with "I am" (égô eïmi) in the Septuagint, which neither Mark (12:26) nor Luke (20:37) noted. Jesus had certainly not forgotten these two highly important words.

even the crowd could remind them with conviction of what Jesus had said.

O my soul, it is good for me to draw your attention to another detail. Have you noticed the way Jesus introduces this word from God? He says, "Haven't you read what God said to you?" What he said to "you," he specifies. These were words spoken to Moses, of course, but words of such power and life that they are eternal and addressed to "you" Sadducees. This is so clear and wonderful! It enables further understanding of what Jesus said to the Sadducees: this was a word from the living God addressed to you who are alive. It's as true that you are alive and that God is alive as it is that Abraham, Isaac and Jacob are alive. God doesn't speak to the dead but to the living, and he doesn't speak about the dead but about the living.

O my soul, this word has such power and such life that it also speaks to us today, to we who live. It's a word we should know inside out because it is an eternal revelation which opens up eternity before us. The Jesus speaking to the Sadducees is the only one who could truthfully say, "I am," and one day he would state more specifically, speaking to us all, "I am the resurrection and the life" (Jn 11:25).[13] These words should perhaps be listened to without our sandals on because they are equally holy and eternal.

O Jesus, my Savior and my God, you are blessed for what you are revealing to us here in these few words of such power that they silenced those who didn't believe in the resurrection. You are blessed for your words that shine like the bush from which they were spoken, for your words that brought Moses to his knees, the depth of which you

13. Jesus' statement begins with the same égô eïmi ("I am") as Exod 3:6.

now reveal. You are blessed as you comment on your own word because you were in truth there in the burning bush with the Father and the Holy Spirit when Moses removed his sandals. Before him you said, "I am," just as you did before the Sadducees, the disciples and the whole crowd, and as you still say before us today. You are blessed, and you will say it again, united with the Father and the Holy Spirit in the eternal Kingdom. Remember us too when you come into your Kingdom, and in your grace, give us your welcome. Grant that we may know how to prepare ourselves for the day of your coming. Protect us from every spirit of dispute, from every spirit that would contest your word, and as you dealt with the Sadducees who were in error here (v 29), please guard us in the truth of your word and in adoration before you who are the resurrection and the life, one God with . . .

22:34–40

O my soul, what a strange conversation this is that we sit in on here. Really a strange conversation, because the person who steps up to Jesus is a lawyer who questions him about the Law, which is to say, the field in which he was a specialist. He was one of those you would address as "master" with questions about the Law, knowing that he would have the right answer because he knew the Law perfectly; he knew all its difficulties, all its secrets and all its mysteries; even the Pharisees and the Sadducees would address a lawyer as "master." But here, it is this man who speaks to Jesus with questions about the Law and calling him "master." The roles were reversed.

Matthew tells us that the man wanted to trap Jesus. No doubt this is true, and the trap he wanted to catch him was pride; the lawyer sought to flatter Jesus so that he would really take himself for a master. If Jesus was to respond by accepting the title, he would fall straight into the trap, a disciple taking himself for a master. Jesus ought to have replied, "Why are you calling me master when you are the real master?"

O my soul, this lawyer didn't know that he would have done better to keep quiet. He didn't know that he didn't have before him a disciple but the Master of the Law, not a disciple of Moses but Moses' Master. Standing before him was the one who gave the Law to Moses, and it was he who formulated it; standing there was God himself, the one who conceived it and gave it to us.

O my soul, if this man thought he could trap Jesus, he was like the fool who wanted to trap a ray of sunshine! It was certainly a strange discussion; this man found himself faced with the sun itself, not a ray of sunshine; in fact, the one who gave the sun existence and created it. Who could possibly shut him up in a trap?

O my soul, this man left without a word; he had no further question to ask. Like him, I am silent in Jesus' presence; this is not someone you try to trick; no, you bow before him in contemplation and adoration; there are no traps for him and instead you listen and receive each of his words as a word from God.

However, Jesus gave an answer! He had the humility to reply to someone who wanted to trap him. Blessed be God, because humility alone escapes every trap; Jesus responded, the sovereign Sun but humble beyond all other humility.

O my soul, let's not waste time trying to capture the light; instead, let us simply open our heart to Jesus for him to illumine it; he comes to write his Law on our hearts in love (Heb 8:10) and to snatch us from the grip of darkness.

Jesus answered, the one who is greater than the greatest commandment, who alone does more than just command us to love and who alone has the right to give us a new commandment (Jn 13:34). He not only invites us to love but he is love (1 Jn 4:8), and he alone is able to lead us along the way of love; he doesn't just pass comments about love but instead lives it in a way so humble that he joins love and humility indissolubly together.

O my soul, the lawyer went away with his trap empty! I am now here alone in Jesus' presence and am silent in contemplation before him as I open my heart to him and allow him to shine in and chase away the darkness from its most hidden corners; he leads me along this way of love, along the way of indescribable love, he who is both the way (Jn 14:6) and humble love itself, greater than all other love.

O my soul, Jesus answered, and what he said is said to me personally and touches me deep in my heart. "You shall love the Lord your God with all your heart, with all your soul and with all your mind; but you shall also love your neighbor as you love yourself. I am not saying this to you as an order but as a promise; I am now setting you on a way which I am opening before you as a future that has no end, a way which will lead you up a mountain which is higher than any other, a way on which you wear out if you try it alone. But don't be afraid, I am speaking these words to you as a promise in which I engage myself to bring it to pass and to experience it with you, to love along with you the one who is above all."

O my soul, blessed is the one who opens up this way and is himself in reality the truth and the love, the Lord God, and who is present in my closest neighbor . . .

22:41-46

This short passage is truly extraordinary, in a few words immersing us in the infinite mystery of the most holy Trinity. Jesus asks a small number of questions without providing any answer; he steps out of the way and is silent so that the Holy Spirit can come and place answers in our hearts and open us up to contemplate this mystery.[14] In fact, no one was able to respond, not the Pharisees, not the disciples and no one else; only the Holy Spirit answers by leading us into the mystery, opening before us the silence of worship.

In his grace, the Holy Spirit had begun by leading David as he composed Psalm 110, which Jesus is citing here. In this grace of the Holy Spirit, David speaks about the Father and the Son, both of them as Lords. It's marvelous to see David, enveloped in the Holy Spirit, contemplating the Father and the Son, a profound mystery!

The Holy Spirit led not only David but, later, Paul, as he meditated the psalm, revealing to him that the right hand of the Father is in heaven, inaccessible (Eph 1:20), and that on Ascension Day, Jesus was raised into the heavens to sit down at the right hand of the Father. The Holy Spirit similarly inspired Peter; using the same verse from the psalm, he preached the Ascension to the crowd (Acts 2:34). Here, Jesus quotes the psalm to the Pharisees, but also to the disciples to prepare them for the Passion. Many times he had announced his death and resurrection (16:21; 17:22; 20:19); here, he makes it a little clearer for

---

14. In his meditation on the parallel text in Mark (12:35–37), Philemon develops the Trinitarian dimension of the text.

them by revealing that after being raised he would respond to his Father's invitation to come and sit at his right hand.

The Holy Spirit continued his work in Paul's heart by revealing to him who the enemies in the psalm are; he lists them as placed under Jesus' feet and subject to his authority: the dominations, authorities, powers and dignities (Eph 1:21). What a revelation! A gross error is thereby done away with: the enemies were not the Romans, the Sanhedrin, Pilate or Herod, but spiritual powers. The last enemy to be made subject is named: death (1 Cor 15:26). What grace and blessing that we too should be granted light!

Who was Jesus to be thus seated at the right hand of the Father? The Holy Spirit states this very clearly: he is Lord and Christ (Acts 2:36); he is God and also perfectly man, the new Adam, whose authority we see is likewise exercised over the animals when we note that in addition to Psalm 110, Psalm 8 is invoked.[15] The Holy Spirit also opened the eyes of Paul to the continuation of the psalm, specifying that, seated at the right hand of the Father,[16] Jesus was a priest after the order of Melchizedek (Ps 110:4; Heb 7:1). After giving his life for us in his one sacrifice, our high priest has gone to sit at the right hand of the Father forever (Heb 10:12). How marvelous!

The Holy Spirit didn't just inspire David, Peter and Paul as well as us as we meditate the psalm, he actually came to accompany Jesus in his Ascension to the Father. We

15. Curiously, when he cites Psalm 110, Matthew replaces "footstool" (*hupopodion*) with "beneath" (*hupokatô*), which is borrowed from Psalm 8 (v 7), "beneath his feet" prior to the list of animals made subject to Adam in Paradise. This emphasizes the perfect humanity of Jesus.

16. Philemon thinks that Paul wrote this letter, though this was not the unanimous view either in his day or now in ours.

are told that a cloud came to lift Jesus up (Acts 1:9); it was the same cloud that enveloped Jesus in his presence at the Transfiguration (Matt 17:5), in the same silence of incomparable humility.[17] The Holy Spirit was thus united with the Father who too was raising the Son to his right hand (Eph 1:20).[18] This was wonderful Trinitarian communion!

O my soul, let's not stay with the disciples on earth, their eyes turned to heaven, as we contemplate the mystery of the Trinity! No! We are the objects of an infinite love, revealed by Jesus himself when he reassured and comforted his disciples, saying to them: "I am going to prepare a place for you; and when I have gone and have prepared a place for you, I will return and will take you with me so that where I am, you will be too" (Jn 14:2–3). We too will be with the Father! What infinite grace!

As we await his return, the Holy Spirit revealed to Paul, he, Jesus, is there at the right hand of the Father, interceding for us (Rom 8:34).Before we are in heaven with the Father, we are already being carried by Jesus in his prayers, and not only by the Son but also by the Holy Spirit who intercedes for us too (Rom 8:26). The Son and the Holy Spirit pray to the Father for us! What infinite love the Trinity has for us!

O my soul, what grace it is to be able to contemplate the work of the Spirit in the hearts of David, Peter, Paul and all of us. And what grace to be able contemplate the

17. There was "a cloud" at Jesus' ascension, as at the Transfiguration, a cloud that that is revealed to have been the Holy Spirit, as at Matt 17:1–13.

18. We read, "Having sat down at his right hand" (Eph 1:20), meaning that the Father caused the Son to sit at his right hand. We are told the same thing in Phil 2:9: "He was raised sovereignly." Evident here is the synergy between the Holy Spirit (Acts 1:9) and the Father (Eph 1:20; Phil 2:9).

profound communion of love of the Father, the Son and the Holy Spirit. How marvelous to see David already enveloped in the infinite mystery of the Trinity. What grace to now be able to continue . . .

MATTHEW 23

23:1–12

"WHOEVER HUMBLES SELF WILL BE EXALTED." THESE wonderful words of Jesus present us with humility as a way of life in which our part is to abase ourselves and God's part is to lift us up, as signaled by the divine passive "be exalted." It's clear: it's our place to humble ourselves, God's to lift us up.

The Fathers threw themselves energetically into this wonderful way and very quickly noted that our pride comes to mix itself up in matters; we go astray in delusions and make it our objective to be exalted, with humility merely a transitory post along the way to our goal. This folly incites us to humble ourselves just enough to demonstrate obedience to Jesus' words while keeping our eyes fixed on being lifted up into glory; this clearly reveals our obedience as far from disinterested and that our only real interest is exaltation. What is really motivating us is this rather than humility. The few steps we force ourselves to take with humility are taken so that we can appear humble in the eyes of others, when in reality we are only seeking our own glory. We are therefore totally deluded; humility is not a passing stage towards the heights but a pathway that leads us through incessant steps downwards to unfathomable depths as deep as the heart of God.

"Whoever humbles self will be exalted." It's astonishing to see that this word can be understood in two ways. Satan has us understand it in a way that flatters our pride by telling us we are already humble enough and that we will very soon be lifted up, while Jesus makes the statement to encourage those in danger of losing courage along the long road of humility.

Paul saw this danger and to encourage us further preached humility using Jesus himself as an example and model. Picking up the same expression, he tells us that Jesus "humbled himself" (Phil 2:8) and then presents his exaltation as the work of his Father at the end of the way, not as the objective he envisaged. Jesus' objective was not to be exalted by his Father but to obey him in humble obedience to the Father whose will is to save all (1 Tim 2:4). In the passage in which he takes Jesus as a model, Paul wonderfully defines humility by saying that a humble person abases self with eyes fixed not on self but not on others, regarding them as greater (Phil 2:3–4).This magnificent correction turns us away from our selfish interests and from pride. Paul didn't just teach humility, he practiced it: "abasing myself so that you can be exalted," he wrote to the Corinthians (2 Cor 11:7). When Jesus humbled himself to the point of the cross, it was to save us, not to save himself. He humbled himself to the utmost degree; all his life was lowering of self; humility was not a step along his road but was the road itself all the way to death. And what did he find in the deeps of his humbling? The hand of his Father to receive him, this open hand beneath the greatest depth into which Jesus was able to entrust his spirit: "My Father, I remit my spirit into your hands," he said as he breathed his last (Lk 23:46). The hand of the Father then lifted him to his right hand in the highest heaven (Eph 1:20). What a difference between this and the objective of the proud, always looking to be exalted but who find at the summit the hand of God which brings them low!

Everything Paul teaches here is already present in the words of Jesus I am meditating here, specifically in a very important aspect that is so discreet pride will have us read right over it without noticing. Jesus is speaking here to those he invites to make themselves servants: "The greatest among you shall be your servant." He calls us to follow him along the way of service as one who came not to be served but to serve (20:28). A servant is not a slave concerned only with their salary; a servant lives out their service in a way that is not forced, constrained or pained like a slave, but freely and voluntarily, not out of self-interest but out of love. Service is the voluntary abasement of a son who gives his life for others in love, not the forced abasement of a slave who goes through life centered on self.

O my soul, the eyes of the humble are not fixed on self but on others to lift them up, on God, to obey him, and on Jesus, to contemplate and follow him in the giving of self to others and to God in love, not self-interest. O my soul, let us contemplate our beloved Jesus Christ who humbled himself to the cross out of love for his Father and for us, and who his Father exalted to have him sit at his right hand in the highest. Let us contemplate him and this . . .

23:13–36 (A)

"*Ouaï!*" We have only to hear a word like this to know that it is a cry of pain;[1] this was Jesus' cry and his pain was

---

1. Although the simple translation "Woe!" reproduces the Greek sound, it can still sound like something of a curse, which could cause some confusion; in the Greek it is simply a cry of lament.

so great that it made him cry out seven times. No one else in the Scriptures laments like this as often, with the prophet Isaiah the next most vocal.[2] The amazing thing here is to see that Jesus is not lamenting privately, in solitude, but in the presence of a whole crowd. When a man suffers, usually he finds a place apart. Here, though, Jesus laments in public; his pain was so great he was unable to contain it.

"*Ouaï* because of you!" Jesus' suffering results from the scribes and the Pharisees he is speaking to. He had just been speaking about them (v 1–12), denouncing the suffering they were causing him, but his suffering was so great that now he suddenly challenges them directly. We don't know if they were actually present among the crowd since this is not stated, but perhaps they were there, quietly. Whatever the case, they were so much present to Jesus' heart that he speaks to them directly, unable to contain his great pain even in the presence of the crowd and the disciples.

Jesus laments that the scribes and Pharisees did not themselves seem to suffer. This is not so surprising and was more a sign that Jesus was pained over the suffering they had yet to experience. Just like all the prophets, Jesus was already seeing the suffering that would befall those he was speaking to even as he warned them.

Jesus was not calling down a curse on them but warning them by announcing the curse that was at their door if they didn't change. It was an act of grace towards the scribes and Pharisees to be warned like this since they could now

2. The next longest list of such cries is in Isaiah, with six occasions (5:8,11,18,20,21,22). No lament is as long as Jesus' here with our word used seven times (v 13,15,16,23,25,27,29). An eighth *ouaï* is found at 23:14, but this verse is not found in the main manuscripts or in Philemon's; it seems to have been borrowed from Mk 12:40 or Lk 20:47.

avoid the curse by changing their attitude and repenting before God; he it was who would send the curse that would be removed from them if they repented.

Warning someone, alerting them, is to love them. When we love someone and lament over them, we alert them to the situation if the suffering can be avoided. Jesus' cry of pain here reveals his great love for the scribes and the Pharisees. He did in fact love them! They were occupying the seat of Moses (v 2), a position they had not usurped but which had been granted them by God; but their position was not meant for themselves alone but for the good of all the people they were responsible for before God. Jesus' immense love for them was also a love for the people; his suffering was also compassion for the people who were suffering from the poor behavior of their leaders. Moreover, the scribes and Pharisees' bad behavior touched God, who suffered to see his people's suffering, mistreated as they were by the religious leaders. Jesus' lamentation here shows how he shared his Father's pain; the Father's pain is so deep that it is not described, and, indeed, we are told nothing of God suffering as a result of the scribes and Pharisees, nor of his suffering over his people. Nothing is said because this suffering is beyond anything that could be said; it is absolutely inexpressible.

God's suffering was such that he was not going to act and intervene to help the scribes and Pharisees change. So much was he withdrawn from the situation that Jesus intervenes in his place; he does what, in the Scriptures, God alone is able to do: he sends prophets, wise men and scribes himself (v 34). Jesus' divinity is so full that here he becomes one with his Father, without anything abusive of course but in order to care for his suffering Father. This is extreme compassion from the Son towards his Father!

It is prophets that Jesus will send, not soldiers, enemy armies or raging plagues. He will send those who will preach repentance, who will speak to the people to encourage them and to the leaders to cause them to change. The curse was imminent but not immediate; it was still contained and at this moment was only a threat, but this long chapter is a serious warning, spoken by Jesus who was already suffering from the curse proclaimed. "This will all happen in this generation": this statement still lay in the future; threat rather than implementation was allowing further time for repentance. What patience there is in this lamentation! And what love too!

"You race of vipers." Jesus picks up from John the Baptist (3:7), who was also speaking to the Pharisees and calling on them to repent. "Who has taught you to flee from the wrath to come?" said the Baptist, denouncing their connection with Satan, the fleeing snake.[3] "How can you escape?" Jesus says here. However, while John the Baptist spoke about imminent wrath, Jesus doesn't. He says nothing about it because the wrath wasn't going to strike the scribes, the Pharisees or the crowd so much as it would strike him, Jesus, who would drink the cup alone (26:39). His extreme compassionate love would go so far as . . .

23:13–36 (B)

Lord Jesus, in the same way that you had entrusted your flock to the scribes and Pharisees, who made you suffer with their teaching and behavior, today you entrust young Christians, new converts and catechumens to your

---

3. As in the meditation on Matt 3:1–12.

Church, and you now entrust the novices in our monastery to me, thirsty as they are for good teaching and true witnesses to faith. I therefore humble myself before you, begging you to forgive me when I see how much I too must make you suffer and how much I will do so in the future, causing you more pain than I can believe.

In your infinite mercy, please forgive my infidelities, my acts of disobedience and my lack of love towards my brothers today; may I am not be the same tomorrow with the novices. I am almost reduced to reciting a list of all the bishops in Gaza since the early days rather than attempt to teach by living out the realities of love, humility, obedience, forgiveness, and rather than owning to all the difficulty I have living with the brothers with the constant need to forget and efface self, to refuse to judge, to unendingly extend forgiveness and compassion towards the weakest. In your grace, have pity on me, a sinner.

It troubles me to think of leading them in their life of prayer when I have so much trouble conducting my own. In your grace, have pity on me, a sinner.

It troubles me to think of warning them against vainglory when I know that I am concerned about the way I appear to passing visitors. In your grace, have pity on me, a sinner.

Hypocrisy causes you pain, and what you said about the scribes and the Pharisees could also be applied to me. In your grace, have pity on me, a sinner.

Lord Jesus, with all the novices you are going to entrust to me, I don't know how many that will be but I do know that if just one goes astray it will cause your Father, who is not willing for one of these little ones to be lost, to suffer in the depths of his heart (18:14).

Heavenly Father, I earnestly ask you to forgive me if I have hurt or lost even one of the visitors who come through by my behavior or comments. In tears of repentance, I beg you now to grant me your forgiveness. In your grace, have pity on me, a sinner.

Lord Jesus, as I meditate your lamentation over the scribes and the Pharisees, one word in particular touches me, the word "first," when you call us to "first" cleanse the inside of the cup before touching the outside (23:26). I give thanks for this word that brings me correction, and I pray that you forgive me because I too carefully tend first to the outside while neglecting the inside. To cleanse the inside of the cup means cleansing the inner sanctuary of my heart, your sanctuary; but you know how many evil thoughts, bad memories and desires encumber my heart and dirty it. I am prepared to care for what others see while neglecting what you alone see, everything that is hidden in my heart. In your grace, have pity on me, a sinner.

No one sees when I fast with respect to what I look at,[4] avoiding anything unsuitable or indecent; no one sees when I fast with respect to what I hear, avoiding calumnies

---

4. Philemon on fasting lines up with the teaching of the Church Fathers. Fasting from food is one of the aspects of the asceticism whose goal is to cleanse a person, the better to experience God's presence. The Fathers quickly understood that asceticism does not only concern food and they extended fasting to cover sight, the sense of hearing and touch, everything that tends towards sin, thereby avoiding occasions for sin and focusing above all on whatever strengthens faith: "Happy is he who does not walk in the way of sinners and who meditates in the law of the Lord day and night" (Ps 1:1–2). Philemon doesn't mention it here, but the Fathers also spoke about soul fasting, the soul abstaining from anger, jealousy, judgment, slander . . .

and lies; no one sees my distractions and what fills my thoughts; no one sees the thoughts I have as I go to sleep, or if my prayers turn into daydreams; all of that escapes notice. It follows that I incline not to see all this as so important when, in your eyes, which see everything, it is so important; nothing escapes you, your Father, nor the Holy Spirit. Thrice holy God, I pray, have pity on me, a sinner; in your grace, please forgive me and help me to drive out of my heart every trace of jealousy, evil speaking, lust, judgment, rancor and every other evil thought that soils the interior of your sanctuary; teach me to offer to you a heart in which you can take up residence without suffering, and fill me with your peace in love for you and all who you call me to love; I pray this of you, to whom belong all honor, all glory, now and throughout the ages. Amen.

23:37–39

"As a mother hen gathers her chicks under her wings . . ." What a wonderful image to express the care with which Jesus seeks to keep his own sheltered from storms or any other menacing danger. The simple words suffice to reveal the inexpressible protective attention which watches over us today with a love beyond all love, and which only images can begin to describe.

This wonderful image is very close to the traditional image so well known in Israel. It is found at the end of the Pentateuch to describe God in the protective love he has for his people; he is "like an eagle who protects her brood, watching over her young, caring for them beneath her outspread wings" (Deut 32:11). Jesus is expressing the same protective love here but with extraordinary humility, comparing himself not to an eagle but a hen! No one in

Israel had ever been so humble as to describe themselves like this![5]

"Jerusalem, Jerusalem, I longed to gather together your children, but you would not." The repetition of "Jerusalem" is sufficient indication that Jesus was continuing in a mode of lamentation and that he was continuing the earlier discourse punctuated by so many cries of *ouaï*.[6] His pain results from his protective love not being received. "I wanted, but you didn't": his will comes up against another will that rejects his. This is the sorrow of rejected love, but a sorrow that takes the rejection in the same way that God always, with great respect, receives anyone who doesn't want his love. Here we see true love as respectful of the other person's liberty. Jesus knew the pain of rejected love, and his lament is full of the pain of God when rejected by his children.

"How many times have I longed . . . ?" The number of rejections is beyond counting. Since the beginning of the world, how many times had humanity turned away God's love? How often had God longed to spread his wings and gather his children? Would Jesus once again spread his arms

5. The image of a chicken is too humble to have inspired any biblical poet. In fact, the word *ornis* only occurs once in the whole Bible, in the list of foods on Solomon's table (either 1 Kgs 5:3 or 4:23, according to the version used). The Greek word translates the Hebrew *barbur*, which is difficult to identify, so the translators are uncertain ("poultry," "fatted fowl," "hens," "geese").

6. In Philemon's meditation on a passage in Luke, the brother monk who knew some Hebrew tells him that in the Hebraic culture, repeating a proper noun in the vocative was a very emotional expression of love, as found four times in God's mouth, addressing Abraham (Gen 22;11), Jacob (Gen 46:2), Moses (Exod 3:4) and Samuel (1Sam 3:10). Jesus does the same with Martha (Lk 10:41) and Peter (22:31). This is worth emphasizing so that we understand the extent of Jesus' love for Jerusalem. See also the note above on the use of *ouaï*.

to take in those who spurned him? It may seem incredible to us, but his love is indeed so great that he would do this yet again. High on Golgotha, his arms would be extended on a cross to gather in his children; he would extend them with infinite tenderness and say in all the pain of crucified love, "Father, forgive them, they don't know what they are doing!" (Lk 23:34). Once again, Jerusalem would mock, sneer, blaspheme and reject the love so magnificently offered it.

However, we then have presented to our contemplation an extraordinary miracle of the Holy Spirit, the very same who from the beginning of the world has hovered over creation like a protective bird (Gen 1:2).[7] He began right here to bring together a new covey, a new flock, a new people beneath the wings of the Crucified. On Golgotha, a man heard his prayer and perceived Jesus' love, and this man, a bandit, spoke to him this wonderful prayer: "Jesus, remember me when you come into your Kingdom" (Lk 23:42).[8] Jesus heard and answered, and the thief came to

7. In the Septuagint we read that the Spirit of God settled on or moved over the water (Gen 1:2). Philemon has a bird in mind, no doubt because of the account of Jesus' baptism where the Holy Spirit is likened to a dove. He may also have been influenced by the Syriac Fathers like Ephraim who read the verb in Gen 1:2 in a way that makes the Holy Spirit a mother bird brooding over her young, an interpretation favored in the Syriac by the Holy Spirit being feminine. This can change the way we see the Trinity and the wings of God if we see the Father as an eagle, the Son as a mother hen and the Spirit as a dove, each image being one of protection.

8. Different translations phrase this verse in two different ways; some have, "He said to Jesus, 'Remember me . . .'" while others have, "He said, 'Jesus, remember me . . .'" This difference derives from the vocative and dative forms of "Jesus" being the same in Greek, so it can be taken either as the complement in the dative of "he said," or the vocative opening the request. Philemon takes it as a vocative: "He said, 'Jesus, remember me.'"

place himself under the wings stretched out above him and found divine protection.

Then others too came to place themselves silently under the divine wings. Jesus heard the silent prayer of his mother, Mary, and John, his beloved disciple, as they stood near the cross; he brought them together, receiving them into his humble protection: "Woman, here is your son," "And you, here is your mother" (Jn 19:26). The centurion, Longinus, and others with him, knew the dead man for who he was, his arms spread out on the cross, and they too came to put themselves under his protection (Matt 27:54).[9] Then the women from Galilee who had stood at a distance also perceived the call and the divine protection; they found refuge beneath the nail pierced wings; among them were Mary Magdalene, Mary the mother of James and Joseph, and the mother of the sons of Zebedee (Matt 27:56–57).

In this manner, the Holy Spirit brought together and continued to bring together a new people for the one the Father made to sit at his right hand.

O my soul, how good it is to say, with David and with all the redeemed people, this wonderful prayer: "Lord, keep me as the apple of your eye; hide me under the shadow of your wings" (Ps 17:8).

O Jesus, here I am, the least of the least. It's my turn now to say, "Remember me when you come into your Kingdom; in the shadow of your wings, keep me as the apple of your eye . . ."

9. The Bible doesn't give the centurion's name, but by the 4th century he was known as Longinus. Matthew mentions others along with him so there were many who confessed together with him, "Truly this was the Son of God." Longinus' name is found in the Synaxarium for October 16 (Hieromonk Macarius, *Synaxarium*, Simonos Petra at Mount Athos, vol 1, p.498).

MATTHEW 24

24:1–14

WHEN I FIRST READ THIS TEXT IN ORDER TO MEDITATE IT, I was overcome and then overwhelmed, firstly by the multitude of catastrophes and trials it announces: wars, famines, earthquakes, persecutions, hatred . . . Surely all this is unbearable for our poor human strength? Of course, Jesus calls on us to face all this with perseverance, holding fast in prayer and to do so until the end in order to be saved — and this is our daily task as monks, our part in the Church's task. But what affects me even more is to see another task added to this, that we preach the Gospel throughout the inhabited earth. This is what discourages me. Jesus had already sent out his disciples to preach, but that was only to the lost sheep of Israel, not to the pagan Gentiles or the Samaritans (10:5–6), whereas now he was sending them throughout the earth, to all people, to the most savage, to the ends of the earth. This is really beyond our strength! If we need to pray for those who will be crushed beneath this excessive load, then our prayer as monks will also be beyond bearing. So I was discouraged on reading this text in which God seems to be strangely absent, but, at just that moment, in God's grace, a detail touched me to the core and filled me with deep joy, renewing my strength for my role in the Church.

O my soul, did you notice a discreet divine passive which reveals the presence of God in this text where he seemed absent? Here, for the first time Jesus doesn't tell us to "preach the Gospel," but changes the expression and tells us that "the Gospel will be preached"[1]; he doesn't specify by whom it will be preached, but the answer is clear because of the divine passive. It will certainly be preached by the disciples but not only by them, and this is wonderful.

When Jesus first sent the disciples out to preach to Israel, he had already told them that the Holy Spirit would speak in them (10:20), and this is what came to pass. The Gospel was indeed preached by the disciples and by the Holy Spirit in synergy with them in that harmonious collaboration which is a source of great joy. Blessed be God for such harmony and co-operation!

What else did Jesus say to the disciples? That without him they could do nothing (Jn 15:5); nothing, not to preach, not to pray, not to accomplish the least little task in the Church. He accompanied this with a wonderful promise, telling us that he would be with us to the end of the world (Matt 28:20), and it is just a fact that the disciples and we too see the Lord working with us (Mk 16:20), offering us this wonderful collaboration with the Holy Spirit. May he be blessed eternally!

---

1. Until this point in Matthew's gospel, the verb "to preach" (*kérussô*) has always been in the active voice. John the Baptist preached (3:1), Jesus preached (4:17,23; 9:35; 11:1) and the disciples preached (10:7,27). Suddenly, where we might have expected "you will preach the gospel," Jesus changes and uses the passive, "The gospel will be preached."

O my soul, do you believe that the Father will rest without doing anything? Certainly not! He too will join the work of evangelization, in particular by sending angels, as he did when they announced Jesus' birth to the shepherds (Lk 2:10);[2] the angels too are preachers, joining in with the work of the disciples. But this is not all; the Father has other servants, of whom he can also make preachers of his Kingdom, as Jesus has just discreetly been reminding us. He invites us to preach throughout "the inhabited earth," using a word he hadn't used before and wouldn't use again, one that suggests a wonderful reality. While we certainly don't know the language of every nation, there is a psalm in which we are told that the whole universe, the day, the night and the heavens also preach a mysterious message addressed to the whole of "the inhabited earth."[3] This is wonderful! The whole universe joins with us to preach to all peoples the wonders of God; it too collaborates with us, and what we don't understand of its language, the Holy Spirit can enable all peoples to grasp, as the disciples would find on the day of Pentecost (Acts 2).

O my soul, prayer for preachers of the Gospel is a wonderful task when I see that not only the whole universes preaches the Kingdom to the ends of the earth, but that it also praises the Lord and joins in with the prayers of the Son

2. The angel, we are told, "announced good news" to the shepherds. The verb *euangélizomai* means both "announce good news" and "announce the Gospel," and here Jesus speaks of an *euangélion* which means both "good news" and "the gospel."

3. Philemon is referring to Psalm 19 which states that the message from the cosmos is addressed to "the inhabited earth" (*oïkouméné*). This is the word used by Jesus here and nowhere else (other than the parallel passage in Lk 21:26). We might note that Paul cites the psalm as well (Rom 10:18), bringing together the sound of the cosmos and the witness of the disciples.

and the Holy Spirit who intercede for the preachers with the Father (Rom 8:26, 34) and encourage us too to persevere.

O my soul, no one goes alone to preach the Gospel to the ends of the earth because the Father, the Son and the Holy Spirit are alongside them to work with them and mysteriously encourage them with infinite love. Neither is anyone alone in prayer because the Son and the Holy Spirit, heaven, earth and every creature both seen and unseen cause incessant prayer to rise up to the Father. So I am here alone in my cell, borne up by the prayers of the Son and the Spirit in concert with heaven and earth . . . What wonderful grace, and what encouragement!

24:15–25

"You see, I have told you beforehand," Jesus says to conclude this passage in which he enlightens us on two very important points, with the goal of helping us in the last times.[4]

The first point has to do with Satan, who Jesus doesn't name as a person since his name is so repugnant; instead the reference is as if to a thing, "the Desolation," to denigrate him (v 15)[5] and uncover the destructive effects of

---

4. In this meditation, I sense that Philemon is including everything Jesus says from the moment he sits down to teach on the Mount of Olives, so, from verse 3 of this chapter.

5. Philemon takes up the phrase "the abomination of Desolation" which comes from Daniel 12:11, and which is found again in the first book of the Maccabees (1 Mac 1:54, the apocryphal/deutero-canonical book), where it designates the altar built by Antiochus Epiphanes IV in the Jerusalem temple to honor Zeus the Olympian; this was in 168 BC. According to the Greek of the Septuagint, it was not the Desolator/Destroyer but the Desolation, a feminine term which thereby mocks Zeus and so too Satan, who Jesus makes fun of here.

his works which lead only to desolation. The evils begin with him when he is installed in the temple with the manifest intention of taking God's place and he says, "I am the Christ" (v 5). Just these words are enough to tell us that he sets himself up as God because only God can say with truth, "I am" (Exod 3:14). By stating that he is the Christ, he wants to appropriate the divinity of Christ. All of this of course is lies because he is truly the father of lies (Jn 8:44), and all his envoys are nothing but liars, christs of the lie and prophets of the lie (v 24).[6] His works are arrogant (v 24), intended to impress, seduce and lead astray, and in a hidden way they cause love to grow cold and spread anguish and pain. In order to show us the way Satan works in secret and to help us refine our discernment, Jesus uses passives that are similar to divine passives but which might better be termed malign passives.[7] To say that love will grow cold (literally, be made cold; v 12) leaves no confusion: it is Satan who endeavors to freeze out love and extinguish it, while God fans the flame of love in our hearts. This then is the devious work of Satan, producing devastation and nothing else: wars (v 6), murders (v 9), hatred (v 9), scandals (v 10), distress (v 9, 21, 29). O my soul, how precious it is for us to have been forewarned by Jesus so that we don't fall into Satan's traps!

6. "False-christ" and "false prophet," or "pseudo-christ" and "pseudo-prophet": the Greek here uses words preceded by "pseudo" which means "lying," hence the link with Satan, "the father of lies," according to Jesus in Jn 8:44.

7. There are not many of these "malign passives" in the gospels, but they abound here: "don't be alarmed" (v 6), "a people will be raised" (v 7), "many will be offended/scandalized" (v 10), "false prophets will be raised up" (v 11 and 24), "love will be chilled" (v 12), "iniquity will be multiplied" (v 12). Each of this passive leaves as understood their accomplishment "by Satan."

The second point has to do with God, who, again, Jesus doesn't name, but for quite different reasons: his name is too holy for our human lips and he is beyond anything we could say of him. Where Satan needs to be unmasked and denounced, God is to be revealed and revered. To show how inexpressible God is, Jesus uses two expressions which allude to him: he speaks of "the Gospel of the Kingdom" (v 14), which could only be the Kingdom "of God, and also of the "elect" (v 22, 24), who are the elect "of God"; he also calls on us to "pray" (v 20), with the understanding that prayer is to God. While he is not named, God is nonetheless present and at work now in wonderful ways. In order to say that his work is humble and discreet, Jesus prefers to speak with divine passives, which, this time, are undeniably divine passives. Thus, we are told that the Gospel of the Kingdom "will be preached" throughout the world (v 14). Who will it be preached by if not God who alone can preach to the entire world, he who is Father, Son and Holy Spirit? He it is who will do this but working discreetly through us, in synergy with us, in a communion that is so humble we can almost miss it. I looked at this wonderful grace just now.

With another divine passive, Jesus tells us again about the infinite love God has for us: the days of distress "will be shortened," he says (v 22). While Satan endeavors to spread distress and to extinguish love, God will intervene and put an end to his activities. "Then will come the end," Jesus tells us, and this is wonderful because it means that this will be the end of Satan's work. Who is it that will shorten this time if not God? He will do this, Jesus tells us, when he sees that the elect themselves are at the point of being led astray by prophets of the lie (v 24). If this time was not shortened, no one "would be saved" (v 22), again with a divine passive which says that the work of salvation is accomplished by God. We need to be very attentive here: Jesus doesn't say that only the elect will be saved but that "because of the elect" everyone will be saved.[8] It is because there are the elect of God that we will all be saved. Who then are these elect? They are not necessarily numerous; it was enough for a few like Moses to stand in the gap before God (Ps 106:23). The Chief Elder spoke in this way of John of Rome and Elias in Corinth.[9] God knows how many there are, but even if there is only one left, and that one is at the point of being led astray, then God will intervene out of love for all and save everyone. The love of God is so great that he fully respects our liberty; but this tremendous respect of God's for us will not go so far as allowing Satan to destroy us; God will intervene sovereignly against the destroyer. Then the end will come . . .

"You see, I have told you beforehand," Jesus says. What mercy! And what infinite love for us!

24:26–35

The coming of our Lord Jesus is so important that Jesus himself devoted the whole of this passage to help us prepare in the best way possible. To do so, he makes us aware that deceivers will come pretending to be him (v 5,

8. The text says "all flesh," an expression which here means all human beings. [Translator's note: we might want to be careful here. Virtually every translation, both French and English, says that if it were not for the elect "no flesh" would be saved, implying only that some (but perhaps all) flesh will be saved. The Greek says literally "not was saved all flesh"; Wuest renders this as "all flesh would not be saved." It seems that Philemon's understanding is possible.]

9. Intercessors who might, as above in the meditation on Matt 22:1–14, be considered the elect of God.

24); this should be enough for us to understand that we should not so much as listen to them and that we should be very vigilant.

Jesus also calls on us, insistently, not to go looking for him where they tell us he is (v 23, 26); we are not to listen to such statements, nor to go out of our way to check on them. I conclude, with this awareness, that it is best for me not to go anywhere, whatever happens, but to stay in the monastery. Since, moreover, he announces his coming is from heaven, on the clouds of heaven, how foolish it would be to want to go and meet him! Wisdom does not promote gadding about; I will therefore stay here in my place of service.

Jesus' announcement of cosmic signs is beyond my understanding; however, I do respond to the parable of the fig tree, which is easier for me to think about thanks to the fig trees here at the monastery. I am most challenged by Jesus' statement at the end of all these signs when he tells us that he "is near, at the doors."[10]

This mention of doors particularly touches me, having been entrusted with the role of doorkeeper. The day Jesus comes, he will present himself at the door and knock, humbly waiting for us to open to him. Jesus knocking at the door of the monastery! How lovely and how impressive! I recognize his humility in this, and I am even more touched to think that it is I who will open the door to welcome him! What emotion. Will I be awake at the moment he knocks? I am very aware of the degree to which we need to be vigilant! He will stand "at the doors," he specifies, but we may

10. In the Greek, the word for "door" is plural, a way of suggesting each of our doors, all doors. Many English translations have this plural, which is helpful to a reading of Philemon's meditation.

ask which doors, given that nothing is said of this, and in fact they are introduced without a definite article, so really it is "at doors." The clearest texts in the Scriptures on this give me to understand that the lack of precision means simply that we are talking about the doors of whoever is being spoken to. "I stand at the door," Jesus says to the Church at Laodicea, talking about the door to this church (Rev 3:20). "The voice of him who knocks at the door," says the beloved, speaking of her own door (Song 5:2). The doors Jesus is talking about are ours, in our everyday life; I am called to await the Lord at the door to the monastery as well as at the door to my cell, since there are many doors. I find myself full of emotion because among the doors mentioned here by Jesus, there is my cell door, the very door that one day he spoke to me about closing so that I can pray in the presence of the Father (Matt 6:6). What a mystery! When he comes, he will come to join me and also join his Father who is there in secret in my cell. What an inexpressible mystery! I weep with emotion to think that they will both be there, the Father and the Son, there in my presence, in my cell.

Jesus' words to the Church at Laodicea direct my meditation in a still more wonderful and overwhelming way because they reveal why he stands at the door: it will be to share a meal, which is to say the Holy Supper.[11] O my soul, how wonderful this is! He will come to celebrate the Divine Liturgy!

The text of the Song of Songs reveals something else about the Lord. In today's text, Jesus says simply, "He is

11. The word for the meal of Rev 3:20 (*deïpnon*) is the same used for the meal during which Jesus instituted the Holy Supper (Lk 22:20).

close, at the doors," without putting a name to who this "he" is.[12] The context gives us to understand that it is the Son of Man, but in the Song of Songs we are given another term to designate this person: the one who stands at the door is "the beloved" (*adelphidos*).[13] The humble Jesus, who will come to join our Father in my cell, presents himself as my "beloved brother"! What extraordinary humility this is, confirming that Jesus and I are sons of our mutual Father! More, in the Song of Songs this "beloved brother" is none other than the well-beloved, the espoused.

O my soul, rejoice and stand ready in prayer; it is your beloved who will come to knock at the door of your heart[14] with his inexpressible love and waits for you, his beloved, his espoused, to open to him . . . Nevertheless, O my soul, pay attention, because in the Song, when the beloved knocks at the door, his beloved is asleep, and you know that when she finally comes to open the door after making herself ready, he is no longer there; he left (Song 5:5–6)! O my soul, make sure you're ready!

24:36–44

After describing the work of the men in the fields and the women at the mill, Jesus says, "Watch," inviting us to watch while we work, with our hearts absorbed not by our

---

12. "He is close/near." There is a mixed witness in English translations, some (KJV) have "it is near," which seems to be incorrect; some have "he is near," which seems to more closely follow the Greek; and some have "the Son of Man is near," which is not wrong, but doesn't fit with Philemon's meditation.

13. In Hebrew, we have *dôd*, "beloved," correctly translated as *adelphidos*.

14. Philemon discreetly suggests a third door after the doors to the monastery and his cell, the door to his heart. This fits well with the plural "doors."

work but by the Lord whose return we await. We are therefore called upon to watch and pray during our work,[15] which was the way of Abba Lucius as he applied himself to doing as Jesus asks.[16] To keep our spirit turned towards the Lord as we work is a great challenge because it involves an unending struggle against thoughts that lead us into distraction; but there is great grace too because prayer opens our hearts and directs them beyond our work and beyond the horizon towards he who will fill us with his love on the day of his coming. What grace this is because our watching fills us with peaceful hope and surrounds us with the activities of grace.

"Watch," Jesus tells us, and then illustrates this with an example set at night, thereby calling us to continue watching during the night. This type of watch is also very demanding because it exposes us to the tricks of the thief who looks for any failing as an opportunity to pillage our hearts! It requires of us constant struggle against the evil thoughts that are always more numerous at night then during the day! But what grace there is too! When we watch at night, we sense our thirst grow for the coming of our Lord to deliver us from the thief. There is also grace in being able

15. It is interesting to note Philemon speaking here of prayer when Jesus only mentions watching. He was a monk to the core and automatically associates watching with prayer; he had good reason to do so because Jesus later makes the same association, telling his disciples to "Watch and pray" (26:41). Jesus says, "Watch" here, but after saying, "Pray," (24:20) in the same passage. Philemon had rightly understood that watching and praying are inseparable. To tell the truth, to watch without praying makes no sense.

16. Here, Philemon is referring to Apophthegm 446, which tells of how Abba Lucius prayed as he worked; he prayed seated since he was obliged to sit while he worked: "I sit before God, wetting my little strands of palm and plaiting them into rope as I say, 'Have pity on me, O God, according to your great pity' . . ."

to turn during the night to our Father who neither slumbers nor sleeps (Ps 121:4) but who watches with us in our cell to protect us from the thief and cleanse our hearts from the effects of his aggressions! What grace and what beauty to pray heart to heart with the Father in our cells while the world sleeps and is silent! We have this inexpressible presence of the Father who watches beside us in our cells, awaiting with us the coming of his beloved Son! Therefore, let us watch, just as he invites us! Let us watch, awaiting the day of his return!

We discover that our watching is filled with an infinite mystery because the one we await is also the one who is always with us! What a mystery it is to hear Jesus say to his disciples on the very day he left, "I am with you always, to the end of the world" (28:20). This is clearly confirmed at the end of Mark's Gospel, where we are told that "the Lord was taken up to heaven" (16:19) and "he was working with the disciples" (16:20). Here, Jesus is in heaven while we are on earth; and we await him while he is with us every day. What a paradoxical mystery! Each of our days is filled with his presence, and each of our days is a day that we await him, a day when he might return! All our watching, all our praying is marked by this profound mystery, both night and day.

It is hard and demanding to persevere as long as his absence impinges on our hearts and causes us to suffer! How tough, how demanding, to pray without ceasing without him! But how good it is to take refuge in the Father who constantly comforts us with his presence in our cells! How good it is to open up to the Comforter Spirit who spreads his wings over us day and night, and settles upon us to comfort us with his tenderness! And what joy to pray, knowing that the Son is effectively here with us at all times, in accordance with his promise, taking upon himself the burden of our faults and the pain of our struggles; he bears the burden of our everyday together with us, under the same yoke! Our watching is then filled with peace, both day and night, with a peace the world cannot give; this unspeakable peace then leads into thanksgiving.

The one we await is "the Son of Man," Jesus tells us here, emphasizing that he is the unseen, heavenly being now seated beside the Father in the highest place. We also await the one who is "your Lord," as Jesus says, here emphasizing the bond of love between us and him, the one who accompanies us every day and to whom we can say, "my Lord and my God" (Jn 20:28), as we marvel at being able to look to him.

O my soul, we don't know the day or the hour of his coming, but I give thanks because Jesus doesn't know the day or hour any more than do we; he too, like us, is preparing without knowing the day but knowing our thirst and sharing in it; it is his thirst too, the thirst for reunion which is growing in his heart as it does in ours. O my soul, what grace it is to know that we will share with him the infinite joy of his reuniting with us to celebrate together the Supper in the Kingdom beside the Father . . .

24:45–51

"Happy is that servant, who when his master returns is found so doing; in truth, I tell you that he will be set over all his goods."

O my soul, happy indeed is that servant because his master will have proved his faithfulness, entrusting him first of all with lesser tasks, all of which were carried out perfectly, then with greater tasks, again faithfully fulfilled, until the day came when he could be entrusted with a still greater task and the master left without any disquietude. He left, putting full confidence in him and leaving him to fulfill his role.

As for the servant, he was touched by the confidence his master placed in him, deeply touched. He had been touched by the first tasks committed to him because he saw this wonderful trust, and this touched him more and more with each new assignment; he thus began to love his master and to trust him in return. In order not to betray his master's trust, he always and increasingly sought to meet every requirement, and when his master left, he honored him even more because he realized how completely he was being trusted; he then wanted to be prepared so that at his return his master would be totally satisfied when together they looked over the results.

Nevertheless, during the master's absence, questions arose when he needed to put particular details into practice; he had to draw upon his memory to work out how his master had proceeded and then copy him. Later, when no memory came to his aid, he asked himself what his master would have done in a similar circumstance and then applied himself to acting likewise so that his obedience would be as faithful as possible. Obedience is the right term here; happy obedience is a precious ally which allows us to always keep alive the word we have heard; in fact the word of the master is of such importance that obedience to it enables the master to be honored in the most faithful way possible.

Then, when nothing else helped the servant decide how to accomplish this or that task, he even dared to improvise, doing what he thought was the best and the closest to what his master would have done; he did this continuing to honor his master's trust. "My master," he thought, "has put so much confidence in me; I hope that he will be satis-fied with my decisions, happy for me to take the initiative." The trust placed in him by the master brought to birth the servant's trust in him, and it nurtured him; this reciprocal trust led on to love and caused it to grow.

It might be that the servant made mistakes, but if so, it would always be with the best intentions and in the hope that the master would appreciate that. If he did make a mistake, he knew that he could confidently ask forgiveness, expecting that forgiveness would be granted out of deep respect for his intentions.

The master's absence mysteriously brought about a lively bond between the two, thanks to which the servant kept the master always in his heart and prepared himself for his return. The servant knew neither the day nor the hour of this return, but he prepared with joy and with a sort of impatience which helped maintain his joy; he did everything so that at his return, his master would share in his joy when he found what he had done. He sought consis-tently to honor his master more and more so that nothing could tarnish the trust placed in him. The servant therefore awaited his returned and prepared to rejoice in it as a feast day to celebrate their reciprocal trust, a day in which no shadow would be cast over their love.

Happy indeed is the servant whose master's arrival will find him with all this done.

You are blessed, Lord Jesus, the master in this parable, you who spoke this beatitude for us to meditate. You are blessed for the faithfulness of the servant you celebrate here and for your silence over the faithfulness of the master. Lord Jesus, it's my place to discuss this, to discuss how wonder-ful your faithfulness is towards me, far beyond anything I can say because it is full of a love for which the servant

had no word either. You are blessed because in your presence the words "servant" and "master" are just not enough
to describe the relationship you establish and live with us.
Lord Jesus, I await the day of your return, but I know I
won't be able to say a thing; I will simply fall on my knees
before you and bow to the ground to hide my tears of joy,
guarding in my heart the final words of Abba Agathon.[17]
Lord Jesus . . .

17. An allusion to Apophthegm 111 concerning Abba Agathon:
"At the point of death, he lay for three days with his eyes open but
fixed. The brothers sought to help, saying, 'Abba Agathon, where
are you?' He told them, 'I am standing before God's tribunal.' They
said, 'How is this? Do you too have fear, Father?' 'I have certainly,'
he replied, 'done all I can to keep God's commandments, but I am just
a man; how can I know if my works have pleased God?' The brothers said, 'Aren't you confident that you work has been according to
God?' The elder replied, 'I won't be content until I have appeared
before God because God's judgment is different to men's.' And he
died joyfully.

MATTHEW 25

25:1-13

HERE ARE TEN WOMEN, ALL VIRGINS, BUT THEIR FINAL
outcome was not the same because they were judged on
their virginal virtue. Similarly, they were all expected to
watch but all fell asleep and all needed to be woken up, so
they were not judged on their ability to stay awake. The
difference between them lay elsewhere, in their provision of
oil; the wise were careful and made sure to fill their lamps,
but the foolish didn't. The parable thereby enlightens us
to what awaits when it comes to enter the wedding feast
of the Kingdom: will we have enough oil? The parable
does, nevertheless, present us with a difficulty which might
prevent us getting ready because Jesus doesn't tell us what
the oil corresponds to! How are we to understand this
important aspect of the parable?

Jesus doesn't specify the meaning of the oil because it
wasn't necessary; just the mention of oil was enough because
the word carries a deeper meaning. When the foolish virgins
said to the others, "Give us some of your oil" (élaïou), the

word for mercy (éléou)[1] would be heard. The oil therefore represents mercy. With this, things become clear: the difference between the two groups lay in the exercise of mercy, and the same applies to us. Mercy is a great virtue which opens the way for us to enter the bridal chamber of the Kingdom, and those who don't exercise mercy will hear the terrible words, "I don't know you!"

A feature of the parable that may surprise is that when the foolish virgins ask for oil, the wise don't give them any! Did they lack mercy towards them? Not at all! The wise virgins' reply simply means that mercy can't be shared. We can be merciful towards others but not in their place. This applies to all the virtues; they are not goods that can be shared. It's a characteristic of mercy to forgive and not judge, and the truth is that I can't forgive in someone else's stead or abstain for judging on their behalf.

"Happy are the merciful because mercy will be given to them," (5:7)[2] says Jesus, and now this encouraging beatitude is magnificently illustrated in the parable, but it also helps us understand how unhappy those who are not merciful will be when the door of the Kingdom is shut against them.

---

1. In the Greek, oil is élaïon. When the foolish virgins say, "Give us some of your oil" (25:8), the word takes the form élaïou, which sounds almost the same as éléou, from éléos, meaning "mercy." The same interpretation of oil is found in Philemon's close contemporary John of Gaza, who writes in one of his letters: "Behave like a wise and not a foolish virgin, those who were excluded from the nuptial chamber because they lacked the fruit of mercy and good deeds." For him too the oil was "the fruit of mercy" (Barsanuphius and John of Gaza, *Correspondence*, Letter 638). The interpretation of oil as mercy is found earlier in John Chrysostom, Homily 23 on John's Gospel.

2. In the Greek of this beatitude, the final verb is a divine passive, meaning "mercy will be given to them," it is understood "by God."

"Mercy will be given to them": this expression using the divine passive tells us where the oil of our mercy comes from. The perfectly merciful one is God (Exod 34:6), and by his grace, we are merciful too because we are made in his image. However, from day to day, the oil of our mercy runs down in our lamps and needs to be regularly renewed, and it is in God's presence that it can be; we have particular need of this whenever we sin. As we repent we appeal to the mercy of God, and because he forgives us we have the wherewithal to forgive others. Similarly, because he doesn't judge us, we learn not to judge others. We never, however, stop sinning, so we always need to repent. If the foolish virgins had no more oil, this is doubtless because they had not been through repentance and so failed to receive from God the mercy of his forgiveness.

We receive mercy from the merciful God, and this encourages us too to forgive, but at the same time the beatitude tells us that it's because we are merciful that we receive God's mercy. There is an enigma here that has to be maintained, that God forgives us because we forgive others, but we also forgive others because we receive God's forgiveness; the two aspects are inseparable.

Every instance of forgiveness received from God is a miracle proceeding from his divine mercy and is wonderful to behold when compared to our poor human mercy. Further to this, when God forgives us, he deposits his divine mercy in our heart and mingles it with our human mercy and thereby renews us into his image. What extraordinary grace! And since divine mercy can't be measured against human mercy, we can see the extent to which the beatitude points to an unfathomable depth: "Happy are those who exercise mercy humanly because the divine mercy will open the door of the Kingdom to them . . ." O my soul, let us never cease to repent because God's mercy fills our lamp with oil so that we can both await him and welcome him when he comes . . .

25:14–30

In this parable, my attention is drawn to the confidence the master has in his servants, revealing the confidence that the Lord Jesus, our master, has in us.[3]

This confidence or trust of the master causes me to marvel in a very particular way because it is absolute, having nothing to do with any kind of contractual agreement. Nothing obliges a master to entrust his goods to his servants, and it's not a servant's role to manage his master's goods. Matthew, as a tax-collector, knew this very well; if a master was going to entrust management to someone it would be to a banker. The confidence Jesus puts in us is in no way requisite because of some circumstance but comes from pure grace towards us, his servants. And whether we are good or bad, his confidence is the same. How wonderful!

The master hands out his goods to each of us in a different way, not arbitrarily but in line with our competencies. It follows that he knows us perfectly; he knows what we are capable of and wonderfully takes full account of this. No one can complain of receiving too much or too little. The talents entrusted to us are his and not our own. This too is wonderful; before him, I am in fact poor and I remain poor. Every good thing that he entrusts to me is not given; it remains his and will remain so throughout my life; I am its provisory manager! Before Jesus, I have no personal riches;

---

3. The Greek *kurios* means both "master" and "Lord." In our translation of Philemon it is taken to mean both, indiscriminately.

I am just a servant. All I have is his; all I have ever done is to receive from him. This is really wonderful!

The master leaves, without any record of the transaction and no indication of his expectations! He isn't expecting anything specific from my obedience! This is really surprising to me as a monk! In the parable of the tenants to the vineyard, there was a contract with the master (21:33): they were supposed to give him his part of the fruit at harvest time, and they knew that he would return for the vintage. But there is none of that here; the master could return at any moment. What is to be done when there is no clear indication? What is to motivate the servants' behavior?

The wicked servant stated what motivated him; it was fear. He was afraid because, in his view, his master was a hard man who reaped where he had not sown. The master agreed while rejecting the idea that he was hard; that is, he did reap where he had not sowed, but was not hard; the servant's fear was not justified, and the master was right to speak about him as lazy. The wicked servant had done neither evil nor good; he had done nothing; nothing!

What about the others? What had motivated them?

Well, they don't state their motivation but we can work it out. They knew their master, and they too knew that he reaped where he hadn't sown; but they then wished to please him and offer back to him what he had not required. They weren't acting out of obedience but out of love. They were doing nothing for themselves but everything for him. Their love was genuinely disinterested because they didn't yet know anything about any reward he might bring with him. Their love was so great that they took various initiatives and did so "immediately" after his departure. Their love didn't wait before getting down to work; they acted in order to honor the immense trust they had received from their master. On his return their master would say that they were good, but, if so, it was because he was first good to them. Their goodness was a fruit of his; they were in his image. Their love too was according to their capacities and the master didn't congratulate one more than the other; for him, the two servants were both good and faithful, and he wasn't measuring their love. The tax-collector, Matthew, must have marveled to see that the servants had made no effort to enrich themselves! The master's love had excited his servants' love, not egotism!

When the master returned, his attitude is again very unusual. All that his servants had done for him with goodness and faithfulness, despite everything was "a few things" (v 23)! But we mustn't be mistaken here; in his eyes it was not something great, but he doesn't speak to denigrate; it was only small in comparison with what awaited them, with the "abundance" (v 29) that would be given them. In fact, what they would be entrusted with was incalculably, disproportionately, infinitely more and indescribable! And that's not all; the master's announcement might seem no more than a recompense the servants might have foreseen; they might indeed have thought that their loyal service would be rewarded. However, they could not have imagined what the master says to them finally: "Enter into the joy of your lord!" This is pure grace, infinite love, because to enter into joy is like entering into the Kingdom of heaven or into the bridal hall.[4] Entering into the master's joy, for a servant, is beyond price, indescribable, utterly unknown, above anything he could think. This is so great that even the master says nothing further; his love is inexpressible . . .

4. "Enter into the joy of your lord," is said to each of the good servants using the same verb as elsewhere: "enter into the Kingdom of heaven" (7:21) and "enter into the wedding hall" (25:10).

25:31-46

When our Lord sets at his right hand those who have given food to the hungry, he is surely speaking about physical hunger, but I believe he is also speaking about those whose soul is hungry; a soul can hunger for appreciation or respect. He knows this very well; on the cross he knew this hunger in the midst of insults and blasphemies but heard one of the two thieves speak his name with infinite respect: "Jesus, remember me when you come into your Kingdom" (Lk 23:42). These blessed words brought him calm in his hunger to be respected. Look at the cross, O my soul, and care for the hungry, even the least of them, if only by speaking their name with great respect so that they taste your words as a taste of blessing.

When our Lord sets at his right hand those who give a drink to the thirsty, yes, he was speaking about the thirsty throat only a drink can quench, but I believe he was also talking about the thirst a soul can know; the soul can thirst, whether for justice, compassion or kindness. He knows this very well; on the cross he knew thirst in the midst of mocking smiles, and as he saw his mother shed silent tears (Jn 19:25). They were blessed tears that slaked his thirst for compassion. Look at the cross, O my soul, and care for those who thirst, even the least of them, so that their souls can find something that brings relief through the tears of your compassion.

When our Lord sets at his right hand those who welcome strangers, yes, he was speaking of those who come from other nations, but I believe he was also speaking of those who are strangers in their own land, who no one welcomes. He knows this very well; on the cross he was rejected by his own people but found refuge in the heart of John, the beloved disciple (Jn 19:26). Blessed John, who stood at the foot of the cross, his heart open to welcome his Master. Consider the cross, O my soul, and care for those who no one welcomes, even the least of them, so that their souls can find in your heart a welcome as warm as a fire in the hearth.

When our Lord sets at his right hand those who have given out clothing to those who were naked, yes, he was speaking about physical nudity, but I believe he was also speaking about souls that have been stripped bare of their dignity. He knew this very well; on the cross he knew this nudity both physically and in his soul, but Joseph of Arimathea came to take him down from the cross and wrap him in clean linen cloth (Matt 27:59). That blessed cloth, whose purity wrapped his denuded soul in love! Consider the cross, O my soul, and care for the despoiled, even the least of them, so that their souls can recover their dignity in your attention and your words so full of goodwill, like a lovely warm coat.

When our Lord sets at his right hand whose who care for the sick, yes, he was speaking about the physically sick, but I believe he was also speaking about those whose souls suffer and languish as though dying. He knows this very well; his soul was so weakened that he stumbled on the way to Golgotha, but suddenly felt the weight of his cross lightened thanks to the beneficent help of Simon of Cyrene (Matt 27:32). Blessed Simon, who lovingly gathered all his strength to relieve this man whose body and soul were so weakened. Look at the cross, O my soul, and care for the sick, even the least of them, so that their souls can find in you new strength to stand tall.

When our Lord sets at his right hand those who care for prisoners, he was surely speaking of those who are detained in prisons of stone, but I believe he was also speaking of those whose souls are prisoners, pitilessly judged and confined. He knew this very well; his soul was imprisoned by those who condemned him to death, but he saw something different in the eyes of Longinus the centurion, who looked at him and recognized in him the Son of God (Mk 15:39). That blessed look of acknowledgement touched him in the depths of the mystery of his being. Look to the cross, O my soul, and care for prisoners, even the least of them, so that their souls can find in you the loving, kind eyes and attitude of a brother.

You are blessed Lord Jesus. You gave food to the least of your brothers when you fed a whole crowd. You are blessed; you give your body again as food and your blood as drink to the least of your brothers to restore and strengthen them in the very depths of . . .

MATTHEW 26

26:1–13

ALL OUR FATHERS SAY THAT THIS WOMAN WAS A SINNER, while Matthew only lets this be known very discreetly. The Fathers say this so clearly because, in Luke's Gospel, Jesus himself said that she had sinned greatly (7:47). So why is Matthew so discreet about this that we could read the passage and take from it only the woman's act of worship? It seems to me that Matthew was full of respect for her because he knew himself to be just as much a sinner as her. In addition, the difference between the two gospels comes from Matthew reporting only the words Jesus spoke to everyone, while Luke also records all that was said personally, first to Simon the leper (7:40) and then to the woman (7:48).

If the woman was really a great sinner then her action was more one of repentance than adoration. Matthew very discreetly gives us to understand that by pouring the perfume over Jesus' head, she was pouring out all her sins onto him. The verb for "pour/tip" he uses has a very interior aspect which fits with the meaning that she "poured out her shame."[1] Another element is that, distinct from Mark (14:3), Matthew doesn't say that the perfume was "pure," because for him it was as impure as the woman was impure; but in his respect for her, he kept quiet about this; he does say that the perfume was of great price, and this must be because it represented all the money the woman had gained by her sinful practices. So what she was pouring out on Jesus was indeed the price of her sin. While she didn't confess her sins openly in front of everyone, they were silently confessed in the perfume of her impurity which she poured out on Jesus. Moreover, the fact that she didn't react to the criticisms made of her by the disciples is because she felt unworthy to say anything in the presence of the Lord. Her whole being was taken up in silent repentance; it's wonderful, because she knew that Jesus understood, that he saw everything going on in her heart.

Jesus response is truly magnificent; he said nothing reproachful to her but, on the contrary, before everyone present he said that she had done a "good work" for him. This was really very beautiful and full of delicacy; in saying what he did, he gave the woman to understand that he wasn't keeping any record of her evil actions and that therefore she was forgiven. By not speaking about her sins, Jesus didn't humiliate her before them all but let her know that,

1. Matthew and Luke use different words for the woman "pouring out" her perfume. Luke uses *aleïphô* meaning the sort of action used in washing oneself or applying cosmetics (Ruth 3:3; 2 Sam 12:20); Matthew uses a very unusual verb (*katachéô*) meaning that she poured out her perfume in the same way that one might "pour out one's shame" (Ps 89:45). It is this expression from the psalm that Philemon picks up here, which is why I have added quotation marks. With *aleïphô* there would be a physical aspect, but with *katachéô* there would be no contact, giving us to understand that knowing herself to be unclean, the woman dared not touch Jesus' head.

far from being judged, she was forgiven. She could feel even more forgiven because Jesus said that he would carry her perfume with him into the tomb so that her sins would be buried with him in the place of the dead, never again to appear in the light for anyone to see. This is so beautiful!

Matthew must certainly have been deeply moved because he could see himself in what had just been going on. He hadn't, of course, sinned in the same way as the woman, but all the money he had received or, rather, stolen, at his tax office made him a great sinner. He hadn't confessed his sins publicly any more than she had, but one day he must have opened his heart to Jesus, who was able to express his forgiveness with infinite delicacy. Matthew knew himself to be forgiven just as this woman knew herself to be forgiven, and he kept himself all the more discreetly hidden as he knew himself to be a greater sinner than her. In fact, is anyone Jesus has forgiven in a position to criticize this woman? The criticism came from the disciples, Matthew specifies,[2] so this must have included him. This is so serious because it shows that he was still attached to money and undoubtedly even sick from this bond. Was he more aware of the financial value of the perfume than the value of the woman's repentance?

Jesus' final word, spoken as a promise, is wonderful. It opens up the horizon to include the whole earth as unable to contain the beauty of this act of the forgiven woman, whose repentance is mingled with adoration. This is what all the Fathers say; they all preach her repentance and adoration with great admiration. And with so much discretion, thanks to the divine passives, Jesus announces that

2. The same criticism is there in Mark's Gospel, but is made by "certain among them" (14:4), while Matthew specifies that it was "the disciples."

everything that would be said of this woman would also be said by God himself.[3] As she heard Jesus speak, the woman would have understood that her sins were forgiven both by Jesus and by his Father.

O my soul, not only is this woman's repentance admirable but so is Jesus in his extreme care not to humiliate her even as he helped her understand the truth of his and his Father's forgiveness. Matthew didn't provide a conclusion to this passage, so as to leave us simply contemplating our Lord shining forth the light of his divine mercy and . . .

26:14–25

How can we not be overwhelmed by this text that is so full of the love that filled Jesus? That said, Matthew's pen makes no mention of the word love; however, this paradox reveals the way Jesus' love is beyond everything else, too great for our impoverished human vocabulary. In this text for us to meditate, everything to do with Jesus is love.

Judas' betrayal is the principal focus, but Jesus speaks about it with infinite delicacy. The disciples all found out which of them was the traitor, but Jesus' delicacy is so great that he revealed Judas to them without denouncing him; this constitutes an invitation to us not to judge. Jesus laments over him, saying *ouaï*,[4] because he could already see in him a disciple who was spiritually dead; he was thereby inviting the other disciples, and us too, to do the same and weep with him over Judas.

3. This woman's act would be spoken of by preachers throughout the world, but the divine passive adds that God too would announce it, which is to say, the Holy Spirit would speak through the preachers.

4. As above, *ouaï* is a mourning type lamentation.

With the announcement of the betrayal, the disciples were filled with sadness, but in his love for them, Jesus was at pains to reassure them by, in a way, making sure that Judas identified himself. It wasn't the disciples that would betray him; Jesus helped them move from sadness to lamentation by calling on them not to weep for themselves but to weep with him over Judas without judging him. How much love there is in this!

"You have said so." With these words, Jesus turns Judas back to himself, to examine himself and discover that he could still call a halt to the process, repent and not hand Jesus over. Jesus sent him back to himself but without abandoning him since that would be terrible; immediately after this he offers him the Holy Supper with an infinite love which goes far beyond anything I can say, and always with absolute respect for his personal liberty. Judas, all the same, was not going to change and would hand him over; yet, still, on the cross Jesus would pray again for him, asking the Father to forgive him (Lk 23:34). What love this is, full of infinite mercy!

And Jesus, how would take the betrayal? The verb "hand over" is found throughout this text from beginning to end and makes Jesus the one victim;[5] but we have already seen that he inserts into the betrayal the offering of his life, an offering of love so great that the betrayal is turned around.[6] He takes on, assumes, all this murderous hatred on the cross, making the cross an altar on which he

5. Just in these verses, "hand over/deliver up/betray" occurs six times (v 15,16,21,23,24,25). The subject is always the same: the traitor. The victim is always Jesus, except for once (v 24), where it is stated to be the Son of Man, though with a passive verb, which leaves the meaning unchanged.
6. Philemon has already gone into this, in particular in his meditation on Mk 10:32–45.

offers his life to deliver us from death, even as he asks his Father to forgive us our denials and rejections (Lk 23:34). Everything in this offering is infinite love.

There is something new here, and it is the announcement of his departure: "The Son of Man is going," he says discreetly. He had never before spoken of the Son of Man in this way. What he says is barely even veiled; we understand that he is speaking of himself. Where though is the love in his leaving? Jesus says no more at this point because Judas was still there; he was waiting for him to leave to say a little more, and in John's Gospel Jesus enlightens the disciples.[7] There we find that the goal of his departure was to rejoin his Father (Jn 16:10); it was his infinite love for his Father that motivated his leaving.

And what of us? Was Jesus abandoning us? Surely not! With so much love, Jesus would reassure his disciples again, telling them that they could not follow him just yet (13:33) but that they would follow him later (13:36). He was not abandoning them, was not leaving them as orphans (14:18), and was going to prepare a place for them (14:2). All of this was filled with love for them. What, though, were they to do while they waited? Before we follow him, Jesus calls us to a wonderful task, to read the Scriptures and discover the meaning of his departure: "The Son of Man goes in accordance with all that is written of him in the Scriptures." Our place is to read and to search, and it's amazing that we be left with this as a task because nowhere in the Scriptures is the departure of the Son of Man mentioned! This shouldn't discourage us, but it does call us to pause! What are we to

7. After Judas' departure (Jn 13:30), John's Gospel records Jesus' lengthy farewell discourse, in which we find the same verb "go away" (*upagô*) as used here. Philemon now turns to the usage of this verb.

understand? Before bowing our heads over the Scriptures, we do well to understand that Jesus has entrusted the Holy Spirit to us (14:26) as the master of the Scriptures who will lead us as we read and make everything clear. By giving us the Holy Spirit, Jesus opens the door very discreetly to an infinite mystery of love, the mystery of the Trinity. The Son was going to the Father, and we follow him under the guidance of the Holy Spirit. In the first place, we follow him by allowing ourselves to be led by the Holy Spirit in the Scriptures; and, in the Scriptures, we can join the Son and the Father who are wonderfully to be found there. What a mystery! In the Scriptures, led by the Holy Spirit, today we can contemplate Jesus in his divinity as in the vision of the prophet Daniel, the Son of Man coming to the Father (Dan 7:13–14); and we can contemplate Jesus in his humanity in the wonderful text from the prophet Isaiah who describes for us the Passion of this mysterious person who God presents as his Son . . .[8]

26:26–29

The Holy Spirit provides in a few words a precise point not given us in either the parallel accounts in the other gospels or the exposition of the Holy Supper passed on by the holy apostle Paul to the Corinthians (1 Cor 11). This might leave us thinking that the point is secondary, which is not the case; each word and each detail of the Holy Scriptures is of great price, and this is all the more

8. Philemon is referring to the great text of Isaiah 52:13–53:12 devoted to the personage we know today as "the suffering servant." The Hebrew text does indeed refer to a servant (52:13); however, the Hebrew word 'evèd is translated in the Greek by païs which means firstly "son" and then also "servant"; in the Greek, then, God says "my Son" in 52:13.

true here; our point is not repeated elsewhere because it has to do with a mystery hidden from catechumens and is not common currency for the ears of the crowd.[9] The specific point the Holy Spirit provides us here through Jesus' words reveals that the blood of Jesus is shed "for the remission of sins."[10] It's this that I wish to dwell on in my meditation.

For me there is a mystery of love of such infinite depth here that I marvel to the highest degree. If Jesus went so far as to shed his blood so that we can be forgiven for our sins, this means that he loves us with an infinite love which is so powerfully effective that it accomplishes the miracle of forgiveness in us. He must surely be God to bring such a miracle to pass.

Jesus gave his life, he died "for the remission of sins"; not only did he die but he descended into the place of the dead to free them too from their sins. He died for the forgiveness of the sins of both the dead and the living and then rose again, giving his new life to all, so effectively that by drinking his blood we are discharged of our sins but also watered by his new life. It is the life of the Risen One that we drink! What a profound mystery! This is really so extraordinary! The blood of Jesus has inestimable value. Peter was right to say that his blood is "precious" (1 Pet 1:19); it is more precious than the blood of all the lambs ever sacrificed since none of them had given their blood out of love, while Jesus, the true lamb who takes away the sin of the world (Jn 1:29), gave his life out of love for all those

9. In the Orthodox Church, catechumens can be present for the first part of the Divine Liturgy which includes intercession and listening to the Word of God but are then invited to leave when the Eucharistic liturgy begins, along with all who are not baptized.

10. "For the remission of sins" (Mt 2:28). This expression is not found in the parallel accounts (Mk 14:24; Lk 22:20; 1 Cor 11:25).

whose sins he bore. How precious is this blood, of which we are truly totally unworthy!

As I consider my unworthiness, I am troubled, as we can indeed be, by Paul's words when he warns anyone who approaches "unworthily" to participate in the Holy Mysteries (1 Cor 11:27). What exactly did he want to say? The truth is that we sinners are all unworthy of blood as precious as this, and yet it was for sinners that Jesus died. Are there therefore worthy sinners and unworthy sinners? Well, I give thanks to God for Abba John the Prophet's answer when questioned about this. He said, "No one can propose that they are worthy to participate in the Mysteries, but each person can say: 'I am unworthy, but I believe that I will be sanctified by participating.' And that is how it will be, according to their faith in our Lord Jesus Christ."[11] O my soul, anyone who doesn't take seriously the invitation of Jesus to repentance (Matt 4:17) and fails to repent is unworthy; they are not taking seriously the forgiveness of sins that Jesus gives in his blood; they are approaching unworthily.

To enjoy fellowship in the Holy Mysteries is an immense grace offered to the sinners that we are. We therefore cannot approach other than with the greatest respect and deep wonderment, confessing in our hearts the sins they are charged with or simply confessing our condition as sinners like the tax-collector (Lk 18:13). We can draw near in deep repentance and with a great thirst to be disburdened and forgiven, a thirst to receive a new life, the very life of the Risen One; and as we receive, it is Jesus who comes into us to live in us, forgiving, transforming and uniting us with

11. Letter 464.

himself, making us participants in his divine nature (1 Pet 1:4). What mystery! What extraordinary grace is granted us simply by drinking this precious blood!

O my soul, on the way between my cell and the church, I confess my sins to the Lord, just as Abba Ireneus taught me in reference to Abba Poemen, panting after the body and blood of the Lord like the deer pants for the springs of water (Ps 42:1; Apophthegm 604). And when I return from the church, I do all I can to be like Abba Isaac the Theban, who fled after communion so as to keep alive in his heart the little flame he received through the body and the blood of Christ (Apophthegm 423). Then there is blessed Abba Marcellin who shed floods of tears during the Divine Liturgy, mingling tears of repentance with tears of thanksgiving (Apophthegm 1567). O my soul, the Lamb of God who takes away our sins tell us himself that "whoever eats my flesh and drinks my blood has eternal life, and I will raise him up on the last day . . ." (Jn 6:54).

26:30–35

"No, I won't deny you!" Peter knew very well that if he was to deny Jesus, he would be denying his love for him. He therefore insisted because he loved Jesus; his heart told him so. It was out of love for Jesus that he dared speak against what Jesus had just announced. He would also have remembered another day when he spoke out against Jesus and had been treated as though he was Satan; but today he knew he was full of love, not Satan, which is why he dared to speak, knowing that his love was sincere. This was true, but, however sincere his love, it didn't prevent him denying Jesus; however sincere it was, it was also a sick love which would be swept away by the fear of death. It is good to know that sincere love can be diseased; not blameworthy, just diseased, which is far preferable because Jesus came not to judge but to heal the sick. And Jesus would indeed heal Peter; he would heal him by granting him forgiveness (Jn 21:15–17) after he had shed bitter tears of repentance (Matt 26:75).

So it's true, sincere love can be diseased; I marvel to see Peter here in the presence of a whole, sound love, the love of Jesus, who would have no fear before death and would not recoil in the way that Peter would. Peter's diseased love was face to face with the wholesome love of Jesus; this is what gives to rise to my meditation here. What is to be said about this?

Peter was leaning on his own love as grounds for refuting Jesus, and that's where the difference with Jesus lies; Jesus leant on his own love but also on his Father and the Holy Spirit; in fact he was leaning on a word from his Father transmitted by the Holy Spirit through the Scriptures: "I will strike the shepherd."[12] Jesus was relying on this word,

12. There are a number of occasion when Philemon expresses surprise at not finding the Greek text in the Septuagint to which the gospel refers, and here too surprise is appropriate because the text is not there. Philemon doesn't express such surprise at this point, no doubt because he has already stated his confidence in Matthew, but on this occasion the reference is difficult to find, even in the Hebrew. The reference is to Zechariah (13:7), with the difference that in Hebrew the verb is imperative ("strike the shepherd"). This imperative is masculine so that it cannot be addressed to the sword which was the object of the preceding imperative ("arise," a feminine form). The masculine is strange because it is not said to whom or what it is addressed. However, Jesus understood that the Father was addressing it to him, and shows this by replacing the imperative with a future with his Father as the subject: "I will strike." This understanding was not Matthew's but Jesus' and is taken from Mark's Gospel (14:27), which Matthew is citing. Matthew, then, was doing no more than repeat what he had found in Mark, and since Mark would never allow himself to alter the Scriptures, it had to have been Jesus who brought this understanding, which Peter heard, understood and then relayed to Mark. It is wonderful to see Jesus shedding light on his Father's word. It is a sign of them understanding each other beyond words, in the infinite transparency of their communion.

not superficially but totally; this word from the Father directly concerned him and he was ready to obey with his whole being. However, this word was terrible, announcing that the Father would kill him, the shepherd! Very humbly, though, Jesus didn't speak against this where Peter simply opposed it. The difference between the two is right there: Peter stoutly and proudly was against it while Jesus just humbly accepted. Jesus had already consented when he told his disciples that he was ready to give his life (20:28); he was prepared to receive death, not only from the hands of men but also from his Father's hand. This is absolutely inexpressible! That he accepted this was for the salvation of many, he had said (20:28), to save the world, both others and those he loved, certainly including Peter. This is sound, wholesome love, love untouched by pride, egotism or any other disease; this is the greatest love (Jn 15:13).

Jesus accepted death, not from a murderous Father who lacked love, but from a Father who was full of the same love as his own, just as he so wonderfully stated, "God so loved the world . . ." (Jn 3:16). The Father's love for us is this same greatest love, the infinite love which gives the most precious thing he has, his Son, just as the Son gave the most precious thing he had, his soul, his life.[13] No one could take it from him, not even his Father; he gave it (Jn 10:18).

"I will strike the shepherd": the Father would kill his Son! And the Son accepted! To hear this hurts us deeply; it is so hard to hear, and it is just this that Jesus is announcing

---

13. "He came to give his 'psuchè' as a ransom for many" (20:28). Philemon is referring to this verse. Since it's hard to know whether to translate *psuchè* by "soul" or "life," as both meanings are correct, it seems best to me to use both so as to provide depth. In the verse from John (10:18) to which Philemon also refers, the same word is found.

here to the disciples, "You will all be scandalized because of me!"[14] We can accept love, but not the love which puts to death; both our reason and our heart are against it. And it's true, the death of Jesus is scandalous; it causes us to stumble. Although Peter opposed Jesus, he would stumble too, just like the others and just like us until such time as the understanding comes that this murder was more profoundly an offering granted us in infinite love.[15]

The remedy against pride and all the other passions is humility. Jesus evinces humility here by effacing himself before his Father and the Holy Spirit, effacing himself out of obedience to his Father's commandment (Jn 10:18), but without any servility, obeying out of love for his Father and for us; he obeyed as we are unable to obey when unaided by the Holy Spirit. The sign of his perfect obedience in love is the cross (Phil 2:8). Peter would recoil at death, but Jesus would not because his love is stronger than fear, stronger than death, stronger than pride, stronger than egotism, because his love is perfectly healthy; it is the divine love that he shares with his Father and the Holy Spirit.

O my soul, Peter said nothing more because he understood that he was in the presence of infinite love; like him, I will say nothing more but just open my heart to this love. O my soul, I stoop and bow, contemplate and adore the one who loves us with a love that surpasses every other love . . .

14. "You will all be offended/scandalized." The verb is sometimes translated as "fall" or "stumble." The associated noun *scandalon* means a stone or obstacle over which one might stumble and fall.

15. It was a double offering, the Father's, handing his Son (Rom 8:32) over to us, and the Son's, handing himself over to us (Gal 2:20). Philemon doesn't develop this theme here because he does so elsewhere, notably in his meditation on Mk 10:32–45.

26:36–46

"Not my will but yours."

In his divinity, the Son had not for one moment opposed his will to his Father's or indeed to the Holy Spirit because their will has been mutually one from all eternity; it is one in the same way that their love is one. Nothing and no one could or ever will divide the unity of the Trinity: this is the faith of the universal Church, and I adhere to this with all my heart and with great thankfulness because this Divine Communion strengthens me in my life and fills me with immense joy and peace.

It is also true that, in becoming human, Jesus was given a human will like ours, and, like us, was given full freedom such that he was perfectly free in whether to submit his human will to God's will, to either obey or disobey him. God gives this magnificent liberty to us all, honoring us to the highest degree, this being true of Jesus as well. The gift of freedom is an extraordinary divine gift that reveals how much God loves us since true love always respects the freedom of others. All of us, Jesus as well, are absolutely free to obey God and to love him, or to reject his love.

This night on the mount of Olives, we witness the moment when Jesus, in his perfect humanity, was faced with the choice of either accepting or refusing the cup proffered him by his Father, of accepting or refusing the cross. The prayer he addressed to his Father is full of his humanity. It wonderfully reflects the inner tension the cross provoked in him, between his entirely human desire not to die and his entirely divine adherence to freely taking the way of the Golgotha. The "yes" he gives to his Father is a sign to us of the profound union of Christ's two natures.

He adhered humanly to his divine "yes." With his whole being, he was now ready to go forward in a perfect unity of his humanity and his divinity. How wonderful it is for us to know that from this moment Jesus would head all the way to the cross deeply at one internally, in full freedom, one in his divine-human love for us.[16] I feel all the more loved by him knowing that he loves me freely and that he loves me in his perfect humanity as well as in his perfect divinity. This touches me very deeply in my soul. He loves us despite our denials and betrayals; he loves us despite the insults and mockery he was subject to. He loves us even though he wasn't strong enough to carry his cross alone and needed to be helped by Simon of Cyrene.

O my soul, to follow him now along his path to the cross is a wonderful opportunity given us to contemplate him in his perfect humanity and his perfect divinity, abandoned by us but in deep fellowship with his Father and the Holy Spirit. We are given this time to contemplate him in his perfect mercy which held him back from judging us in our failings and infidelities towards him, and to contemplate him too in his silence before the Sanhedrin and then Pilate, before the crowd and the soldiers, and then to see the welcome he gives the thief's prayer . . .

O Jesus, you know that it is not always easy to obey the will of your Father; but you opened your heart to your Father in full confidence and total freedom, telling him in your prayer how difficult it was for you too. You are blessed because we in turn can open our hearts to you in

16. "Divine-human" corresponds very well to the Greek *théan-thrôpos*, a composite word from *théos* ("God") and *anthrôpos* ("man"), a Christian neologism to express the divinity and humanity of Jesus-Christ, bringing together the two realities in one word. Philemon use of it is readily understood since it's found as early as Origen's writings (3rd cent.).

full confidence and freedom to tell you our difficulties with obedience, knowing that you understand. You are blessed because we can ask you for help, fully trusting. With my whole heart, I can tell you my profound desire to obey you, but I know that the Tempter will do all he can to have me fold to his will and make me disobey yours and your Father's. I ask you to help me to see his traps, to resist and repel him; you were confronted with him and were able to reject him and stay attached to your Father, in communion with the Holy Spirit. Without you I can do nothing. You fell with your face to the ground to pray to your Father; I too bow to the ground to ask for your help, your succor. You know my heart; you know how weak I am. O Jesus, your disciples were all asleep; not one of them came to your aid in this time of sorrow and pain. But you are blessed. You don't sleep and you watch beside me unfailingly when I pray, and I can look to you for help in full confidence. O Jesus, we are told that you shed tears in the prayers you addressed to your Father (Heb 5:7), and this overwhelms me. You know our tears as well and I know now that you come still closer when we too fall face to the ground and our prayers rise up to the Father; this is why, in . . .

26:47–56

"Judas gave Jesus a kiss." I am challenged here by the difference between the kiss Judas said he would give (v 48) and the kiss he actually gave Jesus (v 49). The difference is apparent in the change of the verb form, which really grabs my attention. Judas first spoke about the kiss with the simple verb, *philéō*, without being more specific about the quality of the kiss he would give except that it was a sign to indicate who it was they should arrest. But at the moment the kiss was given, something happened which meant the kiss is described with a different verb, *kataphileô*, a different kind of kiss,[17] one that is full of emotion, a kiss of the same quality as described by Jesus in the parable of the son who was lost and then found, the kiss of a father welcoming home his repentant son (Lk 15:20). The kiss is also like the kiss of the sinful woman at Jesus' feet (Lk 7:38), also full of great emotion. This is the way Judas embraced Jesus! What a mystery! Here we have Judas, full of his plan of betrayal, now suddenly embracing Jesus with emotion that is quite astonishing. What was going on for there to be such a change?

As long as Jesus was at a distance, Judas could speak of his Master perfidiously, but this all changed when he was in his presence, or, more precisely, when his lips touched him. Don't the Gospels tell us that those who touched Jesus felt power go out of him, a beneficent power able to heal the sick (Lk 6:19)? This power is the power of divine love, such that when Judas came in contact with it he was touched profoundly; in his kiss he suddenly encountered a love that overcame him, the divine love received from the Lord Jesus which invaded him to the point of being overwhelmed.

This overwhelming feeling was so strong that Matthew had no words to describe it. After telling us about the kiss, he says nothing further about Judas' attitude during Jesus' arrest. Everything unfolds without Judas, between Jesus and a crowd armed with swords. A servant of the chief

17. Most of our translations don't observe the difference here, perhaps influenced by the Latin translation of Jerome (4th cent.). Unhappily, subsequent to him, the Latin Fathers could scarcely pause to comment on a subtlety they couldn't see. Some translations do, however, add, in v 49, adverbs such as "tenderly," "ardently," "affectionately," "earnestly." It should be noted that the same distinction is found in Mark's parallel account (14:44–45).

priest had one of his ears wounded, and we learn elsewhere that Jesus healed him (Lk 22:51), and that the healing came about simply by a touch of Jesus' hand to the wounded ear. Wouldn't Judas also have been changed by touching Jesus? We know that Peter wept after meeting Jesus' gaze (Lk 22:61), but we know nothing about Judas' reaction after embracing Jesus; no doubt the kiss touched on the inexpressible. What sort of turmoil must the traitor have been plunged into after embracing his Master like this? Nothing further is said about Judas in the arrest account, but a little later we find that he was filled with remorse (Matt 27:3). This remorse shows that Judas had changed, and doubtless this change was set off by the kiss he had given; but if this is so, his remorse came too late because the crowd had seized Jesus and our Lord was headed for death. Judas could do nothing to intervene! His tragedy was to be gripped by the horror of his actions at the very moment they reached their goal. What a tragedy, to understand the depth of his sin at the moment it was committed! O my soul, isn't this our experience too? Don't we march unreflectingly along the way of sin only to discover the extent of our error the moment we commit it? What wretches we are! We sin and discover too late the consequences of our sin.

I will meditate on Judas' remorse later; here I want to pursue my meditation on the kiss he gave Jesus. Jesus did not just receive the kiss, he also allowed the power that touched his disciple to flow out of him; this power is the power of his love. It was the love of Jesus that touched Judas and brought remorse to birth in him. O my soul, we know that remorse is the first step on the way to repentance. While the consequences of our sins are completely beyond us, a door is always open to us, the door of repentance; it's a door which opens into the heart of God and his forgiveness, a doorway to light. Not only does Jesus open this door, he loves us to the extent of accompanying us along the road of repentance, taking our sins upon himself and uniting his prayers with ours. For him, this road of repentance became the road to Golgotha, and on the cross he turned to his Father addressing to him, on behalf of us all, this prayer: "Father, forgive them because they don't know what they are doing" (Lk 23:34). O my soul, we need to turn, on our knees, to the one we have betrayed.

26:57–68

"Jesus held his peace."

O my soul, what could Jesus say in response to Caiaphas and all the false witnesses with their lies? What could he say to a high priest who had only sought out liars to accuse him, who had only ever told the truth? In his immense love, Jesus would nevertheless reply by proclaiming truth, saying that the Son of Man would come on the clouds of heaven. He would reply, but not immediately; at first, he waited. He was silent as he waited, it seems to me, for Caiaphas to go and find true witnesses in the same way he had sought false. When the true witnesses spoke and the Sanhedrin heard the whole truth, then Jesus could emerge from his silence. As long as he was waiting for true witnesses, he was silent.

O my soul, had Caiaphas met any true witnesses? Perhaps there were two he knew who he could call?[18] Was there even one he had heard who could tell the truth? Had he been there, he would certainly have heard one on Mount

---

18. The testimony of two witnesses was required for anyone to be condemned to death (Deut 17:6), which is why Philemon insists on there being two, noting that Caiaphas had already received the testimony of two false witnesses (26:60).

Tabor when God spoke in the presence of Moses, Elijah and the three disciples (17:5), witnessing that Jesus was his Beloved Son; but Caiaphas couldn't have heard this because Jesus didn't take him up the mountain. He might also have heard the same truth on the banks of the Jordan when God bore witness in the presence of all those being baptized (3:17). Had Caiaphas gone out to the Jordan on the way of repentance to confess his sins to the John the Baptist? Perhaps he thought that he, a righteous person, had none to confess? But, I say to myself, he could at least have asked someone from among those that had been baptized, which was easy enough because all of Jerusalem (Mk 1:5) had been there.

O my soul, the witness of God there on the banks of the Jordan was already old news, and Caiaphas could perhaps have used the pretext that after three years, such witness was not reliable. Perhaps, but without searching so far back, there were more recent witnesses right there in Jerusalem who would no doubt be well disposed to witnessing about Jesus. Wasn't there the man born blind who Caiaphas could call? He had begged for years on the streets of the city until the day he stopped holding out his hand because Jesus had healed him (Jn 9:35). If this man didn't wish to witness out of fear of being excluded from the synagogue (9:22), weren't there all the children of the city who, with palm branches in their hands, had proclaimed even in the temple that Jesus was truly the Son of David (Matt 21:15)? Caiaphas may not have heard them, but everyone who lived in Jerusalem had and could testify to the truth. And if all the children and all their witnesses were afraid of being put out of the synagogue, if Caiaphas would but listen, he would hear the stones cry out the truth (Lk 19:40).

O my soul, if Caiaphas didn't want to hear the witnesses from Jerusalem on the pretext that they were all sinners, if he didn't wish to seek out witnesses from Samaria (Jn 4:29) or from the region of Tyre and Sidon (Matt 15:21) on the pretext that gentiles and Samaritans could never speak the truth, didn't he have to hand the Holy Scriptures whose witness he, as high priest, should have been meditating day and night (Ps 1:2)? He had only to incline his ear to his heart to hear the prophet Isaiah conveying to him God's own message, clearly saying, "This is my Son, my beloved who my soul loves,"[19] or indeed a second prophecy, on which Jesus had commented in Nazareth: "The Spirit of the Lord is upon me because he has anointed me to preach the good news to the poor."[20] He would also hear David saying, "The Lord said to my Lord" (Ps 110:1), thereby testifying that Jesus is Lord and God. He would hear the witness of the prophet Zechariah announcing to Jerusalem the coming of the King seated on a donkey (9:9).

O my soul, if Caiaphas found that these witnesses were not solid enough and if he wanted others that had seen the centuries pass since the creation of the world, he could have questioned the winds and the sea and he would have received from them a twin testimony that would line up perfectly;[21] they would have stated clearly the authority they obeyed and that this authority was God's (Matt 8:27).

O my soul, Jesus was silent in the midst of his accusers, like light in the midst of darkness. He had no reason to

19. See above the meditation on Matt 12:9–21, where Philemon considers this passage from Isaiah 42 as it is in the Greek.

20. This is the prophecy from Isaiah 61:1 commented on by Jesus (Lk 4:18), in which the verb "anoint" (*chriô*) points to him as "Christ" (*christos*).

21. After the two false witnesses who had spoken before Caiaphas, these two true witnesses might now have been heard (Deu 17:6).

speak; it was enough for him to shine in all his splendor, and there he stands for us to contemplate.

O my soul, the true witnesses are a multitude; it suffices for us to call them, let them step forward, and just listen; their song is truly the most beautiful of songs . . .

26:69–75

Peter's three denials were full-blown lies, reported with details that show us that the lies became more and more serious. The first was serious enough because it directly concerned Jesus. The second was more so because it was accompanied by an oath, and the third was extremely serious, so blasphemous that it is difficult for me to talk about it. In fact, not only did Peter deny his Lord, he went further and cursed him.[22] This is horrible! Peter was really sinking, going under and on the way to drowning. He had walked on the sea (14:29) and was now to be submerged in lying; and now he no longer had the hand of the Lord to grab him and lead him back to reason in the boat. On the sea, Peter had implored Jesus' help, but now Jesus wasn't there; Peter wasn't looking to him in prayer and wasn't even praying to God. Peter was sunk. We are told all this very soberly but very clearly, no doubt with horror on Matthew's part but also without passing any judgment. I don't wish to judge either but I would like to understand so that I don't go under one day.

One factor that can explain drowning in lies like this is fear of death. This is a terrible fear, but no doubt there is

---

22. Matthew doesn't just use the word for "swear" (*omnuô*) but adds a second verb that is found nowhere else in the Bible (*katathéma-tizô*) and seems to be a neologism; the prefix *kata* gives an extreme meaning to the word for "curse": it is truly a terrible term!

more than this. In fact, if we go back to the moment Peter first declared that he would never deny Jesus (26:33), we discover something else, a detail given discreetly because Matthew had no wish to judge Peter but a detail that makes everything clear. At that moment, Peter said two things, that he wouldn't deny Jesus and that he wouldn't be offended. When he said this, he did so in way that included a significant redundancy: he didn't just say, "I will never be offended," but, "Me, I won't be offended" (26:33). This "me" clearly shows pride. Unhappily this was not the first time because it had already been apparent when Jesus repulsed him, calling him "Satan" (16:23). Peter's now sinking into these lies was undoubtedly out of fear, but above all it was because he was full of and was being led by pride. Pride is Satan's accomplice that threatens us all, including, unhappily, me. However, I do give thanks to be enlightened here about this formidable enemy, against which the best weapon is humility. May the Lord keep me always beside him and lead me into humility.

What happened, though that enabled Peter to survive? Who came to save him, because something stronger than pride was certainly needed for him to be saved? There is another detail in the account which shows us the answer. We are told that Peter "was reminded,"[23] a remarkable passive which could only be divine. It wasn't the cock crowing that saved Peter but God, who awakened the memory of Jesus' words, pulling up from the depths of his heart this memory which was buried by pride. The statement about his denial was not in fact very old. In fact it had only been made a few hours before, but pride had immediately taken the upper hand because it was well established in Peter's heart.

23. My translation shows that the verb for "remember" (*mimnèskô*) is in the passive and not the middle voice.

Therefore, God had acted, or, more precisely, the Holy Spirit had effected a work deep in Peter's heart and driven out the pride. It was certainly the Holy Spirit because Jesus himself had made the following promise to his disciples in his final teaching: "The Comforter, the Spirit of Truth, who the Father will send in my name, will bring to your mind everything I have said" (Jn 14:26). How wonderful! Without saying a thing, even when Peter had not called upon God, the Holy Spirit came, not because Peter was calling on God but because Jesus had. I can't say it any other way. Jesus had announced that the Father would send the Holy Spirit "in his name," which is to say in answer to his request. He knew Peter was in danger of denying him. He decidedly had not reached out his hand to save him from this drowning, but he had prayed to his Father, asking him to send the Holy Spirit. Jesus had prayed for him just as he said he would (Lk 22:61). We are told elsewhere that the moment the cock crowed, Jesus looked at Peter (Lk 22:61). At that moment, freed from pride, saved from drowning, delivered from his lie and led back into the truth by the Spirit of Truth, Peter left the courtyard and began to weep bitterly, with bitter tears that were themselves affected by the poison of pride; he emptied his heart of the pride with his bitter tears which were all the more bitter because he knew he had denied the one he loved and by whom he was loved so truly.

He left to weep, but he didn't leave alone. The Holy Spirit went with him; how wonderful once more! I give thanks because when Jesus announced the work of the Holy Spirit "bringing to mind," he named him as the "Comforter." Blessed be God because Peter left in tears but with him in his heart was the divine Comforter who, mysteriously . . .

MATTHEW 27

27:1–10

Judas' death is so painful that it leaves us feeling naked when we have to discuss it. I note that the Holy Spirit speaks about it very discreetly because he only entrusted the task to Matthew, and he does so with just one brief statement without any commentary: "He hung himself." That's all! When we are told about the death of John the Baptist, we learn that his disciples carefully buried him (14:12); here, however, nothing is said of what became of Judas' body; we can well understand because the two deaths are very different. John the Baptist's death was dramatic but there was great respect surrounding it because it was the death of a faithful servant of God. Judas' death wasn't on the end of any commentary from Matthew, whose disquiet is seen when we note that immediately afterwards he describes at length what became of the silver, the price of the betrayal, without another word about Judas himself.

In the book of the Acts of the Apostles, the issue of Judas' death arises again, but we are not told there that he died at his own hand (1:18) because this is precisely the most painful aspect to it; he did, however, kill himself. The Chief Elder used a particular word to comment: he said that it was done in "despair,"[1] which is unhappily true. This helps me understand Jesus' attitude; without saying anything, he had discerned Judas' despair and had done so early on, while the disciple was still alive. Jesus' response to this despair witnesses to his great love for Judas, a deep love which he maintained to the end, a true love which unfailingly left Judas really and entirely free; he did this in a wonderful way because he didn't just leave him to himself without doing anything for him, but, on the contrary, showed him his love in multiple forms. Thus, during the meal, when Judas had already betrayed him, Jesus delicately let him know that he was aware of the betrayal, and Judas understood. "Is it me, Rabbi?" he said. Jesus answered clearly, "You have said so," (26:25), without bringing any judgment to bear at all.

The cause of wonder to me is that Jesus immediately gave him his body and his blood with the infinite love that filled his actions (26:26). Earlier he had washed his feet, witnessing to him by this beautiful act his inexpressible love that could not fail to have touched him (Jn 13:2). Then later, when being arrested, Jesus received Judas' kiss with such love that Judas felt it and was touched to the point of feeling real remorse. However, as the Chief Elder saw, Judas continued in remorse without coming to repentance.[2] Repentance is always filled with the hope of forgiveness, while remorse may consist of despair, which was the case with Judas, whose confession of sin was only a matter of remorse. Jesus left him free, but Judas was unable to

1. Barsanuphus speaks of Judas' "despair" (*anelpistia*) in Letter 465.

2. In letter 465, Barsanuphus specifies that Judas did not repent (*métannoéô*). He notes that Matthew mentions remorse (*métamélêô*) not repentance. Some modern translations have "repent," unhappily so, because Matthew clearly says *métamélêô* ("to be seized with remorse"), not *métannoéô* ("to be seized by repentance").

keep his freedom; indeed he lost it, allowing himself to be enchained by the terrible despair which is Satan's work.[3] Shackled in this way, Judas then went away and put a rope around his neck, which we may well take as a sign of the chain that had him bound.

O my soul, what really overwhelms me is the immense love of Jesus for his disciple, a love which impelled him to give Judas his body and his blood, to wash his feet, and more besides. Previously, indeed, Jesus had lamented over him. He said, *"Ouaï!"* (26:24), his heart full of tears[4] since such a thing can only be spoken with a tearful heart. It overwhelms me that Jesus didn't say this when Judas was absent but in his presence. Judas heard him and must have perceived the love that filled this lament, and he must also have been touched by the rest of the lament: "It would be better for that man never to have been born" (26:24). This fateful statement was so overwhelming that Luke didn't have the heart to include it in his gospel.[5] O my soul, I can only lament with Jesus over Judas. Saint John the evangelist didn't record this statement of lament either, putting things in a different way, telling us that when Jesus announced his betrayal to his disciples in Judas' presence he was "troubled in the Spirit,"[6] though this is even stronger because

---

3. Philemon mentions Satan since this is attested to by Luke, who tells us that Satan entered the disciple before he handed Jesus over (22:3; also Jn 13:2).

4. Again, *ouaï* is lament.

5. Mark tells us the whole of Jesus' lament (14:21), but Luke doesn't go beyond its opening (22:22).

6. We are told that as he announced his betrayal to the disciples, Jesus "was troubled" (étarachthè, Jn 13:21). The divine passive tells us that the Father was conveying to him his own sense of being troubled.

the divine passive tells us that the Son was troubled by the Father, which means he was sharing his Father's trouble in the Holy Spirit. It was therefore the Holy Trinity that was being troubled and that lamented. I can only now be silent and entrust Judas to the merciful love of the Holy Trinity who alone is able to save from despair . . .

27:11–31

Lord Jesus, the chief priests and the elders led you before the governor, Pilate, to have you put to death (Matt 27:1) when your rightful place was to be conducted on the clouds of heaven into the presence of your Father, the God of the universe, there to receive from him authority over all the peoples of the earth (Dan 7:13–14).

You are blessed in the love of your Father; forgive our lack of love.

Lord Jesus, the only witnesses before the governor were these same chief priests and elders, and they were all against you, when rightfully you should have been receiving the witness of your Father for you (Jn 5:37), the Father who beside the Jordan proclaimed in the presence of heaven and earth that you are his Beloved Son (Matt 3:17).

You are blessed in the love of your Father; forgive our lack of love.

Lord Jesus, the night-time crowd cried vehemently for your crucifixion when rightfully you should have been receiving the luminous acclamation of the multitudes of the heavenly army, who, also at night, had announced your birth to the shepherds (Lk 2:13).

You are blessed in the love of your Father; forgive our lack of love.

Lord Jesus, you said nothing, when rightfully we should have been witnessing in your favor, but we said nothing, we who had abandoned you and left you alone (Matt 26:56; Jn 16:32), and then you were judged, you whose rightful place is to judge the living and the dead (2 Tim 4:1).

You are blessed in the love of your Father; forgive our lack of love.

Lord Jesus, the soldiers plaited a crown of thorns for you and placed it on your head with accompanying derision in the presence of their entire platoon when rightfully there belongs to you the crown of glory and honor (Ps 8:6), which you Father has woven for you, to be placed tenderly on your head in the presence of the heavenly multitude.

You are blessed in the love of your Father; forgive our lack of love.

Lord Jesus, the soldiers wrapped you mockingly in a scarlet robe when your rightful clothing is a garment of light your Father has woven for you to wrap you round with infinite love (Ps 104:2).

You are blessed in the love of your Father; forgive our lack of love.

Lord Jesus, the soldiers mocked you as they bowed before you when rightfully every knee in heaven, earth and hell should bow to you, with the praise of every tongue confessing that you are Lord to the glory of God your Father (Phil 2:10).

You are blessed, before whom I too now bow my knees, confessing with all others that you are in truth my Lord and my God (Jn 20:28).

You are blessed in the love of your Father; in your grace please forgive my lack of love and grant that I may love you in truth. I pray this of you to whom belongs all honor and glory together with the Father and the Holy Spirit, now and throughout the endless ages. Amen

27:32–56

Darkness covered the earth for three hours during which no one moved and nothing happened. What is the meaning of this darkness that came at such an unexpected hour, in the middle of the day? An important detail makes it clear: the darkness is described in a very odd way which somewhat overturns the normal rules of grammar![7] This out of place construction reveals that the mystery of God cannot be stated in human languages other than by twisting them out of shape. This is how the inexpressible nature of God is evoked, and here we learn that the darkness came from God. When God comes down and draws near to the earth, he hides in the darkness to keep himself unseen (Ps 18:11).[8] What was God coming to do, thus hidden in darkness?

Thanks to the darkness, God could cover Jesus nakedness that was exposed on the cross to everyone. The soldiers had stripped him of his clothing, but to cover his nakedness no clothing was suitable anyway because his beaten, bloody

7. In Greek, the verb "to be" is a verb of state not a verb of movement. Here, Matthew uses *ginomaï*, which serves in the aorist as a substitute for the verb "to be," but he uses it as a verb of movement. Instead of saying that the darkness "was on the earth" with a genitive as would be normal for a verb of state, he says that the darkness "was onto the earth," with an accusative as though of a verb of movement; this is a grammatical mistake but a happy one because it enables us to say that the being of God is a being of movement and his love an indescribable pulse of love.

8. Psalm 18 describes a magnificent intervention of God to save David when in deadly danger: "He bowed the heavens and came down with darkness under his feet; he rode upon a cherub and flew, he flew on the wings of the wind and made darkness his hiding place" (18:9–11, as in the Greek).

body (v 26) couldn't bear them; the wounds and welts were open sores and even the robe the soldiers had put on him would have been unbearable on his bloodied skin (v 28). However, the impalpable darkness in which God wrapped him was softer than any cloth could be. In this way and with infinite delicacy, the Father was caring for his Son. What compassion! And what love!

Thanks to the darkness, God quickly and lastingly reduced to silence the crowd with their insults, the leaders of the people with their mockery and one of the thieves with his blasphemy. The Father was giving three beneficent hours of silence to his Son whose ears were scorched by so many evil words. What compassion and what infinite love!

This magnificent silence then provided Jesus another benefit; just before, he had been silent before Caiaphas, Pilate, the leaders of the people and everyone else with whom no word served any purpose; in the silence, Jesus could now speak out, saying the only words of any value, a prayer. No doubt he had not stopped praying internally, but now he could pray in a loud, clear voice before everyone, speaking to the only one really able to listen, his Father. For three good hours, the silence of the beneficent darkness was a wonderful invitation to Jesus to pray; his Father was very near in his infinite tenderness to listen.

Jesus prayed, but strangely he cried out his prayer; he cried out as never before.[9] The strength of his cry reveals a vigor beyond the ordinary for a dying man, the vigor of his divine strength. But why cry out when his Father was so

9. Matthew uses the composite verb *anaboaô* ("to cry out") derived from the simple verb *boaô* and conveying a more intense cry; the verb is accompanied by an expression that further reinforces this, "with a loud voice." Jesus had never previously cried out in such way, so intensely; the cry is all the more surprising in that he was dying.

near and no one was troubling his praying with mockery or other form of speech? Jesus cried out so that those around could hear, so that the mockers could hear and so that everyone who was looking for his response would discover that he wasn't responding to them but to God; he cried out so that everyone who heard would know that a word addressed to God is of greater price than any other. Above all he cried out to be heard by all who believe themselves to be abandoned by God; he made their cry his own by saying "my God," whereas his prayer was habitually "my Father." In this way he came wonderfully close to them, even becoming one of them, to show that they are not alone, to strengthen them by showing that he is with them, solid in their suffering and compassionate towards it. His prayer is a marvelous miracle of compassion, which can be heard throughout the earth and thereby bring together all who have no strength to pray, who have stopped praying, thinking that God doesn't listen to them. At the heart of the silence that was now covering the earth, Jesus prayed in a way that was so clear that not a word of his prayer was lost. Even someone who, like Peter, weeps in the darkness can hear and understand him. What infinite compassion of Jesus towards us when we are gripped by the pain of being abandoned by God.

Then, with a final cry that again testifies to his divine strength, Jesus remitted his Spirit to the one who alone could receive it and who was so close to him in the darkness. In the darkness, the Son remitted the Holy Spirit to the Father; there, hidden in the darkness was the holy Trinity. There was then a sudden formidable outbreak of life, magnificently described in an impressive list of divine passives: the veil was torn, the earth was shaken, the rocks were rent, the graves were opened, dead bodies were raised and appeared to many, and the centurion along with others was gripped by fear . . .[10] The work of the most holy Trinity was evident, a work of life leaping out of the graves, a work of faith springing up in the heart of the centurion, a work of love and light awakening contemplation in the women who had served and followed Jesus from Galilee . . . O Lord Jesus . . .

27:57–61

"Taking the body of Jesus, Joseph wrapped it in a linen cloth . . ." Everything told us here incites great respect in me; it's a particularly holy scene, instinct with the holiness of our Lord Jesus.

Joseph was a pious Jew and very aware of his actions; he knew perfectly well that to touch a dead body made one unclean (Num 19:11). Nevertheless, neither he nor any of the evangelists seem to be have been concerned with this issue since they were all convinced that the body of Jesus, far from making unclean, did just the reverse. The body was of such holiness that contact with it was enough to sanctify Joseph. Matthew notes carefully that the linen cloth used by Joseph was "clean,"[11] but this detail was almost superfluous and was not touched on by the other evangelists on the basis that it could not be otherwise; the

10. Our translations typically don't give the passives of the Greek full expression, which are very impressive straight from Matthew's pen. Translators tend to pull back in order to make the text easier to read, but this does, unfortunately, detract from the accumulation of divine passives which can so feed our meditation.

11. Most translations say the linen cloth was either "clean" or "white," but we may note that the word Matthew uses means in the first place "pure" (*katharos*).

linen cloth was of necessity clean if it was wrapped round the holy body of Jesus.

Joseph touched Jesus' body with the infinite respect needful for everything pure and holy. Everything he did was done in perfect silence, in the contemplative state that is God's due. None of the evangelists reports a single word from Joseph. He certainly spoke to Pilate and doubtless also to Nicodemus,[12] but nothing he said is recorded; everything he said concerned Jesus and so touches on the inexpressible. It is all shrouded in silence because Joseph's words and deeds are beyond words. Mary Magdalene and the other Mary watched and were present with him throughout, but nothing is known as to whether they helped him; no doubt they were restrained by the sanctity of the scene.

Joseph's immense respect for the body of Jesus was surely full of a love that is just as inexpressible. Who could describe the love with which Joseph bent to wipe from Jesus' forehead the drops of blood the crown of thorns made flow? The women who were there and saw all this never spoke of it; no words could be adequate. Joseph's infinite love and respect for Jesus are because he was one of his disciples. He was present at the crucifixion right up to the death of his Lord; he heard the cry of his prayer and the final cry he could never forget. In silence and with infinite respect, with his hand he tenderly brushed clean Jesus' mouth. The women saw but, again, never spoke of it. Who could express this disciple's heart as he wrapped the body of his Lord in linen and then laid him in his own tomb? He gave him his place with the thought he was receiving him into his own house, and that in giving him first place he was himself honored to be receiving into his own home his

12. Philemon mentions Nicodemus because John's gospel points to his presence alongside Joseph (19:39).

Lord and his God. He gave him this place he had reserved for himself which no one else had previously occupied (Lk 23:53), knowing that from that time throughout the ages this place would be holy. After laying out Jesus' body in his tomb, Joseph rolled the great stone over the entrance and, always in silence, went his way. No one knows where he went or what he did next. No one knows how many tears he shed as he cared for his Lord's body or if perhaps he was remembering Jesus' words about the resurrection of the Son of Man. He rolled the stone into place and left. The women observed as Joseph tended to his Lord with an infinite love.

O my soul, one day I saw Abba Georges on his knees at the entrance to the church. It was the day after Easter and he was scraping away the mud left by visitors on the floor mosaic. He did so with wonderful application, with the infinite respect due to a holy place; he was silent, a silence which was certainly full of his inner prayer. I think of him now as I meditate all we are told of Joseph. The greater our respect for the Lord, the more we are led to respect anything to do with him, both in the church and in the most miserable hovel where one of his creatures lives. As he fashioned us with his own hands, our Lord sanctified us, and this invites us to respect everything his hands have touched. Joseph's respect for Jesus' body, Abba Georges' respect for the furnishings of the church, the respect of all the faithful who receive the body and blood of Jesus in the Divine Liturgy, this all invites me to extend the same respect to the least object in my cell, especially because of the day he indescribably told me that he was right there with me in my cell. Since that day I saw Abba Georges cleaning the mud away from the mosaic in the church, I have taken care to keep my cell clean; I do so in silence like him, making efforts to fill the silence with prayer. Now, after watching and contemplating Joseph caring for Jesus' body, my desire is never again to leave this silence and never cease to tend to everything that concerns Jesus, filling the silence with the same love and the same . . .

27:62–66

The aspect I take from this, and a cause of wonder to me, is the extreme delicacy of the evangelist Matthew in his mercy towards the chief priests and the Pharisees, all adversaries to Jesus. This mercy is so fine that time fails me to comment; it's as if Matthew wished to hide it so as not to draw any glory from it. What humility!

Matthew's delicacy is first apparent in his designation of the day of these events, "the day after the preparation." Which day was this? Thanks to Mark's Gospel, we know that the day of the preparation was the day before the Sabbath (15:42), so it follows that the day after the day of the preparation was the Sabbath itself. Why then this somewhat complicated way of presenting things? Well, it would be simply to avoid saying that the Pharisees' actions took place on the Sabbath day; specifically, Matthew abstained from mentioning the Sabbath so that it wouldn't be apparent that the Pharisees had broken the Sabbath day commandment by going to seal the rock over the tomb, which was work. He carefully avoided saying this so as not to give the impression of denouncing the people who had so many times accused Jesus of not respecting the Sabbath (Matt 12:2; Mk 3:2; Jn 9:16); this would have been a form of revenge which Matthew was trying to preclude. What delicate mercy this is!

Matthew reports, with the same delicacy, the interview between Pilate and the Pharisees, who had to suggest the hypothesis of a theft without saying anything further if they were to carry out their plan. They certainly didn't say anything else, but we discover later that they had bought off the guards so that they would spread the lie of the body being stolen (28:12–13). Before Pilate, they said nothing of this, but this lie was in their spirit. Moreover, even in the following passage (28:12–15), Matthew restrains himself from denouncing their dissimulation in lying to Pilate. Again, the same delicate mercy!

Finally, Matthew does not unveil as such a terrible blasphemy proffered by the Pharisees to Pilate. We would have to be very well informed to notice this blasphemy Matthew avoids denouncing; we would need to know that the title "deceiver" the Pharisees attributed to Jesus is one that in the Scriptures is reserved for Satan. Only Satan is designated in this way,[13] but I don't wish to insist here because it is very painful for me to hear such a blasphemy against our Lord Jesus. Again, with great delicacy Matthew demonstrates great and praiseworthy mercy in not denouncing the Pharisees' blasphemy for what it was.

This attitude of Matthew's is really magnificent; it reveals a true disciple who was at pains to lean on the example of Jesus, who throughout his trial kept silent without ever denouncing the lies spoken about him. Without pushing himself to the fore, Matthew simply followed his divine

13. The word *planos*, translated here as "deceiver," is often rendered as "imposter" or "seducer"; whatever the translation, this word, used in the singular and with the article (*o planos*) elsewhere in the Bible only designates the Antichrist (2 Jn 7); to this are added passages in which the participle used as a substantive (*o planôn*) is used for Satan, the devil (Rev 12:9; 20:10). Philemon was right to see this as blasphemy on the lips of Jesus' adversaries.

model; he neither denounces nor disputes the blasphemies, lies and false witnesses; he merely suggests without judging.

The Desert Fathers followed the same route, calling on us not to dispute with heretics and not denounce their errors. "Guard against disputing with heretics when you wish to defend the faith, fearful lest you be wounded by the poison of their shameful discourses," said, among others, Abba Isaiah.[14] To keep quiet like this is not easy; is it even possible to accept hearing the truth of the faith traduced and allow lies and blasphemies to be spread? Nevertheless, Jesus accepted it, the very person of Truth, who was traduced, opposed and crucified without defending himself!

Among the Fathers, there is a very beautiful example of this in Apophthegm 652, which I simply reproduce here. "Certain heretics came one day to see Abba Poemen and sought to denigrate the archbishop of Alexandria on the pretext that he had been consecrated by priests. The elder carefully kept quiet, then he called his brother and said, 'Set the table, give them something to eat and send them away in peace.'" Just as Jesus kept quiet when his adversaries were speaking ill of him during his trial and again on the cross, Abba Poemen too kept quiet with such love that he made sure the heretics were given food. This is the way of truth; Abba Poemen didn't make the truth a subject for debate because truth is not open to dispute but is alive . . . and quiet . . .

O my soul, what a lesson this is for me because among the visitors I welcome to the monastery there are a few heretics. Abba Poemen gave food to such and Jesus gave them his life. May he fill my heart with delicacy, mercy and love!

14. *The Ascetikon* 4:67.

MATTHEW 28

28:1–15

WITH THE STONE ROLLED INTO PLACE AND CAREFULLY sealed, the guards could rest and even sleep; but they didn't know that behind the stone a man slept a different sleep, a sleep from which he would be awakened. Filled with dread, they became as dead men when the angel announced to the bearers of spices: Christ is risen.[1]

Crosses always handed those they had stripped of life permanently over to death and death congratulated them on a job well done; but on this day, today, death was struck dumb before a crucified man who spread life among the tombs and who all acclaim as they say: Christ is risen.

Nobody had ever seen a sacrificed lamb rise; but early on this morning when the women approached to add their spices to the offering (Mk 16:1), they saw the stone rolled

---

1. In this meditation, Philemon adopts the style of the Kontakion, a liturgical hymn composed in strophes that conclude with the same refrain. "The bearers of spices" (*myrophores*) was a term for the women who came to the tomb to embalm Jesus. Matthew says nothing of this but Mark (16:1) and Luke (23:56) both mention the spices. (A note on "Christ is risen": both the original Greek and the French have a definite article so "the Christ" is the literal translation; "Christ" is a title not a name. However, we have opted for the more usual English, without the article. [Trans.])

away and the lamb standing, alive, the scars of immolation still there on his body, but shining like the sun as it rises. They were so troubled that they had no idea what to say when the angel told them: Christ is risen.

No guard could stand in the way of the angel descending from heaven. No seal on the stone could stop the opening of the door to the tomb. Nothing and no one could prevent God fulfilling his promises or Jesus from rising from the place of the dead. Neither could the money given the soldiers prevent the good news being spread all over the earth, no more than the lies of the chief priests could stop the angel telling the women the truth: Christ is risen.

The great rock in the desert knew not that a fountain could gush forth from it; the sea knew not that a way could be opened through it and an entire people pass through it whom it could not hold back;[2] death knew not that it was detaining the Lord who would rise from it with the power of a love stronger than its own and that he would issue forth acclaimed by the song of all its prisoners: Christ is risen.

Until then, death had inscribed into its registers the names of all it received, and no one could erase the names chiseled on its eternal rocks; but when death wished to inscribe his name into its lists, he took hold of the rock to engrave a song of love whose refrain has rung out since that early morning: Christ is risen.

He had announced that he would rise, but our faith faltered when we saw the nails fix him to the wood and the sun be eclipsed; our hope failed when we saw him bow his

2. Since Jesus' resurrection took place on the day Israel celebrated leaving Egypt, Philemon alludes to two great miracles of the feast, the crossing of the Red Sea (Exod 14) and the water from the rock at Massah and Meribah (Exod 17:1–7).

head and give back his spirit; our love succumbed when we heard the rending of the veil and the earth shake. But today our faith has risen with him, our hope is quickened and our love reborn with him. He has vanquished death, and with all our heart we sing with the angel: Christ is risen.

In the evening of all our days, the sun sinks without resistance, always overcome by the night which receives and buries it in its shroud; but today another sun has risen with such majesty that the night knows it is finished forever; it abdicates and bows before him so that he is lifted up into heaven where he reigns for eternity: Christ is risen.

The one we crowned with thorns is now crowned with splendor and glory. From the bloodied wounds the thorns left on his forehead there now streams forth a light so beautiful that the darkness of death cannot dim its rays, but a light so gentle that the women were not dazzled. Laying down their spices, they offered him their adoration in a wonderment answering the angel's words: Christ is risen.

No one had over passed through the door to Paradise guarded by the cherubim, and every son of Adam had instead entered the gates to the place of the dead wide open before them. But today, he who had left the place of the dead is welcomed by the cherubim who open the door of Paradise to him, bowing before him because he is their Master. They too say with the angel: Christ is risen.

The angels had seen him leave the day of his incarnation, not knowing that he would return with the marks in his hands and his feet; not knowing that they would find him with the wound of a lance in his side; not knowing of the scars left by the crown of thorns; but they recognized him by his royal dignity, the splendor flashing in his eyes and the sweetness of his voice; then they prostrated before him and called heaven and earth to eternal praise: Christ is risen.

28:16–20

When the disciples met Jesus in Galilee, there first reaction is most surprising; the moment they saw him, they were prostrate before him. This is astonishing because they were seeing their brother. When Jesus confirmed the rendezvous in Galilee to the women, hadn't he said clearly that the disciples would meet with their brother (28:10)? Why bow before a brother? When we see Joseph the patriarch and his brothers embrace with such emotion at their reunion (Gen 45:14–15), this might lead us to expect a similar attitude from the disciples; like the father in the parable at the return of his son who was lost and was found (Lk 15:20), so they might have embraced Jesus. The disciples' prostration is truly amazing!

We are also told that the disciples "doubted" when they saw Jesus again, which means that there was some difficulty in recognizing him and that Jesus must have changed in appearance. Why would this be when neither Lazarus, the young man at Nain, nor Jairus' daughter were altered after being raised? The change in Jesus is not told us; the angel who appeared to the women is described (28:3) but Jesus is not, neither when with the women or the disciples. He is not described, it seems to me, because he was beyond description, and this simply because he appeared to his disciples in his divinity. This is why they had trouble recognizing him and why they were on their faces: they were in the presence of God.

As confirmation of this, the reunion took place on a mountain. It wasn't specified that a mountain was where they would meet (26:32; 28:7, 10); but it is wonderful because thus they could all see him as both Resurrected and Transfigured in his divinity.[3]

A final detail seems very significant to me. When the women met with Jesus, they too fell down, but at his feet (28:9) after he came to them. Here, though, the disciples worshiped at a distance; they did so the moment they saw him and it was then that Jesus approached them, not the other way round. The fact that the disciples stayed at a distance from Jesus is because they didn't feel free to go to him, impressed as they were and then held back by his divinity. This is the Risen One, God. Before his indescribable splendor, the disciples were silent and still; they simply listened to the words that become wonderfully clear when we know that they were spoken by God, by one of the three Persons of the Holy Trinity. This final message from Jesus is extraordinary and will carry the disciples and the whole Church through to the end of time.

The Risen One's message is for us too, we who like them can fall on our faces as we receive it since it is in his divine-humanity that he speaks to us, he who is in heaven, the Son of Man who has received all authority in heaven and earth (Dan 7:14) from his Father, and who at the same time is with us every day in wonderful and humble proximity. We are thus invited to walk with him in order to fulfil what he asks of us, to evangelize, baptize and teach.

The future is now wide open before us, but there is a final point which touches and challenges me. The text has no conclusion, wonderfully open, but there is one precise point

3. It's wonderful to see the divinity of the Transfigured Jesus displayed on a mountain; this is the principal location for divine appearances, as in the Old Testament (on mount Sinai, Exod 19:3 . . .). Everything is recapitulated in Christ.

that is lacking. In Luke's parallel account, we are told that Jesus blessed the disciples (24:50–51), a wonderful blessing which gave them an irreplaceable strength for the accomplishment of their mission. Matthew says nothing of this and leaves the disciples on their faces worshipping Jesus.

O my soul, Matthew's silence here is wonderful; he discreetly invites we ourselves to ask Jesus to bless us before we go back down the mountain with him.

Lord Jesus, my Lord and my God, I am here, bowed before you, full of wonderment at you whose majesty and divine splendor are beyond description. You are here and I cannot so much as move; all I can do is rest silently in the unfathomable mystery of your presence. My heart overflows and, before going back down the mountain, I need a lot more time yet to go over again and meditate everything you have shown me and taught me in this gospel. I can only hold my peace and contemplate you in your infinite grandeur with the Father and the Holy Spirit, contemplating also your infinite humility as you announce that you will be with us every day to fulfill with us the mission with which you entrust us; I can only keep silent and allow my heart to overflow with all the love you have placed within it. I bow my head now before you that you may draw near again, reach out your hands over us and bless us; in your grace, please bless me as you blessed the children (Mk 10:16), because really I am no more than a child . . .